HISTORICAL AND MULTICULTURAL ENCYCLOPEDIA OF WOMEN'S REPRODUCTIVE RIGHTS IN THE UNITED STATES

HISTORICAL AND MULTICULTURAL ENCYCLOPEDIA OF WOMEN'S REPRODUCTIVE RIGHTS IN THE UNITED STATES

Edited By
Judith A. Baer

GREENWOOD PRESS
Westport, Connecticut • London

Library of Congress Cataloging-in-Publication Data

Historical and multicultural encyclopedia of women's reproductive rights in the United
States / edited by Judith A. Baer.
    p.   cm.
    Includes bibliographical references.
    ISBN 0–313–30644–3 (alk. paper)
    1. Birth control—Government policy—United States—History—Encyclopedias.
2. Abortion—Government policy—United States—History—Encyclopedias.   3.
Women's rights—United States—Encyclopedias.   I. Baer, Judith A.
HQ766.5.U5 H57   2002
363.9'6'097303—dc21   2001037781

British Library Cataloguing in Publication Data is available.

Library of Congress Catalog Card Number: 2001037781
ISBN: 0–313–30644–3

First published in 2002

Greenwood Press, 88 Post Road West, Westport, CT 06881
An imprint of Greenwood Publishing Group, Inc.
www.greenwood.com

Printed in the United States of America

The paper used in this book complies with the
Permanent Paper Standard issued by the National
Information Standards Organization (Z39.48–1984).

10 9 8 7 6 5 4 3 2 1

Contents

Preface

This one-volume reference work introduces the reader to the subject of reproductive rights through a collection of short articles. It has been planned to be as comprehensive and inclusive as possible. As the title implies, the approach is historical and multicultural. The articles extend both backward and forward in time, attempting to provide insights into both what has changed and what has stayed the same. The article topics—and the authors—were chosen with an eye toward representing American culture in its diversity and complexity, not only with respect to racial and ethnic groups but also in age, class, education, health, religion, sexual preference, and viewpoint. The approach is interdisciplinary as well as historical and multicultural. The encyclopedia includes articles on laws, court cases, political attitudes, prominent activists, and technological advances, and on subjects like race, class, disability, and sexual preference as they relate to reproductive rights.

I have designed this encyclopedia with two purposes in mind. First, I wanted it to do what good, specialized encyclopedias do: provide brief introductions to selected topics and references to guide further inquiry. Second, I wanted articles that would engage and provoke readers. I have worked hard to ensure that this encyclopedia includes opinions other than mine. After I had selected topics on which to solicit articles, I also put announcements on several e-mail listserves, asking readers to suggest other topics. I invited articles from both scholars and activists, and encouraged the authors to incorporate reasoned opinions, supported by evidence, into their articles. Viewpoint was welcome; bias was not. One result of my efforts to include multiple viewpoints is the presence of considerable overlap and repetition in this volume. For example, at least 12 articles deal, directly or indirectly, with the issue of fetal protection policies. Any given item of information is usually contained in more than one article.

Another result of my search for diversity is the absence of uniform terminology. Several contributors had strong opinions about usage, which I respected. These opinions sometimes conflicted. For example, some authors use the term "pro-life" to describe opposition to abortion rights, while others reject the term (as I do.) Labels like "African American" and "black," or "Indian" and "Native American," are used interchangeably.

Few Americans are neutral about reproductive rights. The editor of this volume is not one of those few. In the interests of full disclosure, I will state my own viewpoint. I support reproductive choice, and oppose any official restrictions on women premised on their reproductive role. Not only have I defended abortion rights and opposed fetal protection in my publications, but I have volunteered at the local Planned Parenthood clinic. I have done the best I can to keep my own opinions from taking over this encyclopedia. But readers will have to judge for themselves how well I have succeeded. I do not agree with every statement in this book, and I do not expect all the authors to agree with everything I say in this introduction.

My greatest debt is to the contributors to this volume who endured my nagging, prompting, reminding, revising, nagging, querying, editing, and nagging. The content of their articles, and their suggestions for topics I had not thought of, made my task less arduous and more absorbing. My debt to those who helped me find contributors is almost as great. I had valuable assistance from list moderators who allowed me to post announcements: Jean Shackleford of FEMECON-L, Howard Gillman of LAWCOURTS-L, and Joan Korenman of WMST-L.

The political science department at Texas A&M University provided invaluable assistance. Avis Munson and Brad Epps served as my computer gurus. Matthew Eshbaugh-Soha, Roswell Fichthorn, Jill Nicholson, Phillip Gray, and Carl Doerfler have performed nobly as my graduate assistants.

My association with the Greenwood Publishing Company has now traversed two centuries. Having published my first book, Greenwood has done a remarkable job with my latest. The process of compiling and editing this volume was guided by two exemplary editors. Nita Romer directed the project at the beginning, while Michael Hermann took over at the end. Maureen Melino, Michelle Pini, and the staff at City Desktop Productions in Franksville, Wisconsin ably shepherded the volume from manuscript to book. To all of them, I am truly grateful.

My cousin, Tess, died unexpectedly, a month before her 40th birthday, while this encyclopedia was in preparation. Tess was a vibrant feminist and gay activist, committed to changing the world and to living joyfully within it. Honest, loving, and brave, she inspired me throughout our lives. I dedicate this book to her, in recognition of the ideals we shared.

Introduction

When we speak of reproductive rights, what do we mean? In a literal sense, "reproductive rights" can mean "the right to reproduce." In the American context, the opposite meaning may be more familiar: the right to prevent reproduction, particularly by means of abortion. But the term has additional meanings, which are not included within this familiar dichotomy of the right to have children versus the right not to do so. This volume conceptualizes "reproductive rights" as Mary Lyndon Shanley does in her article: "a range of claims concerning whether, when, and how to have children."[1]

Whatever reproductive rights are, to discuss them is inevitably to plunge into controversy. To speak of reproductive rights is to combine three sensitive issues, any one of which is explosive by itself: sex, gender, and rights. Reproductive rights lie at the intersection of sex and gender. (Social scientists commonly use *sex* to denote physiological factors and *gender* to denote social roles and statuses associated with sex.) The connection between reproduction and sexual activity may seem simple and obvious, but it is complex and dynamic. This is true partly because sexuality itself is complex. It is often regarded as an uncontrollable drive, but society does a remarkably efficient job of channeling it. The French philosopher Michel Foucault called sexuality "an exceptionally dense transfer point for relations of power between men and women, young people and old people, parents and offspring, teachers and students, priests and laity, an administration and a population."[2] The ways society exercises power over sexuality include, but are not limited to, determining what constitutes sex, who may do it, who initiates it, and who enjoys it. In the twentieth century, women's gains in reproductive freedom have done little to increase their control of sexual activity.

The medical advances of the twentieth century made it possible to separate sex from conception. The new technology of the twenty-first century may well separate conception from sex. Artificial insemination, *in vitro* fertilization, and ectogenesis are turning the possibility of reproduction without sexual intercourse into a reality. For the foreseeable future, however, talking about reproduction will entail talking about sex, which entails talking about relationships, which entails talking about gender. As important as reproductive issues are and always have been for men, women's childbearing function gives reproductive rights issues a quantitatively greater and qualitatively different impact on women's lives than on men's. The subject of reproductive rights is inseparable from the subject of sexual equality.

Talking about rights is as difficult and controversial as talking about reproduction. The idea of individual rights is not controversial in itself; it is a basic principle of American government. The founding theory of American politics finds its classic expression in Thomas Jefferson's words in the Declaration of Independence: "that all men are created equal that they are endowed by their Creator with certain inalienable rights; and that among these are life, liberty, and the pursuit of happiness." The agreement starts and ends there.

Jefferson's words articulate a basic tenet of liberalism, the political theory which most influenced the founders of the United States of America. Today, liberal theory has fallen into such disrepute in this country that few political or academic figures will allow themselves to be labeled "liberals." Rights have suffered a similar decline in reputation. Agreement that individuals have rights to do something does not settle moral questions about how they should behave and govern their lives. The idea of rights tends to cease being obvious and starts becoming controversial at about the point that someone tries to exercise a right guaranteed on paper. Things have not changed all that much since Mark Twain wrote that Americans have three precious gifts: freedom of speech, freedom of religion, and the prudence never to exercise either of them.

Specific rights are as controversial as the political philosophy from which rights originate. Americans, as a people, is a long way from any consensus about *what* rights individuals have (abortion? access to reproductive technology?), and *who* has them (minors? prisoners?). Americans also disagree about who should make the decisions about the interests some people call rights. Criticism of the Supreme Court for making an "unwarranted" decision or "usurping" the democratic process began immediately after *Roe v. Wade* in 1973 and continues, virtually without interruption, to the present day. At the same time, other commentators defend the Court for returning the abortion decision to the individual, where, in their opinion, it belongs.[3]

Multiple opinions also exist about what else society needs in addition to rights. Conservatives welcome freedom of expression and religion as means of enhancing their political activities and spiritual lives, but many of them—particularly members of the "religious right," a potent force in American politics since the 1980s—emphasize duty, "family values," and obedience to authority (often to divine law) over freedom. Communitarians, many of whom share liberals' enthusiasm for the welfare state, often echo conservatives' assertions that American culture puts too much emphasis on rights and too little on responsibilities. While communitarians do not reject the idea of individual rights, they fear that cultural stress on rights frustrates societal efforts to agree on and pursue a common good.[4]

Not all critiques of liberal rights theory come from the right or center. Although it sometimes seems that there is no left, left—that liberalism now occupies the extreme left of the political spectrum in the U.S.—radical analyses have long been part of American political thought. The fact that most Americans who know anything about Marxism reject it has not stopped scholars from using the structure and concepts of Marxist theory. American scholars do not uniformly reject Marx's argument that "the meaning [concepts like 'rights'] take on usually reflects the nature of the society of the theorist or commentator, usually in a way which serves the interests of the dominant classes and elites." Thus, "liberty" under capitalism has been defined as the right of entrepreneurs to market commodities, not the right of workers to earn a living wage. "What is really a particular historical product, the nature that 'liberty' takes on in a capitalist society, is presented as something universal."[5]

A Marxist influence is apparent in some feminist critiques of rights. "A focus on rights ignores *needs*," writes Barbara Katz Rothman.[6] Catharine MacKinnon asserts that rights such as privacy and free speech facilitate men's domination of women: "abstract rights authorize the male view of the world."[7] Deborah Rhode suggests that only a legal system devised and administered by men would offer "extensive protection to the right to bear arms or to sell violent pornography, but not to control over our reproductive lives."[8] One does not have to be a student of Marxism or a radical feminist to agree that rights as defined in American law have a male bias. "Difference" feminists, like Carol Gilligan and Robin West, argue that an emphasis on rights prioritizes male interests: that men's ethics emphasize abstract rights while women give priority to care and connection.[9]

Reproductive rights is a complicated subject as well as a controversial one. Discussions of reproductive issues must confront two crucial facts. Each fact seems obvious when stated; but, at least in the U.S., public discourse often seems able to grasp only one of these facts at any one time. The first fact is that reproduction is essential; the second fact is that reproductive capacity is plentiful. Like every other species, *homo sapiens* must reproduce in order to survive. Like every other culture, American society depends on reproduction for its continued existence. Therefore, to have a child is to perform an essential biological and cultural function. But for most people, most of the time, fertility is a commodity the supply of which exceeds the demand. In this country, at this time, this abundance exists not only for individuals but for society as a whole. Society needs babies, but it does not need every baby born, or any particular baby.

Some discussions of reproductive issues emphasize the value of fertility without acknowledging the surplus. Words like "precious," "unique," and "miraculous" recur, suggesting that fertility is the exception rather than the norm. But, how-

ever valuable it is, fertility is not scarce. Most women face the possibility of pregnancy as long as they are heterosexually active during the long interval between
menarche and menopause. In consequence, most women can have—and, without
some means of fertility control, will have—many more pregnancies than they
want. Limiting family size is beneficial not only for most families but also for
society. Yet laws prohibiting contraception and abortion are almost as old as safe,
reliable, and accessible contraceptives and abortifacients.

On the other hand, some discourse over reproductive issues emphasizes the
oversupply of fertility while downplaying its importance. The fact that society
needs babies means that women who become mothers—who bear children, raise
them, or both—are making a vital contribution to society. The fact that society
does not need all its babies may help explain the dissonance between the contribution these women are making and the treatment they and their offspring receive.
Some babies are not welcome at all. In Elaine Cleeton's words, "the phenomenon of 'children having children' is widely believed to cause crime, poverty,
welfare dependency, illiteracy, and a host of other social evils."[10] Terms like "illegitimate child" and "unwed mother" indicate the attitudes encountered by women
who have children outside of marriage. Phrases like "race suicide" and "the propagation of the fit" have vanished from our political vocabulary, and the abuses
these attitudes encouraged have been curbed. But disabled women may still be
discouraged from having children—whether or not their disability is hereditary—
and women whose unborn children have or might have disabilities may encounter
pressure to terminate their pregnancies.[11]

So reproduction is sometimes valued, sometimes not. It depends on who is having what baby—and concerns about health, age, and marital status all too often
serve as proxies for race and class issues.[12] The constant is gender. As important
as human rights have been American political culture, the relationship between
bearing rights and bearing children has not been a comfortable one. Women, the
child-bearers, have not had rights coexistent with those of men. The U.S. has been,
and remains, a male supremacist society—whatever the causes of this dominance
are—and society has rarely hesitated to limit women's freedom. Women's reproductive roles have often been the official justification for these limits. Male
supremacy has limited and threatened the reproductive autonomy of American
women.

BEARING RIGHTS AND BEARING CHILDREN:
AN INTRODUCTION TO REPRODUCTIVE RIGHTS

The cluster of claims we call "reproductive rights" identifies issues that are as
old as human history. However, the term itself is a relatively new addition to political language; it did not come into common usage until the 1960s. This timing is
no coincidence. Custom, technology, law, and politics combined in that decade
to bring reproductive rights issues to the forefront. The 1960s brought a change
in social norms so fundamental and radical that it was called the "sexual

revolution." The old "double standard," which permitted men to experiment but expected women to be chaste outside marriage and monogamous within it, yielded to attitudes which encouraged sexual experimentation by both men and women. This social change was accompanied and accelerated by a major technological innovation: the development of "the Pill" or oral contraceptive. Birth control pills were first marketed in the U.S. in 1960. This method, and later inventions like the intrauterine device (IUD) and Norplant, provided safe, reliable, and reversible methods for women to control their fertility independently of the sexual act itself. Both the sexual revolution and the new contraceptives vastly increased women's freedom by mitigating the physical and social consequences of sex.[13]

At the same time that ideas about sex and parenthood were changing, so were ideas about rights and the law. The 1960s were characterized by what has been called a "rights explosion." Rights discourse was even more prevalent in the United States than it usually is, and that is saying a great deal.[14] The African-American civil rights movement was in full swing by 1960. Within 10 years, the student, Hispanic, gay, Native American, disabled, and poor people's movements were in various stages of development. Reproductive rights issues comprised an important part of all of these movements. But it is the women's movement—the resurgence of feminism which began in the late 1960s—that has had the greatest impact on reproductive rights.

Except for the feminists, who had to wait until the 1970s, rights activists got strong support from the judiciary. Under the leadership of Chief Justice Earl Warren, the Supreme Court issued many landmark decisions protecting rights to equality, liberty, and fairness.[15] One of these decisions, *Griswold v. Connecticut* (1965), ruled that several constitutional guarantees established a "zone of privacy" that protected the right of married couples to use birth control.[16] *Griswold* pre-dated second-wave feminism by a few years, but this gender-neutral ruling obviously had some gender-specific effects. Since public opinion overwhelmingly favored birth control by 1965, *Griswold* did not provoke much controversy—but eight years later, the Court extended the right of privacy to cover a limited right to abortion.[17]

These extraordinary developments brought reproductive rights issues to the forefront of American politics by 1970. However, the concept of reproductive rights that prevailed at that time was narrow and incomplete. Public discourse emphasized women's control over their fertility, specifically, their ability to have conventional heterosexual intercourse without having children. But fertility control includes the right *to* have children as well as the right *not* to do so. For some women, it was the former right, not the latter, which was threatened—and these distinctions had a great deal to do with class, race, and socioeconomic status. Until the late 1960s, women who wanted to be sterilized confronted the "Rule of 120." The American College of Obstetricians and Gynecologists recommended that their members perform this operation only on women whose age, multiplied by the number of living children they had, reached that figure.[18] This rule made it difficult for many middle-class women to choose this permanent and relatively safe means of fertility control. Yet for poor women, the situation was the opposite. In one public hospital, doctors wore buttons saying, "Stop at two, damn it."[19] It was not until 1979—six years after *Roe v. Wade*—that the U.S. government prohibited sterilizations without informed consent in federally funded clinics.[20]

A second group of claims pertains to the use of women's fertility as a justification for, and means of, controlling them. (In the United States, childbearing has not yet been used as an official justification for *benefitting* or *rewarding* women.) From the "protective" labor legislation of the 1900s to the workplace restrictions of the 1980s, government and employers have used women's childbearing functions as a justification for limiting their employment opportunities. The fetal protection movement has attempted to extend the reach of governmental power into all of women's lives. Efforts to impose lifestyle restrictions on pregnant women or to force them to undergo medical treatment are draconian restrictions on women's rights.

A third cluster of reproductive rights issues involves the official control and regulation of motherhood. Government and society structure the contexts in which women mother. It makes an enormous difference in a women's life whether or not she can deliver her child at home rather than in a hospital, consult a midwife rather than an obstetrician, breast-feed at work or in public, or take maternity and/or family leave, with or without pay, mandatory or optional. Women who adopt children, birth mothers who relinquish children for adoption, and mothers in special circumstances face a host of legal and social difficulties.

Once a woman becomes a mother, the state interferes with her freedom in many different ways. (This is also true for fathers, of course.) Few Americans quarrel with state regulation in general, or in principle; society has a crucial interest in the treatment, upbringing, and education of children. But specific instances of state interference often provoke disputes. One example among many is the question of whether grandparents (and possibly other relatives) should have a legal right of access to their grandchildren, even against the wishes of the children's parents. By 2000, all 50 states had "grandparents' rights" statutes. (Considering that many state legislators are of an age to have grandchildren, this unanimity may not be surprising.) In June of that year, *Troxel v. Grenville* invalidated a Washington state ruling that gave a couple the right to visit their grandchildren. However, the Supreme Court avoided a ruling on the constitutionality of these laws.[21]

All three of these different but related groups of reproductive rights have been the subjects of political struggles over the last 150 years. These struggles are still ongoing; few victories have been made invulnerable to attack, and no defeat has been accepted as permanent. Women have struggled to win control over their fertility, in both a positive and a negative sense. At the same time, women have confronted society's efforts to control them *through* their fertility. Finally, women have fought to change the relationship between the mother and the state, to make it less adversary and more co-operative. In this contest, no victory has been won outright and complete; no defeat has been accepted as permanent. The battle for reproductive freedom goes on.

WOMEN AND THE CONTROL OF FERTILITY

Efforts to prevent pregnancy, and to end unwanted pregnancies, are as old as *homo sapiens*. But there were no significant advances in birth control until the 1870s, and it was not until the twentieth century that safe, reliable methods of female contraception and elective abortion became widely available. States began passing laws against birth control and abortion at about the same time technology began making them available and safe: the latter half of the nineteenth century. Many statutes prohibiting the sale or distribution of contraceptives and abortifacients were essentially "little Comstock laws." They mimicked the federal Comstock Act of 1873, which prohibited the importing or mailing of "obscene" material, including these devices. By the 1960s, only Massachusetts and Connecticut still had these (rarely enforced) prohibitions on the books.[22] But only two states, New York and Hawaii, had legalized elective abortions by the time *Roe v. Wade* was decided in 1973.

While the vast majority of Americans regard birth control as an important individual right, opinion on abortion is sharply divided. No more than half the population supports abortion for non-medical reasons.[23] Most abortion opponents believe that the fetus is a human being. The unborn have never had the *legal* status of persons, but that fact does not settle the moral issue. A belief that "life begins at conception" is compatible with support for the right to abortion—human beings do not generally have the duty to use their bodies to keep others alive, not even their own children—but many people who believe the fetus is human equate abortion with murder.[24] Pro-choice opinion is equally vehement. Many pro-choice Americans share the views of an abortion rights activist interviewed by Kristin Luker:

We can get all the rights in the world—the right to vote, the right to go to school—and they don't mean a doggone thing if we don't own the flesh we stand in, if we can't control what happens to us, if someone can get us pregnant by accident, by defeat, or by force. So I consider the right to elective abortion, whether you dream of doing it or not, the cornerstone of the women's movement . . . because without that right, we'd have about as many rights as the cow who is brought to the bull once a year.[25]

As eloquent as this defense of reproductive choice is, it does not express a consensus among women—not even among feminists, and not even if the reference to abortion is omitted.[26] The U.S. has a long history of dispute about the relationship between women's rights and fertility control. The women who gathered in Seneca Falls, New York in 1848 to write the Declaration of Sentiments and Resolutions, the founding document of American feminism, were painfully aware of the effects of repeated pregnancy and childbirth on women's health and lives. These women could not have imagined the fertility control which is possible today, and might not have wanted it if they could. As late as the 1920s, many feminists opposed both abortion and artificial contraception.[27] "Voluntary Motherhood advocates," wrote Linda Gordon, "realized that while women needed freedom from excessive childbearing, they also needed the respect and self-respect motherhood brought." These women believed that sexual abstinence was the best method of birth control: "while women needed freedom from pregnancy, they also needed freedom from male sexual tyranny, especially in a society that had almost completely suppressed accurate information about female sexuality and replaced it with information and attitudes so false as to virtually guarantee that women would not enjoy sex."[28]

"Male sexual tyranny" is an accurate description of women's situations during the first wave of feminism. Until the end of the twentieth century, laws and customs essentially gave control of women's fertility to men. Women's sexual status was defined by their relationship to a man. Unmarried women were expected to remain celibate. Laws against fornication and adultery reinforced these prohibitions. Wives were obligated by law to "submit" to their husbands. Marital sex was even exempted from the law against rape, on the grounds that "by their mutual matrimonial consent and contract the wife hath given up herself in this kind to her husband, which she cannot retract."[29] Before emancipation, women slaves were vulnerable to being used by their owners as sexual outlets and as producers of new slaves.[30]

This description recounts what men *could* do, not what they invariably *did* do. Husbands could and did decide to abstain or to limit sex to prevent pregnancy, to please their wives, or because they were uninterested in sex—at least with their wives. But in an agrarian society, like the U.S. in the nineteenth century, children were useful as a source of farm labor. Farmers had an incentive to have large families. No wife, urban or rural, enjoyed anything resembling a right to say "no." Dutiful sex was a fact of life for many married women. The only check on a husband's power was his own self-restraint.

By 2000, the law approached sexual equality. The marital exemption has been removed from the rape laws; husbands have been convicted of raping their wives. The Supreme Court effectively invalidated the traditional law of marriage—in 1981.[31] On paper, the wife's duty to submit has gone the way of other rules based on traditional stereotypes about sex roles. New cultural perspectives on sex began reducing women's ignorance and revolutionizing their attitudes long before the sexual revolution of the 1960s. Explicit information about male and female sexuality and concrete, practical advice for the ignorant and inexperienced have been available in the mass media since the 1920s. After 80 years of mass-market sexology and 40 years of liberalized attitudes, we know that a woman's capacity for sexual pleasure is at least as great as a man's. Women have access to all sorts of information to help them enjoy sex. But male sexual tyranny has not yet given way to equal sexual autonomy.

Fertility control has vastly improved women's lives. However, the alternative of avoiding pregnancy through sexual abstinence is not without its appeal. No method of birth control is safe, reliable, and convenient for everyone. Many women are in situations where their sexual pleasure has little to do with the conditions of their sexual activity. A woman who does enjoy sex need not give it up to avoid pregnancy. She need only avoid conventional intercourse—and the information about sex which is now widely available includes many ways in which men and women can achieve sexual gratification, including orgasms, without the penis entering the vagina. But many women still lack the freedom to prevent pregnancy by controlling their sexual activity rather than controlling their fertility.

A perception of sex as something men make women do, or something women do to please men, unites women divided by time, place, and politics.[32] Pro-life activists and radical feminists alike assert that the sexual revolution, the Pill, and the legalization of abortion have made women more vulnerable to pressure from men to have sex. These developments did make it more difficult for women to justify avoiding pregnancy by avoiding intercourse. Anselma Dell'Olio has described the sexual revolution as a change in social norms from "sex never" to "sex always."[33] Similar pressure exists within many ongoing relationships. Even in relationships where neither partner dominates and both are equal, a woman may have sex she doesn't want in order to please the man she loves; this becomes one of the many compromises that relationships involve. (A man may do the same, but he doesn't risk pregnancy.) Catharine MacKinnon writes, "the availability of abortion removes the one remaining legitimized reason that women have had for refusing sex besides the headache."[34]

What if a woman wants to restrict sexual expression to acts which do not involve the risk of pregnancy? This may be a tough sell for both her and her partner. Sexual behavior is not instinctive for human beings; we learn it. Culture shapes our perceptions of what sex is and what happens during it. Linda Gordon gives an example of this phenomenon in her article in this volume. She discusses "male continence," a contraceptive method practiced by utopian communitarians in the nineteenth century, in which men refrained from ejaculation. "The fact that this method sounds so bizarre today," Gordon writes, indicates the way "our culture has internalized the notion that the male climax is an irrepressible urge."[35] Today, our culture has internalized the notion that "sex" involves a penis penetrating a vagina. For many people, only conventional intercourse counts as sex. But there are plenty of other forms of sexual activity that are at least equally satisfying, and allow people to dispense with pills, condoms, diaphragms, IUDs, and Norplant, each of which has its own limitations and disadvantages.

Nevertheless, today most American women value birth control for the freedom it gives them to have sex without getting pregnant. Attitudes toward artificial contraception have changed drastically since the days of Voluntary Motherhood. By the 1910s, feminists' attitudes toward sexuality were changing. Margaret Sanger, for example, was sexually active for most of her adult life.[36] By the 1910s, some feminists had joined the birth control movement she led. By the 1920s, Emma Goldman and other socialist feminists celebrated women's sexuality and welcomed the development of safe, reliable contraception. The early feminist movement lost energy after it achieved its primary goal—the vote—through the ratification of the Nineteenth Amendment in 1920, but the birth control movement continued to gain strength. After all, you did not have to be a feminist to support family planning and population control. By the time *Griswold v. Connecticut* was decided in 1965, birth control was widely available and generally accepted.[37]

By 2001, legal, safe, and widely available birth control had long been a reality in the U.S. But easy access to contraception is not yet a certainty for everyone. Some people cannot afford what they need. The going rate for the Pill in central Texas is now $17 a month—quite a dent in many household budgets. Many health insurance plans do not cover birth control—even if they do cover Viagra, the anti-impotence drug for men. The Supreme Court invalidated state laws prohibiting the sale of contraceptives to minors in 1977, but many young people still have difficulty getting access to contraception.[38] Four decades ago, college infirmaries typically prescribed pills only for married students. These practices have changed, but women younger than 18 do not always find it easy to obtain contraceptives, especially without their parents' co-operation. Physicians may refuse to prescribe birth control for minors. The Reagan administration went so far as to propose a "squeal rule" that would have required federally funded clinics to notify parents or guardians.[39]

For birth control, access is the rule, unavailability the exception. The same cannot be said for abortion. The right to terminate a pregnancy still exists—barely—but a powerful, well-funded single-issue interest group has threatened it virtually from the moment *Roe v. Wade* was decided. The "pro-life" movement has not succeeded in making restriction the rule and access the exception, but it has won major victories in all three branches of government and in both federal and state levels. The decriminalization of abortion was followed by laws and court decisions limiting access to abortion. Anti-choice forces have persuaded the national government and most of the states to prohibit the use of public funds and facilities for virtually all elective abortions.[40] Forty-two states have laws that require either parental notification or a "judicial bypass" before a minor can get an abortion.[41] A federal "gag rule" prohibited federally funded clinics from even discussing abortion with clients until the Clinton administration repealed it in January 1993.[42] The Supreme Court has upheld several regulations aimed at discouraging women from getting abortions, such as mandatory waiting periods and "counseling" requirements. *Planned Parenthood v. Casey* (1992) effectively demoted abortion from the status of a full-fledged constitutional right; the Supreme Court ruled that discouraging abortion was a valid legislative purpose as long as restrictions so motivated did not place an "undue burden" on the choice.[43] The protracted controversies over RU-486 (a drug which induces non-surgical abortions) and procedures misleadingly called "partial birth abortions" indicate that reproductive freedom has yet to be a reality for all American women.[44]

Roe v. Wade was greeted with an onslaught of criticism. Many commentators argued that the decision was bad law: that it had little or no support in constitutional doctrine. An equally common and vehement criticism held that *Roe* was bad politics. By legalizing abortion, this argument ran, the Court had usurped the democratic process. It substituted judicial fiat for public deliberation, accommodation, and compromise. In this view, the Court is responsible for the anti-choice backlash: gradual legalization, through democratic decision-making, would not have provoked the opposition *Roe* did. Perhaps; but gradual change would have denied abortions to many women who wanted them. "Having an unwanted child can go a long way toward ruining a woman's life."[45]

I have already discussed the fact that not all women believe that fertility control is an essential freedom. It is equally true that not everyone who supports access to birth control and abortion does so in the interests of sexual equality. For example, the Playboy Foundation has provided financial support for abortion rights—but it is a safe bet that the foundation is less concerned with women's interests than with men's. Women, too, have been known to advocate fertility control for reasons that had little to do with anybody's rights and a great deal to do with coercion. When these activists supported birth control, they did not necessarily mean for women like themselves. Many of them shared the racism of early feminists like Elizabeth Cady Stanton, who declared that white women were better qualified to vote than African Americans. And many, like Sanger, were "eugenics" advocates who advocated measures like the compulsory sterilization of the poor and "unfit."

From the "New Deal" of the 1930s to the "Great Society" of the 1960s, the growth of the welfare state made many women vulnerable to official coercion. The medical advances that enhanced women's control over their fertility could also be used to control their fertility for them. Women (more often than men) who were poor, black, Native American, Hispanic, disabled, incarcerated (in prisons or mental institutions), or "feeble-minded," whatever that meant, were often sterilized without their knowledge, let alone their consent, and threatened with the loss of government benefits if they refused the operation.[46]

American feminists of the "second wave" did not repeat the mistakes of their predecessors. The new feminist movement joined with an emerging consumer health care movement to oppose sterilization abuse. Feminists welcomed the federal prohibitions on forced sterilization as enthusiastically as they did *Roe v. Wade*. Feminists have also discovered that these prohibitions are no more self-executing than *Roe* has been. The federal government does not monitor compliance with the rules; nor do the rules apply to the states' use of their own funds. The new technologies, which have enhanced individual freedom, can also facilitate societal control. Preventing the coercive use of contraception, sterilization, and abortion demands increasing vigilance now that Norplant is a convenient alternative to the Pill, a tubal ligation is minor surgery, and fetuses can be examined *in utero*. Procedures such as amniocentesis can reveal genetic defects in fetuses. Negative findings may be an enormous relief to parents and professionals. If defects are present, parents may choose either to terminate the pregnancy or to prepare for the birth of a disabled child. But whatever choice they make, these parents may find themselves subjected to pressure and criticism: accused of wanting "designer babies" if they choose abortion, or urged to abort if they decide to continue the pregnancy.[47]

So far, this discussion of reproductive rights has left out a substantial minority of the population: those to whom nature has denied the privilege of safe, healthy parenthood. The fact that the supply of fertility exceeds the demand is scant comfort to anyone who is infertile, who risks passing on a genetic disease, or whose health might be damaged by pregnancy. People in these situations have often enlisted the state's help in becoming parents. Their demands raise a host of reproductive rights issues. In the twentieth century, adoption was the most common solution to these problems.[48] Before *Roe*, a common argument against the legalization of abortion was that it would reduce the number of children available for adoption. There is no clear relationship between these two variables. The difficulties attendant on quantifying such a relationship include the fact that many adoptable children do not appeal to prospective adopters, the increasing popularity of international adoption, and the factors which influence a birth mother's decision to keep or relinquish her baby. But there is a very real perception of conflict between the interests of pregnant women and those of would-be parents.

Today, many abortion opponents continue to advocate adoption as the best solution to unwanted pregnancy. The first George Bush made this plea in one of the presidential candidates' debates in 1988. While Bush could sympathize with would-be adoptive parents—his son and daughter-in-law have adopted two children—it is unlikely that he realized how much he was asking of reluctantly pregnant women. The ordeal of going through a pregnancy, giving birth—with all the physical and psychological effects these processes entail—and then relinquishing the baby, is so great that urging a woman to subject herself to it is difficult to justify. Activists who promote this choice do not always try to imagine themselves in the same situation. Prospective adoptive parents who have experienced the pain of infertility may not think much about the feelings of birth mothers.

Adoption is no longer the only solution to infertility. Medical advances have helped many people to have their own biological children. Consumer demand has stimulated the development of new procedures that offer hope to the infertile. But these techniques present troublesome legal and ethical issues. They are controversial; their use is controlled by the state and the medical establishment; and they are available only to those who can afford them. Worse still, some new developments raise the possibility of conflict and exploitation.

Artificial insemination (AI), for example, presents difficult questions even though it is not new; it has been practiced since the late nineteenth century. But in the last generation, AI has been medicalized to the extent that some states prohibit it without the involvement of a licensed physician, refined to the extent that semen can be inserted directly into the uterus, and commodified to the extent that sperm can be bought and sold. Artificial insemination by donor (AID)—more commonly, by seller—enables women to become mothers without male partners. The use of AI by single women and lesbian couples is increasingly common, but not universally approved.[49] The use of AI in "surrogate motherhood" agreements involves another set of controversies. Typically, the birth mother is artificially inseminated with the sperm of the man who will become a custodial parent to the child she will bear, and give up, if the procedure is successful. The cases of Mary Beth Whitehead and Alejandra Muñoz, two mothers who became pregnant this way, received wide publicity when the women fought to keep their babies. White-head was a high-school dropout with two children and an alcoholic husband when she agreed to bear a child for a middle-class, professional couple. Muñoz was a Mexican immigrant who had entered the U.S. illegally, was dependent on the relatives who wanted the baby, and claimed she could not read the contract she signed. Similar disparities of class and socioeconomic status exist between the parties in many, if not most, surrogacy arrangements.[50]

In vitro fertilization and embryo implantation are as ethically problematic as artificial insemination is. IVF has enabled previously infertile women to bear children. When IVF is used in conjunction with embryo implantation, women can donate their ova to infertile women. But neither law nor bioethics has even begun to resolve the question of which woman is the mother: the one who provides the ovum or the one who bears the child.[51] A value hierarchy which gives priority to "ownership" might favor the former; an ethic which ranks maternal feelings above property interests might favor the latter. A woman who gestates and bears the genetic offspring of another woman is as vulnerable to exploitation as a surrogate who undergoes AI. This exploitation has implications for class, race, and ethnic issues. "Embracing reproductive technology," Anne Waters writes in this volume, "would be self-defeating in the Indian community."[52]

Should we worry that the new technology will be used to oppress vulnerable women, or welcome these techniques as enhancements of women's freedom? Except for artificial insemination, these techniques require professional expertise; the state and the medical establishment could legally forbid their use. But such an outcome is unlikely. Few if any societies have halted the development of new technology when demand for it exists among those able to pay for it; in a capitalist economic system, such an outcome is unlikely. Is it possible to reach a compromise which encourages choice but discourages coercion? The process of reaching an understanding of reproductive rights which applies to all women and all situations is still going on.

FERTILITY AND THE CONTROL OF WOMEN

Why is women's status secondary to men's? There are many explanations for the ubiquity and prevalence of male supremacy. These range from the economic (male dominance creates a subordinate group which can be relegated to mundane but necessary social tasks) to the psychoanalytic (men are afraid that women can unman them) to the physical (man "established his control at the outset by superior physical strength.")[53] But the most common explanation is physiological. Women's role in reproduction is the factor most commonly invoked to explain male dominance. It is impossible to state with certainty that women have been disadvantaged relative to men *because* they bear children. But it is certainly true that male supremacy has been *defended* on the grounds that women bear children.

Considered in the abstract, this social arrangement may seem bizarre. A group is disadvantaged relative to another group because the first group can perform an essential function that the second group cannot. If we continue to think in abstract terms, we might expect that the people who performed this function would have high social status, or at least that they would get tangible benefits and rewards. But when these generalizations are applied to reproduction, they describe a situation familiar to us all. Many controversies over reproductive rights originate in society's efforts to use women's childbearing function as a justification for depriving them of rights or burdening them with duties. It is important to remember that these restrictions are not imposed only on women who are actual or potential mothers. They are imposed on all women.

"Protective" labor legislation is an early example of this kind of policy. These laws, enacted by many state legislatures in the late nineteenth and early twentieth centuries, limited the number of hours women could be required to work, regulated their working conditions, established a minimum wage, or barred them outright from certain occupations. The difficulty with protective legislation is that it is simultaneously, and inevitably, restrictive. Any rule which protects an individual by forbidding or requiring certain actions also denies that person freedom. If women may not work more than 10 hours, or at night, or in some occupations at all, these jobs are reserved for men.

Labor laws in the U.S. arose in response to the Industrial Revolution. As job after job was relocated from the home to the factory, working conditions worsened for most Americans. Hours were long, wages low, and workplaces were, at best, unhealthy and, at worst, dangerous. Labor organization and collective bargaining began early in the nineteenth century. But, with no established right to organize and bargain, unions' status was precarious and workers' progress slow. Workers and their supporters also turned to legislation to achieve their goals.

Activists gave special attention to women's labor for at least three reasons. First, the women needed protection more—not because of their physical differences from men, but because they worked even longer hours, for even less pay, and in even worse conditions than men did, and had even less power to improve their situations. Women rarely worked alongside men in the same occupations; the workplace was even more sex-segregated than it is now. Essentially, there were men's jobs and women's jobs, and there were fewer women's jobs than men's. The minority of women who worked outside the home was concentrated in a female job ghetto (as most women workers still are). Far fewer women workers were organized than were men; therefore, women were not in a good position to make demands on their employers. These differences in men's and women's job situations led to a second reason to support special legislation for women. Labor leaders saw an opportunity to reserve jobs for men. In many occupations, the displacement of male by female labor was a real possibility, because employers could pay women less. (This actually happened more than once; clerical work, a man's job in the 1800s, is a famous example.)

The Supreme Court's ruling in *Lochner v. New York* (1905) provided a fourth reason to concentrate on women; laws applying to men would be invalidated. *Lochner* ruled that a general hours law violated the due process clause of the Fourteenth Amendment: Laws "limiting the hours in which grown and intelligent men may earn their living," wrote the Court, were "meddlesome interferences with the rights of the individual." [54] Reformers saw some wiggle room for workers who did not completely fit this description. Reformers pushed laws applying only to women, and defended these laws by emphasizing gender differences. This approach worked. In *Muller v. Oregon* (1908), a unanimous Supreme Court flatly stated that women's rights were less extensive than those of men because women bore children. "Woman's physical structure and the performance of maternal functions" justified limitations "upon her contractual powers" which would be unconstitutional if imposed on men.[55]

Muller ushered in the era of protective legislation. This era lasted well into the 1960s. Early in the century, these laws probably did provide some real protection in the female job ghetto by limiting the extent to which employers could exploit workers—although the women were deprived of the choice between shorter hours and more pay. But the laws also made it harder for women to move into the better-paying men's blue-collar jobs—a feat which would have been difficult enough without laws. In general, these laws have protected male workers from female competition better than they have protected women workers or their children.[56]

Protective labor legislation no longer exists. Title VII of the Civil Rights Act of 1964, which prohibits employment discrimination on the basis of sex, invalidated these laws. But it took less than 20 years for protective policies to reemerge in the guise of "fetal protection." By the late 1970s, employers were barring women from jobs requiring exposure to hazardous materials in order to prevent birth defects. These policies did not apply only to women who were, or were planning to become, pregnant; they affected all women of childbearing age, a term the employer got to define (in one corporation, it ranged from five to 63). Most of the occupations covered by fetal protection policies were not part of the female job ghetto. Instead, they were skilled, well-paying, blue-collar jobs, the sort of work once reserved for men and now slowly becoming available to women. Thus, fetal protection threatened the opportunities that antidiscrimination law had begun to open up to women workers.

Feminists' attitudes toward protective legislation changed as these conditions changed. Opinion among early feminists was divided. Social feminists emphasized women's role in the family; egalitarian feminists stressed equal legal rights with men. As you might expect, social feminists supported protective legislation—in fact, it probably could not have been enacted without their support—while egalitarian feminists opposed it.[57] But the "second wave" feminists included few if any advocates of protective legislation. Late in the twentieth century, the women's movement recognized fetal protection as "a new assault on feminism."[58]

Like the old protective legislation, fetal protection policies were challenged in court. But there was an important difference between the new controversy and the old one; this time, the unions and the government opposed the regulations. The Supreme Court reached the obvious conclusion that they violated Title VII— but not until 1991, after some workers had undergone employer-mandated sterilization *and* lost their jobs. The legal victory was something less than a cause for celebration. Many women still must choose between making good money and risking their and their children's health.[59]

Workplace restrictions are not the only policies premised on women's child-bearing role. Several articles in this volume document the use of criminal prosecutions and forced medical treatment against pregnant women who fail to follow medical advice.[60] Medical research in the last half of the twentieth century extensively documented the potential harmful effects of tobacco, alcohol, and drugs on the fetus. The belief that the placenta created a barrier which kept these substances away from the fetus has been replaced by the knowledge that any substance ingested by the mother may affect the fetus. Although none of these substances invariably harm a fetus—as many mothers know from experience—there is no minimal level of intake that is considered safe.

Physicians have responded to this new information by routinely advising against smoking or drinking during pregnancy and urging pregnant women to take no medication without their doctor's permission—a change from 50 years ago. This sensible change in medical practice has not been enough for many "fetal protection" advocates (not surprisingly, since many women get little or no prenatal care.) Warnings about possible birth defects now adorn advertisements, packages containing tobacco, alcohol, and medicines, and places where they are sold. Fetal protection advocates have also sought to criminalize these behaviors, with some success. Women have been sentenced to prison for drug use during pregnancy.

Dramatic medical advances in the 1980s and 1990s lowered the age of fetal viability and made it possible to perform fetal surgery *in utero*. These developments have led to efforts to force women to submit to cesarean sections or to operations on their unborn children. The case of Angela Carder is probably the worst of such violations of women's autonomy. Desperately ill with cancer, Carder was subjected to a court-ordered cesarean, although there was no clear evidence of her wishes and her husband, parents, and doctor protested. Neither Carder nor her infant daughter survived.[61] An appeals court later reversed this decision. Partly because this ruling remains the most authoritative legal statement on forced medical treatment, the practice is now uncommon. However, the possibility represents a grave danger to a pregnant woman's autonomy.

The fetal protection movement has generated its own subfield within the discipline of bioethics. Several theorists have posited a "duty of care" whereby a woman's decision to continue her pregnancy obligates her to "assure that the fetus is born as healthy as possible."[62] What the duty of care obligates her to do, according to these experts, is to follow professional opinion; the woman must be not only conscientious but also obedient (and what happens if professionals disagree?) Another fetal protection advocate goes so far as to declare, "A woman should consider herself pregnant on the first day her period is due and avoid exposure to anything that has been implicated in birth defects."[63]

Ironically, the duty of care doctrine depends on the existence of a right to abortion. The woman has the duty of care *because* she has decided to bear the child.

Duty of care is grounded in the doctrine of "contingent fetal personhood," which holds essentially that the humanity of the fetus is contingent on the woman's decision to continue the pregnancy. This solution to what *Roe* called "the difficult question of when life begins" is ingenious, but it causes more problems than it solves. Leaving aside the question of whether a *de facto* right to terminate a pregnancy exists, the duty of care doctrine uses a woman's right as a justification for imposing duties on her. Although this union of right and duty suggests the familiar cliché that "rights imply responsibilities," this is not in fact the way constitutional rights are treated in law. While rights like the First Amendment freedoms of expression and religion are less than absolute, people retain these rights no matter how responsibly or irresponsibly they use them. The very existence of the fetal protection movement is a grave threat to women's reproductive freedom.

THE MOTHER AND THE STATE

The United States is often called a "child-centered society." If you took politicians at their word—especially during election campaigns—you would think that children's welfare, education, and safety were our society's most important concerns. The quality of the health care and schooling children actually get, and the conditions in which many of them live, reveals the gap between rhetoric and reality. In the United States, children are essentially the responsibility of their parents. This responsibility devolves primarily on mothers. To become a mother is to assume an enormous task, to make a huge, long-term commitment of energy, care, time, and resources. To bear a child, in addition, is to subject oneself to physical risk. Women who become mothers are performing an essential function. Knowing these things, a naive observer might expect that society would reward motherhood. It does not.

The teenage mother, the mother who is disabled or whose baby is at risk, the lesbian mother, and the mother in prison do not benefit from the social rhetoric surrounding motherhood.[64] But "ordinary" mothers also find that society refuses to put its resources where its mouth is. Maternal subsidies, routine in advanced industrial democracies, are unknown in the U.S. Paid maternity and family leaves are a rarity, granted by only a few employers. Children and expectant mothers are not even entitled to subsidized health care. The benefits the state does afford are grudging, limited in scope, and accompanied by constricting requirements: unpaid family leave, Medicaid, and welfare, for example.[65] The history of protective legislation and fetal protection policies shows that, far from being rewarded or even compensated for having children, women have often been punished for it.

Thus, "society's entrenched disapproval of women who do not form nuclear families is not matched by rewards for women who do."[66] This disregard for motherhood pervades American law. The history of child custody law, for example, is particularly troublesome from a maternal viewpoint. American law has changed dramatically in this regard since the 1700s—but never in response to the needs and interests of mothers. In the eighteenth and nineteenth centuries, when divorce was rare and children were an important source of farm labor, the father got custody unless he was unfit. After the Industrial Revolution, paternal preference yielded to the "tender years" doctrine: the mother, who was virtually always the primary caregiver, was the best parent unless she was unfit. While this doctrine worked to the advantage of many divorced mothers, it was not adopted in recognition of their needs, but of their children's needs. It has been replaced by the "best interests of the child" doctrine, which prefers neither parent. In practice, fathers who seek custody get it about half the time. The mother is still usually the primary caregiver during the marriage, but the law does not entertain the possibility that this experience may give her the primary need for the company of the child.[67]

Legal rules, social norms, and medical practices affect women's ability to become mothers and the conditions under which they may do so. Women have the legal right to birth control and abortion, but medical insurance need not pay for either. Similarly, the right to become a mother does not entail the right to adopt, or rights of access to fertility treatments and advanced reproductive technology. Women have more obstetrical choices now than they did forty years ago. In the 1960s and 1970s, a consumer movement led and organized by obstetrical patients effected significant changes in medical practice. For example, many women are now encouraged to reject pain medication in favor of techniques of pain control like the Lamaze method; the presence during labor and delivery of people chosen by the mother, once forbidden, is now routine; and episiotomies and pubic shaving, once routine, are now discretionary. But government and organized medicine still constrain the choices women can make.

Suppose that a woman wants to deliver her baby at home rather than in a hospital or birthing center. If her physician refuses to attend a home delivery—and most are no more eager to do so than to make other house calls—the woman may hesitate to take the risk. Since midwives do attend home deliveries, this hypothetical woman might prefer to have a midwife assist her in labor. Midwives attend the majority of births in developed countries today, and their success rates compare favorably with those of physicians. However, an expectant mother in the United States may not be able to find a midwife. Deborah Fiedler and Robbie Davis-Floyd recount the difficulties that midwives have faced in winning acceptance as childbirth professionals. The refusal of physicians to cooperage with midwives has left midwives without backup in case of complications, increasing the degree of risk in midwife-attended births and making midwifery less attractive both as a career and as a consumer choice. This official discouragement has reduced both the supply of midwives and the demand for their services.[68]

The changes in medical practice in the last generation include a reversal of expert opinion about infant feeding. The routine discouragement of breast-feeding has been replaced by its routine encouragement. Medical and nutritional experts agree that in virtually all cases, breast-feeding is superior to bottle-feeding. Organizations like La Leche League International provide valuable advice for nursing mothers. A woman who chooses not to breast-feed may encounter medical and social disapproval. But the reverse is not true. A woman who does breast-feed cannot count on society to accommodate her needs. She may encounter difficulties if she nurses at work or in public places, or if she is separated from her child's father and must accommodate his rights of access to the child. A nursing mother may find that her choice is approved only when she stays out of sight, or during the first few months of the baby's life.[69]

CONCLUSION:
THE FUTURE OF REPRODUCTIVE RIGHTS

A historical perspective allows us to assess the development of women's reproductive rights throughout U.S. history. There is no doubt that women have infinitely more reproductive freedom now than they did when the Constitution was ratified. The most noticeable, and dramatic, change is women's enhanced control over their fertility. While it would be premature to declare victory in this struggle, it is clear that the historical trend has been toward increased autonomy. But this progress has not been unidirectional. The Reagan years and the first Bush administration brought severe setbacks to reproductive rights. The inauguration of George W. Bush as president in 2001 put into office a man who has sent conflicting signals about these issues and who lost no time blocking federal aid to international agencies who used their own money for abortions. However, 2000 also brought two encouraging developments. The first was the decision of the Food and Drug Administration to allow the use of the abortion drug RU-486; the second was a ruling by the Equal Employment Opportunity Commission that employee health insurance plans which excluded coverage for prescription contraceptives violated Title VII of the Civil Rights Act of 1964.

Technological change has been at least as important as legal and social change in protecting reproductive rights. But technology can work against women as well as for them. It has been used to limit women's autonomy as well as to enhance it. Safe, reliable contraception and sterilization helped many women avoid unwanted pregnancies; but the new procedures and devices also made it necessary for women to fight against their imposition by force. Likewise, the advances in obstetrics and neonatology which helped women gain control over their medical treatment during pregnancy and childbirth have also been used to enforce medical control over women. While government has less control over women's reproductive autonomy than it once did, the same cannot unambiguously be said about the medical establishment. Nor has the control women have gained over their fertility been accompanied by control over their sexuality. Access to birth control, sterilization, and even abortion has proved easier to win than sexual autonomy.

Significant gains have been made in repulsing efforts to use women's childbearing capacity as an excuse for curtailing their freedom. Both protective legislation and fetal protection regulations have been invalidated. Policies that restrict *all* women because *some* of them *might* give birth are dead. And even efforts to coerce individual women who are actual or potential mothers—for instance, by forcing them to accept medical treatment or punishing them for behavior condemned by the medical establishment—are suspect. Very few women have been prosecuted for their conduct during pregnancy, and even fewer convicted; as troubling as these cases are, they do not appear to represent a trend. However, pregnant women still face intense social pressure to obey medical authority. The fetal protection debate rarely acknowledges the possibility that actually or potentially pregnant women, like all autonomous adults, have the right to accept or reject advice.

But, so far, the best women workers can hope for is the ability to choose between a workplace that may expose them to toxic substances and a less desirable job in a safer work environment. And this choice is by no means a guaranteed right. As some of the pregnancy discrimination cases show, a woman who requests accommodations to which she is legally entitled may risk extralegal retaliation.[70] The actually or potentially pregnant worker is certainly not entitled to a risk-minimizing environment, any more than other workers are. The state and the employer may not deprive her of her right to choose to assume risk, but they need not protect her or her family. Parents have no right to official assistance, cooperation, or accommodation in their performance of a difficult, often risky, and socially essential task. It is a telling commentary on American political culture that the Family Leave Act of 1993—guaranteeing *unpaid* parental leave—was widely regarded as progress. In fact, it is a significant improvement over the policies it replaced.

The New Deal and the Great Society are things of the past. The Republican takeover of Congress in 1994 has led to the contraction, not the expansion, of the welfare state. American families are on their own. The 2000 election, in which the Republicans won control of all three branches of the national government, bodes ill for any reversal of this trend. Americans have no such thing as a reproductive right to the state's cooperation, help, and accommodation in performing the socially essential function of parenting. The truncated version of reproductive rights that American society recognizes preserves significant inequalities between women and society and women and men.

NOTES

1. "Marriage and Reproductive Rights."

2. *The History of Sexuality*, vol, 1, trans. Robert Hurley (New York: Pantheon Books, 1978), p. 103.

3. See, for example, Louis Lusky, *By What Right? A Commentary on the Supreme Court's Power to Revise the Constitution* (Charlottesville, Va.: Michie, 1975), and Michael J. Perry, *We the People: The Fourteenth Amendment and the Supreme Court* (New York: Oxford University Press, 1999). For an opposing view, see Laurence H. Tribe, *Abortion: The Clash of Absolutes* (Cambridge, Mass.: Harvard University Press, 1992).

4. See, for example, Mary Ann Glendon, *Rights Talk: The Impoverishment of Political Discourse* (New York: The Free Press, 1991).

5. See, for example, Richard Nordahl, "A Marxian Approach to Human Rights," in Abdullahi Ahmed An-Na'im, ed., *Human Rights in Cross-Cultural Perspective: A Quest for Consensus* (Philadelphia: University of Pennsylvania Press, 1992), pp. 162-187, 164.

6. Barbara Katz Rothman, *Recreating Motherhood* (New York: W.W. Norton, 1989), p. 249.

7. *Toward a Feminist Theory of the State* (Cambridge, Mass.: Harvard University Press, 1989), p. 248.

8. "Feminist Critical Theories," *Stanford Law Review* 42 (February 1990): 617-638, 633.

9. Respectively, *In a Different Voice* (Cambridge, Mass.: Harvard University Press, 1982); "Jurisprudence and Gender," *University of Chicago Law Review*, 55 (Winter 1988): 1-72.

10. See "Teenage Pregnancy."

11. See "Disabled Women and Reproductive Rights;" "Eugenics;" "Lesbians and Reproductive Rights;" "Sterilization Abuse;" "Youth and Reproductive Rights."

12. See "African American Women and Reproductive Rights;" "Class and Reproductive Rights;" "Hispanic/Latina Women and Reproductive Rights;" "Native American Women and Reproductive Rights."

13. See "Norplant," and "Oral Contraceptives."

14. See, for example, Mary Ann Glendon, *Rights Talk*, note 4 above.

15. The most important equal protection case decided by the Warren Court (indeed, probably in the entire history of the Court) was *Brown v. Board of Education* I, 347 U.S. 483 (1954). *Griswold v. Connecticut*, below at note 16, was the decision with the greatest impact on substantive rights doctrine. Among the most important cases involving procedural fairness were *Mapp v. Ohio*, 367 U.S. 643 (1961) (exclusionary rule), *Gideon v. Wainwright*, 372 U.S. 335 (1963) (right to counsel), and *Miranda v. Arizona*, 384 U.S. 436 (1966) (police interrogation).

16. 381 U.S. 479. See *"Griswold v. Connecticut."*

17. *Roe v. Wade*, 413 U.S. 110 (1973). See *"Roe v. Wade."*

18. See, for example, Boston Women's Health Collective, *Our Bodies, Ourselves*, rev. ed. (New York: Simon and Schuster, 1976), pp. 211-212; *The New Our Bodies, Ourselves* (New York: Simon and Schuster, 1984), pp. 256-57. Sterilization is available to any adult male who requests it.

19. John D'Emilio and Estelle B. Freedman, *Intimate Matters: A History of Sexuality in America* (New York: Harper & Row, 1988), p. 255.

20. See "Federal Sterilization Guidelines (1979); " "Hispanic/Latina Women and Reproductive Rights;" "Native American Women and Reproductive Rights;" "Sterilization Abuse."

21. No. 99-138 (2000).

22. See *"Griswold v. Connecticut;" "Poe v. Ullman;"* "Restell, Madame;" "Sanger, Margaret."

23. See "Abortion and Public Opinion."

24. For defenses of abortion which presume that the fetus is human, see, for example, Eileen L. McDonagh, *Breaking the Abortion Deadlock: From Choice to Consent* (New York: Oxford University Press, 1996); Judith Jarvis Thomson, "In Defense of Abortion," in *Rights, Restitution, and Risk* (Cambridge, Mass.: Harvard University Press, 1986): 1-19.

25. *Abortion and the Politics of Motherhood* (Berkeley: University of California Press, 1984), p. 97.

26. See "Abortion and Public Opinion," and "Pro-Life Feminism."

27. See "Pro-Life Feminism."

28. Linda Gordon, "Why Nineteenth-Century Feminists Did Not Support 'Birth Control' and Twentieth-Century Feminists Do: Feminism, Reproduction, and the Family," in Barrie Thorne and Marilyn Yalom, eds., *Rethinking the Family: Some Feminist Questions* (New York: Longman Inc., 1982), p. 44.

29. Lord Chief Justice Matthew Hale, a seventeenth-century English judge. Hale is also the author of the (in)famous statement that "rape is an accusation easily to be made and hard to be proved." See Susan Brownmiller, *Against Our Will: Men, Women, and Rape* (New York: Simon and Schuster, 1975). This book remains the definitive work on rape in the U.S., 25 years after its publication.

30. See "Birth Control and African American Women."

31. *Kirchberg v. Feenstra*, 450 U.S. 455.

32. See Judith A. Baer, *Our Lives before the Law: Constructing a Feminist Jurisprudence* (Princeton, N.J.: Princeton University Press, 1999), p. 57; Luker, *Abortion*, pp. 192-215.

33. "The Sexual Revolution," in Wilma Mankiller et al., eds., *The Reader's Companion to U.S. Women's History* (Boston, Mass.: Houghton Mifflin, 1998), pp. 536-39.

34. "Privacy vs. Equality," in *Feminism Unmodified* (Cambridge, Mass.: Harvard University Press, 1987), p. 99.

35. "Birth Control Movement." The "communitarians" Gordon discusses are very different from today's communitarians. See note 4 and accompanying text. The latter are political theorists whose label is derived from the word *community*; the former were social activists who lived in group settings or *communes*.

36. See Ellen Chesler, *Woman of Valor: Margaret Sanger and the Birth Control Movement in America* (New York: Simon & Schuster, 1992).

37. The Roman Catholic Church, which opposed the use of artificial contraception, was the most powerful exception. The church opposed the legalization of birth control in Connecticut and Massachusetts, but abandoned its position after *Griswold* while continuing to expect its own members to obey its doctrines. The church's position has not changed, but non-compliance among individual Catholics is even more common today than it was in the 1960s.

38. See *"Carey v. Population Services."*

39. See Judith A. Baer, *Women in American Law: The Struggle toward Equality from the New Deal to the Present*, 2nd ed. (New York: Holmes & Meier Publishers, Inc., 1996), p. 181. The rule never went into effect because a federal court granted an injunction against it. See *"New York v. Schweiker."*

40. See "Abortion and Public Assistance;" "Hyde Amendment"

41. See "Abortion and Parental Consent and Notification."

42. See "Gag Rule;" *"Rust v. Sullivan."*

43. See *"Planned Parenthood of Southeastern Pennsylvania v. Casey;"* "Undue Burden."

44. See "RU-486;" "Dilation and Extraction."

45. John Hart Ely, "The Wages of Crying Wolf: A Comment on *Roe v. Wade*," *Yale Law Journal* 82 (April 1973): 920-49, 923.

46. See, for example, "African-American Women," "Disabled Women," "Hispanic/Latina Women," "Native American Women," "Prisoners and Reproductive Rights," and "Sterilization Abuse."

47. Martha N. Beck, *Expecting Adam* (New York: Times Books, 1999), recounts such a situation. After tests reveal that her unborn child had Down's Syndrome, she and her hus-

band found themselves surrounded by health care professionals who expected them to terminate the pregnancy.

48. See "Adoption;" "Birth Mothers and Reproductive Rights;" "Child Custody."

49. See "Artificial Insemination."

50. See "Baby M;" *"Muñoz v. Haro;"* "Surrogate Motherhood."

51. See, for example, "Ectogenesis," *"In Vitro* Fertilization," and "Surrogate Motherhood."

52. See "Native American Women and Reproductive Rights."

53. *Muller v. Oregon*, 208 U.S. 412, 421 (1908).

54. 198 U.S. 45, 61 (1905).

55. 208 U.S. 412, 421-23. See *"Muller v. Oregon."*

56. See Judith A. Baer, *The Chains of Protection: The Judicial Response to Women's Labor Legislation* (Westport, Conn.: Greenwood Press, 1978); Theda Skocpol, *Protecting Soldiers and Mothers: The Political Origins of Social Policy in the United States* (Cambridge, Mass.: Belknap Press of Harvard University Press, 1992).

57. See Baer, *Lives,* note 32 above, p. 40.

58. See Katha Pollitt, "'Fetal Rights': A New Assault on Feminism," *The Nation* (March 26, 1990): 409-18.

59. See "Employment and Reproductive Rights;" "Fetal Protection;" *"International Union, United Auto Workers v. Johnson Controls;"* *"Secretary of Labor v. American Cyanamid;"* "Title VII, Civil Rights Act of 1964." The childbearing age policy is found in *Wright v. Olin Corporation*, 697 F. 2d 1172 (4th Circ. 1982).

60. See "Fetal Abuse;" "Fetal Rights;" "Forced Medical Treatment and Pregnancy;" "Lifestyle Restrictions and Pregnancy;" "Substance Abuse and Pregnancy."

61. See *"in re* A.C."

62. John A. Robertson, "The Right to Procreate and In Utero Fetal Therapy," *Journal of Legal Medicine* 3 (September 1982): 352.

63. Margery Shaw, "Constitutional Prospective Rights of the Fetus," *Journal of Legal Medicine* 5 (March 1984): 73.

64. See "Disability and Reproductive Rights;" "Lesbians and Reproductive Rights;" "Prisoners and Reproductive Rights;" "Teenage Pregnancy."

65. See, for example, "Abortion and Public Assistance;" "Class and Reproductive Rights;" "Family and Medical Leave Act;" "Hyde Amendment."

66. Baer, *Women*, p. 301.

67. See "Child Custody;" "Fathers' Rights."

68. See "Midwifery as a Reproductive Right."

69. See "Breast-feeding and the Law."

70. See, for example, *"California Federal Savings and Loan Association v. Guerra."*

A

ABORTION AND PARENTAL CONSENT AND NOTIFICATION. Parental consent laws require an unmarried minor, under the age of 18, to obtain the written consent of one or both parents before having an abortion. Parental notification laws require the abortion provider to inform one or both parents that their daughter intends to have an abortion. Parental consent laws (a term that will be used hereafter to refer to both consent and notification laws) currently exist on the books in 42 states, although the laws are enforced in only 32 of these states. In 2000, the New Jersey Supreme Court invalidated that state's law.

Anti-abortion groups have introduced parental consent laws as part of a piecemeal erosion strategy of women's reproductive rights since *Roe v. Wade* (1973) recognized a limited right to abortion. But even some proponents of reproductive choice argue that minors need their parents' input into their decisions. The arguments for and against parental consent were made clearly and cogently in *Planned Parenthood v. Danforth* (1976), the Supreme Court's first parental consent case, which struck down the law. "Minors," wrote Justice Harry Blackmun for the majority, "are protected by the Constitution and possess constitutional rights." While these rights are not coextensive with those of adults, the majority could not perceive "any significant state interest in conditioning an abortion on the consent of a parent." Justice John Paul Stevens, usually a supporter of abortion rights, dissented. "Whatever choice a pregnant young woman makes . . . the consequences of her decision may have a profound impact on her entire future life." A legislative decision to require that "the advice and moral support of a parent play a part in the decision making process is surely not irrational."

Anti-abortion groups did not give up after *Danforth*. They tried to work around the decision, while judicial attitudes gradually changed. In the 1980s and 1990s, as Reagan and Bush appointees replaced members of the *Roe* majority, *Danforth* suffered the same judicial fate as *Roe*. While neither ruling has been reversed, both have been weakened. The Court has never upheld an absolute parental veto. But after *Danforth*, state legislatures and the Court seemed to make efforts to meet each other halfway. *H.L. v. Matheson* (1981) upheld a parental notification requirement. None of the justices, then or since, indicated any awareness that the line between notification and consent is thin. Since minors have a general legal duty to obey their parents, a notification requirement is a serious threat to a young woman's autonomy.

The Court has also upheld laws which allow minors to seek a judicial bypass (*Planned Parenthood of Kansas City v. Ashcroft* (1983); *Hodgson v. Minnesota*, (1990); *Planned Parenthood of Southeastern Pennsylvania v. Casey* (1992). This procedure allows the young woman to request the permission of a judge, who must decide if she is mature enough to make the decision or if the abortion is in her best interests. The judicial bypass usually results in approval by the judge. However, the court procedure greatly increases the stress and anxiety of young women. Obstacles to a judicial bypass, such as inconvenient hours and location of courts that hear abortion petitions, tend to delay abortion, which in turn carries greater risk for the patient.

Public discourse on this issue reveals some discontinuities between rhetoric and reality. Many supporters of parental consent laws emphasize the fact that parental consent is generally required for minors' medical treatment. This is true as a rule, but relevant exceptions exist. The law protects the privacy of minors in areas of confidential health care, such as sexually transmitted diseases and drug abuse treatment. These protections eliminate parental consent in order to encourage minors to seek help. Seventeen states also allow minors to consent to pregnancy related medical care without parental input, but 13 of these exclude abortion from the services to which minors may consent.

The majority of young women (approximately 61 percent) who become pregnant do inform parents of their pregnancy and plans to seek an abortion, whether or not parental consent laws exist in their state. The laws do not seem to encourage more young women to confer with their parents about their pregnancies. In short, parental consent laws appear to be unnecessary. If a family relationship is unstable or uncommunicative, it is unlikely that the state can legislate stability and communication. The factors that foster communication are longstanding characteristics of the parent-child relationship, characteristics that cannot be modified by legislative actions. Additionally, since young women most often turn to their mothers when confiding in only one parent, the two-parent consent laws that exist in six states can be seen as an attempt to lessen the authority of young women and their mothers and enhance that of fathers.

These laws also have unintended consequences. First, minors travel to states without consent laws in order to have abortions. Second, young women might seek illegal or back-alley abortions. Many teenagers believe that they would use such desperate measures to deal with parental consent laws. Abuse may be another unintended consequence. In one study, 30 percent of minors who did not tell their parents had experienced previous family violence and were afraid of more violence or of being forced to leave home.

Anti-abortion groups that support parental consent laws claim to be acting in the best interests of young women and their families. However, the laws have harmful and unintended consequences to young women's health. Proponents of abortion rights who support these laws are actually playing into the hands of the anti-choice movement. Safe and legal abortion without restrictions and caring, communicative family relations are the best ways to protect young women.

SEE Abortion and Parental Involvement; *Bellotti v. Baird, I* and *II; H.L. v. Matheson; Hodgson v. Minnesota; Planned Parenthood of Central Missouri v. Danforth; Planned Parenthood of Kansas City v. Ashcroft; Planned Parenthood of Southeastern Pennsylvania v. Casey;* Youth and Reproductive Rights.

Further References. Patricia Donovan, "Judging Teenagers: How Minors Fare When They Seek Court-Authorized Abortions," *Family Planning Perspectives*, 15, 6 (1983): 259–267. M.D. Greenberger and K. Connor, "Parental Notice and Consent for Abortion: Out of Step with Family Law Principles and Policies," *Family Planning Perspectives*, 23, 1 (1991): 31-35. Stanley K. Henshaw and Kathryn Kost, "Parental Involvement in Minors' Abortion Decisions." *Family Planning Perspectives*, 24, 5 (1992): 196-207, 213. Jon F. Merz, Catherine A. Jackson, and Jacob A. Klerman, "A Review of Abortion Policy: Legality, Medicaid Funding, and Parental Involvement, 1967-1994, " *Women's Rights Law Reporter*, 17, #1 (1995): 1-61.

ADRIENNE BOUSIAN

ABORTION AND PARENTAL INVOLVEMENT. In the landmark case of *Bellotti v. Baird* (1979) (*Bellotti II*), the Supreme Court indicated that a state can require a minor to obtain parental consent for an abortion, if it provides her with an "alternative procedure," such as a confidential court hearing in which permission can be obtained without parental knowledge or involvement. Since this decision, a majority of states have enacted parental involvement laws. When faced with challenges, the Court has consistently upheld these laws as constitutional, thus making clear that a minor's fundamental right to choose abortion does not include the same degree of decisional autonomy that adult women have.

Bellotti II articulated traditional views about youth and an idealized view of the family. The plurality opinion emphasized the "vulnerability" of teens, their "inability to make critical decisions" and the "importance of the parental role in child rearing." This reasoning assumed that parental involvement would serve as a counterweight to youthful immaturity. By providing mature guidance and emotional support, parents would be able to protect their daughter from the consequences of an impulsive or uninformed decision. Committed to this singular vision of parental nurture and guidance, the justices failed to consider any reasons why a teen might choose not to involve her parents, other than the possibility that they would refuse consent. Another troubling feature of the opinion was that the Court ignored laws that give minors considerable autonomy with respect to other "sensitive" medical decisions, including those related to pregnancy.

Despite the defects of *Bellottti II*, a majority of states now have parental involvement laws that limit the autonomy of teens wishing to end an unwanted pregnancy. Proponents of these laws often express similar views about the immaturity of teens and the benevolence of parents. They assert that without the element of legal compulsion, teens would simply "blow-off" their parents as teens are wont to do, casually assuming that their parents would "flip out" or "kill them." Grounded in this vision, these laws are seen as necessary to ensure family communication.

The idea that disclosure should be legally compelled is problematic on many levels. To begin with, the majority of teens, even in states without a parental involvement law, do tell their parents about their abortion plans. Thus, the element of compulsion does not appear to increase rates of involvement. Instead, it simply forces young women who cannot tell their parents into the court system to seek judicial authorization for an abortion. This process is not only intrusive and frightening, but it also causes delay, thereby increasing the cost of the abortion. Moreover, the idea of compelling communication about such an intimate matter assumes that family closeness can be achieved by legislative fiat.

These views disregard the research which shows that teens who do not tell their parents about their abortion plans are likely to have very good reasons for the decision not to disclose. For instance, in-depth interviews with a small but representative group of minors in Massachusetts who sought (and obtained) judicial authorization for an abortion revealed that the non-disclosure decision is both multi-dimensional and well grounded in the realities of family life (Ehrlich, 2000). Far from being rebellious teens who casually disregarded their parents, these teens took the decision not to involve their parents very seriously.

The interviewed teens had multiple reasons for non-disclosure. The three most frequently given reasons were fear of a serious adverse parental reaction, concern for the parent, and concern that disclosure would damage the parent-child relationship. A number of the young women also feared that their parents would deny consent, thus effectively forcing them to have the baby. Other studies also support the importance of these reasons.

Supporters of parental involvement laws often discount teens' fear of parental reactions; statements like, "they'll kill me," are regarded as typical adolescent exaggeration. However, the teens who feared a serious adverse reaction had generally experienced a history of harsh parental treatment. Some had been subject to repeated physical abuse or kicked out of the house at young ages. For these teens, their fear was not a reflexive, unconsidered justification for avoiding parental input; it was rooted in the realities of their lives.

Other teens based their decision not on fear of their parents' reactions but on concern for their parents' well-being. Attuned to the difficulties and complexities of their parents' lives, they sought to shield their parents from the distress they anticipated disclosure would produce. The problems discussed by the teens include the often combined burdens of physical and/or mental illness, job and financial pressures, and marital difficulties. Describing, often in remarkable detail, how their parents were barely holding on, these young women recognized the frailty of their family systems. The situations confronted by these parents included recent release from a drug rehabilitation program and recurring bouts of destabilizing depression. Non-disclosure was rooted in a protective impulse—in a desire to safeguard rather than risk disrupting established patterns of family life.

Many young women feared that disclosure of their pregnancy and abortion plans would irreparably damage their relationship with their parents. They worried that their parents would never trust them again, would be deeply disappointed in them, would be deeply hurt, and/or that parental expectations would be dashed. For these minors, non-disclosure represented a desire to safeguard connection rather than risk its disruption. Far from dismissing their parents' concerns, these minors were motivated by a profound desire to preserve existing bonds.

It is, of course, possible that the minors' assessment of their parents' probable reactions was incorrect, and that the relationships would have withstood the impact of disclosure. However, the seriousness of the teens' concerns is made evident by the fact that they were willing to go through the burdensome and frightening process of seeking court authorization for an abortion rather than risk damaging their relationships with their parents. The willingness of these young women to entrust such an intimate decision to a robed stranger, closer in age to their parents than to them, underscores the weight both of their beliefs regarding the anticipated parental response and of the desire not to do harm.

Another indication of the seriousness and discernment of the minors' reasoning was the fact that they distinguished between their parents when discussing their reasons for non-disclosure. Rather than indiscriminately lumping mother and father together, the teens saw each parent as a distinct person, and saw their relationship with each parent as having its own dynamic. Thus, for example, a minor might have been concerned both with protecting her recently hospitalized mother from the news and with avoiding her father's anticipated anger. This careful delineation between parents and the corresponding differentiation of reasons for non-disclosure further challenges the image of the rebellious teen who is indifferent to her parents' feelings.

Also significant was the lack of communication about sexuality. Some of these young women who were interviewed had never spoken with a parent about sex; for others, the only communication had been negative, with parents conveying the message that sex is for "bad girls." In the few instances of open communication, conversations halted at the door of the minor's own sexuality. As studies make clear, this relational history shapes a teen's sense of whether she can discuss her abortion plans with a parent. Where there is no context for communication about intimate matters, teens may be unwilling to test the waters at such a critical juncture in their lives. Where parents have not discharged the responsibility of guiding their daughters into adulthood, it does not seem right that the law should reconstruct them as the saviors of their daughters' futures.

These young women who were interviewed were clear that at this time in their lives, they were not ready to embrace the demands of motherhood (or, for those who already were mothers, the demands of a second child). In making the decision to abort, they focused on their need to develop a meaningful future and on their present inability to provide a stable and secure life for a child.

Although they firmly asserted their autonomy, all of the minors drew on existing networks of social support as they made their abortion decision. These networks included at least one trusted adult. As studies suggest, these interactions serve as an important source of advice, support and information. Thus, although not involving their parents, these minors were not isolated in the decision-making process. While accepting ultimate responsibility for the decision and their futures, they nonetheless engaged with others whom they felt they could trust and rely upon for guidance and emotional support.

These interviews suggest a countervailing reality to that of the rebellious teen who casually dismisses her parents' input as unimportant. Situated in their own life histories, these young women made careful and well-considered decisions about why the risks of disclosure were too great, thus challenging the idea that the law can determine the borders of intimacy. In an ideal world, all young women would have parents they could turn to at a time of crisis in their lives. In turn, parents would respond in the wise and loving manner envisioned by the *Bellotti II* Court. It is unfortunate, though not unprecedented, that the Supreme Court's commitment to this ideal vision of parental nurture was not accompanied by awareness of the complex and sometimes ugly, even brutal, reality of daily family life.

SEE Abortion and Parental Consent and Notification; *Bellotti v. Baird II; H.L. v. Matheson; Hodgson v. Minnesota; Planned Parenthood of Kansas City v. Ashcroft; Planned Parenthood v. Casey;* Youth and Reproductive Rights.

Further References. Patricia Donovan, *Our Daughters' Decisions: The Conflict in State Law on Abortion and Other Issues* (New York, 1992). J. Shoshanna Ehrlich, "Minors as Medical Decision Makers: The Pretextual Reasoning of the Court in the Abortion Cases," *Michigan Journal of Gender and Law,* 7, #1 (2000): 65-106. Stanley K. Henshaw and Katherine Kost, "Parental Involvement in Minors' Abortion Decisions," *Family Planning Perspectives,* 24 (September/October 1992): 196-213. Gary B. Melton, ed., *Adolescent Abortion-Psychological and Legal Issues* (Lincoln, Neb. 1986).

J. SHOSHANNA EHRLICH

ABORTION AND POLITICAL CONFLICT. The issue of abortion has given rise to one of the most intense political conflicts in U.S. history, the prototypical "hot-button" issue. Positions are so polarized that activists on both sides of the debate disagree even about so fundamental a matter as what to call one another. The term "pro-choice" is usually applied to supporters of abortion rights, while opponents are called "pro-life." These are the labels the groups have given themselves. But pro-choice activists say that their opponents are not truly pro-life but anti-abortion or anti-choice, while pro-life adherents counter that "pro-choice" actually means "pro-abortion." These names are important in abortion conflicts because the way an issue is framed can affect the ways people respond to a political cause. For example, "pro-life" is a much more positive name and image than "anti-choice." So far, neither side has succeeded in renaming the other.

The abortion issue shows up almost everywhere in American politics: presidential nominating campaigns, political party platform statements, campaigns for federal, state, and local offices, debates about federal and state judicial selections, and controversies over everything from preventing teenage pregnancy and the spread of sexually transmitted diseases to funding for the United Nations. Dozens of bills introduced in the U.S. Congress have abortion riders (amendments) attached to them declaring that none of the money in this program may be spent to promote, encourage, or pay for abortions.

Pro-choice activists insist that abortions will never be eliminated. If they are made illegal again, or difficult to get, desperate women (especially the young, the poor, and women of color) will resort to illegal and often very dangerous methods to end their pregnancies. People of privilege, however, will be able to secure safe abortions, even if it is made illegal, as they did before *Roe v. Wade* (1973). Some legal activists, therefore, have posited an equal protection argument to protect legal abortion. "Equal justice under law" would strongly defend legal abortion, they assert, since it is a deeply valued principle in American law.

Equally forceful are the pro-life efforts to extend human rights under law to the fetus, or in their terms, "the pre-born." The Proposed Human Life Amendment to the U.S. Constitution is one such effort. Seeking to control and punish women for harming their fetuses when they use illegal drugs while pregnant is another inroad pro-life activists have established for treating a fetus like a child. The woman, then, becomes subject in some legal jurisdictions to child abuse statutes.

Activists' views on women's roles are central to conflicts over abortion. Pro-life adherents see women as life givers, nurturers and mothers, roles which are essential to women's nature. These roles are regarded as sacred, powerful, and female-affirming gifts. Pro-life activists assert that women are harmed by legal abortion. Pro-choice activists, on the other hand, regard the affirmation of the complex lives women lead and the preservation of individual rights to privacy, agency, autonomy, and choice as fundamental. Although pro-choice advocates do not denigrate motherhood, they do not romanticize it either. Recognizing the importance of motherhood, they believe each woman should be trusted to make her own reproductive decisions. The pro-choice position seeks to empower women to control their reproductive lives. These activists believe that the availability of safe, legal abortions is healthy for women. In addition to using legal channels and the established political process to affect abortion politics, some activists have resorted to civil disobedience. Dedicated pro-life adherents, led by a group that calls itself "Operation Rescue" (again, names matter; this label implies that there is a person who needs immediate help) staged noisy, disruptive, and newsworthy sit-ins, lie-ins, and blockades at various abortion clinics around the country. The purpose of these demonstrations is both to shut clinics down, even if only for a few hours, and to highlight the pro-life cause and demonstrate the intensity of the demonstrators' beliefs.

From the pro-life point of view, these actions save babies who might have been aborted while the clinic was shut down during their demonstrations. But to pro-choice activists, these demonstrations interfere with the clinics' legal right to perform abortions, the patients' legal right to obtain them, and everyone's right to safe entry and exit from the facilities. Abortion rights advocates have established clinic escort services, whereby volunteers help girls or women seeking abortions (and other patients) and their companions safely enter and leave clinics. Interest group activity by pro-choice activists helped safeguard clinic access in another way by getting Congress to pass the Freedom of Access to Clinics Entrances Act (FACE) in 1994. FACE regulates the distance protesters must keep from clinic patients and staff and tries to balance the free speech rights of the pro-life protesters with the reproductive freedoms of clinic patients and staff. FACE was challenged in the federal courts and found to be constitutional.

Abortion stirs up such heated emotions for some people that they have even resorted to violence and murder. Several clinic workers have been murdered by pro-life activists. Some were shot when entering or exiting their clinics. A security guard was killed and a nurse severely injured and maimed by a bomb at a clinic in Birmingham, Alabama. Late in 1998, a doctor in upstate New York was murdered by a shot fired through his kitchen window. This case has not been solved, but several murderers—like Paul Hill, who shot clinic personnel in Florida—have been tried and convicted. Since Hill and others like him are totally convinced that abortion itself is murder, they justify their actions as a lesser evil. They accept punishment for their crimes, often comparing themselves to Martin Luther King and other heroes of civil disobedience. Mainstream pro-life organizations and spokespersons, however, do not officially support these violent actions, which can be counterproductive for abortion rights opponents. In fact, the violence often taints the pro-life cause for many people.

Political conflict over abortion is a constant in American politics and an illustration of the salience of reproductive issues to people. The politics of abortion also echo our societal battles about women's roles, cultural mores about sexuality, and just boundaries for state monitoring and control of women's bodies when establishing policies on human reproduction.

SEE Abortion and Political Rhetoric; Abortion and Public Opinion; Abortion Providers and Violence; Human Life Bill/Amendment; Operation Rescue; *Roe v. Wade.*

Further References. Mark A. Graber, *Rethinking Abortion: Equal Choice, the Constitution, and Reproductive Politics* (Princeton, N.J., 1996). Kristin Luker, *Abortion and the Politics of Motherhood* (Berkeley, Calif., 1984). Eileen L. McDonagh, *Breaking the Abortion Deadlock: From Choice to Consent* (New York, 1996). Laura R. Woliver, "Social Movements and Abortion Law," in Anne N. Costain and Andrew S. McFarland, eds., *Social Movements and American Institutions* (Lanham, Md., 1998).

LAURA R. WOLIVER

ABORTION AND POLITICAL RHETORIC. The rhetoric used by activists in the abortion debate demonstrates how deeply contested the issue of abortion has become in U.S. culture. Each side rejects the other's terminology while insisting—so far successfully—on naming itself. Opponents of legalized abortion call themselves "pro-life" and their adversaries "pro-abortion;" supporters of abortion rights speak of "pro-choice" and "anti-choice," or simply "antis." Each side seeks to ally itself with moral values held by the general public, offering judgments about what its opponent's value system threatens. Pro-choice advocates appeal to the tenets of liberal individualism, depicting the anti-abortion movement as a threat to self-realization, sexual freedom, and bodily integrity, especially for women. Anti-abortion activists predict the destruction of the traditional family unit by selfish or misguided women and by profit-mongering doctors and clinic workers.

The association between anti-abortion rhetoric and traditional family values has a long history. The tactic of accusing aborting women of neglecting their God-given calling as mothers originated when abortion was first politicized in the mid-1800s in the United States by physicians. Early anti-abortion rhetoric was much more explicitly patriarchal and male supremacist than that of contemporary anti-abortion rhetoric. For example, "abortion represents a threat to male authority and the 'traditional role' of women; abortion is a symbol of uncontrolled female sexuality and an 'unnatural' act. Above all, the aborting woman is selfish and self-indulgent." In 1871, the American Medical Association's Committee on Criminal Abortion wrote that a woman who terminates her pregnancy "becomes unmindful of the course marked out for her by Providence. . . . She yields to the pleasures—but shrinks from the pains and responsibilities of maternity" (Joffe, 1995: 29).

Abortion opponents have supplemented such rhetoric with new rhetorical strategies that take full advantage of technological innovation. With the popularization of sonography and of high-tech enhanced medical photography techniques (like those employed in Lennart Nilsson's film, *The Miracle of Life*), embryonic and fetal images have become ubiquitous; abortion rights opponents take advantage of this technology in their quest to idealize the fetus. They use graphic tactics like the juxtaposition or alteration of pictures of fetuses with pictures of live babies to stress the similarities between them and to convey the idea that the fetus is literally a baby. This relatively recent fetal fetish means that women are increasingly absent from anti-abortion visual rhetoric. Some experts on rhetoric and communication believe that the more accustomed people become to this manner of seeing fetuses, the less likely they will be to notice the absence of women.

Pro-choice rhetoric and representations, in contrast, are legalistic and woman-centered. They follow the lead of the Supreme Court in *Roe v. Wade*, defining the right to abortion as a right to privacy and declaring the question of when life begins unanswerable. Pro-choice activists focus on the gravity of rights and meaning of personhood for women. Consistently with this focus, both abortion law and pro-choice rhetoric are vague about the issue of viability. Pro-choice rhetoric draws on both liberalism and capitalism. It portrays women as individual self-owners entitled to control over our bodies. If I "own" my body, it is mine; anything within it counts as my property. In the words of one pro-choice scholar, "Pregnant women are not merely ingenious containers for growing babies. . . . It demeans motherhood to conflate it with pregnancy in this way. The ultimate corollary of fetal personhood is nothing other than forced motherhood" (Hadley, 1996: 69).

Much rhetorical energy on both sides of the abortion debate is devoted to responses to the opposition. These responses often consist of appeals to the values invoked by the other side. Far from rejecting liberal individualism outright, anti-abortion activists strive to identify themselves as the authentic liberal individualists. They compare their efforts to those of civil rights activists and Holocaust resisters, and employ vivid imagery of themselves as "warriors" employed in just and justifiable battle. For its part, pro-choice rhetoric endorses motherhood as a *chosen* activity. The decision to abort serves as testimony to how seriously women take motherhood. As one physician wrote, "I am an abortion practitioner because of my utmost respect for motherhood, which I refuse to believe is punishment for a screw. I do what I do because I am convinced that being a mother is the hardest job there is" (Karlin, 1998: 287).

Some responses to the opposition consist not of claiming to embody its values but of the opposite rhetorical device: distinguishing oneself from one's opponents. For example, supporters of abortion rights have generally striven to separate their language from that of the opposition and thereby neutralize anti-abortion activists' efforts. Staff members in abortion clinics commonly use clinical terms like, "the pregnancy," "the tissue," "the products of conception," and most explicit, "fetal tissue" in their interactions with clients, even when clients use the word "baby." This kind of unemotional, sanitized language is not always an effective response to anti-abortion rhetoric. The current debate over "intact D&E" (dilation and evacuation), demonstrates how sensational rhetoric introduced by a reactionary group easily slides into public parlance, edging out pro-choice activists' deliberately unprovocative language. This procedure, a rarely used technique for abortion in late pregnancy, has been successfully stigmatized by abortion opponents, who have dubbed it "partial birth abortion."

The acceptance of this term in everyday usage represents an important rhetorical victory for the anti-abortion movement, but not its most important victory. The very term "pro-life" puts the pro-choice side on the defensive: how can one be the opposite? The personalization of the fetus has also proved effective. The anti-abortion movement has the graphic images and the emotional appeal, while the pro-choice side must fall back on abstractions. Even when pro-choice activists use images of women killed by back-alley abortions, adult images do not have the same impact as those identified with babies. Many pro-choice activists believe that the opposition has succeeded in stigmatizing abortion and stifling open discussion of it. People might talk about abortion as a disembodied political or moral dilemma, but they seldom discuss *having* actual abortions. To talk frankly about abortion in this cultural climate is to profane pregnancy and to shame women. Recent poll data indicating that an overall commitment to abortion rights has declined in the 1990s provides some support for this perception.

Recent medical advances have the potential to change the course of the abortion debate. The development of new forms of abortion, in which no instruments are used, no doctor acts on a woman's body, and the abortion process cannot be distinguished from a miscarriage, presents a challenge to both anti-abortion and pro-choice factions. New medical methods of early abortion—particularly the drug mifepristone, a progesterone-inhibitor, commonly known by its French industry name, RU-486—are offered by a number of clinics in the U.S. Research conducted during the U.S. clinical trials of mifepristone suggests that women using medical abortion may experience it as more natural than a surgical abortion: more like a miscarriage, and, therefore, less of a moral offense. Anti-abortion activists call mifepristone "the death pill" or "chemical warfare on the unborn." Their vociferous opposition to medical abortion indicates that they fear it could dilute the persuasiveness of their rhetoric. The availability of medical abortion would also make it much more difficult for anti-abortionists to identify providers and aborting women. While anti-abortion advocates delayed the availability of mifepristone in the United States, the Food and Drug Administration gave final marketing approval in September 2000. Its eventual appearance on the pharmaceutical market, which is now inevitable, may transform the entire abortion debate as dramatically as fetal imagery did.

SEE Abortion as a Reproductive Right; Abortion and Political Conflict; Dilation and Extraction; *Roe v. Wade*; RU-486.

Further References. Janet Hadley, *Abortion: Between Freedom and Necessity* (Philadelphia, 1996). Carole Joffe, *Doctors of Conscience: The Struggle to Provide Abortion before and after* Roe v. Wade (Boston, 1995). E. Ann Kaplan, "Look Who's Talking, Indeed: Fetal Images in Recent North American Visual Culture," in Evelyn Nakano Glenn, Grace Change, and Linda Rennie Forcey, eds., *Mothering: Ideology, Experience, and Agency* (New York, 1994), 121-137. Elizabeth Karlin, "'We Called it Kindness:' Establishing a Feminist Abortion Practice," in Rickie Solinger, ed., *Abortion Wars: A Half Century of Struggle, 1950-2000* (Berkeley, Calif., 1998), 273-289. Wendy Simonds, *Abortion at Work: Ideology and Practice in a Feminist Clinic* (New Brunswick, N.J., 1996).

WENDY SIMONDS

ABORTION AND PUBLIC ASSISTANCE. Supporters of reproductive rights and women's rights welcomed *Roe v. Wade* (1973), which recognized a woman's constitutional right to terminate a pregnancy, as a major victory. Since *Roe*, the right to life movement has worked diligently to weaken the impact of the decision. Anti-abortion activists have pressured Congress and state legislatures to adopt counter-measures to *Roe* to set direct and indirect limits on women's right to choose to terminate a pregnancy, and have challenged the scope of abortion rights in the courts. While the pro-life movement has failed to get *Roe* reversed, a human life bill or amendment enacted, or an absolute parental veto over a minor's abortion established, it has succeeded in narrowing women's right to choose and limiting their access to safe, legal abortion. The passage of state and federal laws prohibiting the use of public funds for abortion is one of the greatest victories of the anti-abortion movement. The exclusion of abortions from Medicaid coverage has been a primary goal of the pro-life movement virtually since *Roe* was decided. This attack on the rights of women who receive public assistance, and depend on Medicaid for their health care, reflected the political reality that the poor are less likely than the affluent to organize to defend their rights. Since most middle class women did not feel threatened by restrictions on public funding for abortions, organized opposition to pro-life efforts was slow in materialize. Missouri and Pennsylvania banned the use of state Medicaid funds for abortions within months after *Roe*. (The federal government and the states share the cost of Medicaid). In 1976, Congress passed the first Hyde Amendment. Its sponsor, Representative Henry Hyde (R—Ill). has introduced a restrictive amendment every year since 1974. The 1976 amendment was attached to the appropriations bill for the Department of Health, Education and Welfare and the Department of Labor. This version of the Hyde Amendment banned the use of federal Medicaid funds for abortions, except for women whose lives would be endangered if they carried a fetus to term. The scope of the restriction has varied over the years. At present (2000), a Medicaid recipient is covered for abortion services if her life is endangered by the pregnancy or if she is a victim of rape or incest.

In 1977, the Supreme Court upheld state prohibitions on public assistance for abortions (*Beal v. Doe; Maher v. Roe*). Over angry dissents by Justices William Brennan, Thurgood Marshall, and Harry Blackmun, the majority insisted that these restrictions did not deny equal protection to women dependent on Medicaid, nor were they unreasonable (even though the ban on abortions forced the states to fund childbirth, which is more expensive). *Harris v. McRae* (1980) upheld the Hyde Amendment. Since 1977, most jurisdictions have limited the availability of funded abortions to public assistance recipients. (New York and the District of Columbia are significant exceptions). Twenty states use their own funds to pay for abortions for women who are Medicaid recipients. In 30 states, there is no Medicaid funding for any abortions. Coverage is severely limited even under the exceptions to the ban. In 1992, for example, Minnesota funded abortions for seven victims of rape or incest, Wisconsin for six, and Pennsylvania and Wyoming for none.

The Supreme Court's increased receptivity to restrictions on abortion, indicated by such rulings as *Webster v. Reproductive Health Services* (1989) and *Planned Parenthood v. Casey* (1992), suggests that it is unlikely to revisit the issue of public assistance any time soon. *Webster* upheld a law banning abortions on state property, while *Casey* gave the green light to any restrictions that did not place an "undue burden" on the exercise of the right to abortion. The Hyde Amendment continues to enjoy broad-based, bipartisan support in Congress. President Clinton, who believes that abortion should be "safe, legal, and rare," has never threatened to veto any version of the amendment. The three branches of the national government have thus made it more difficult for women, especially poor women, to choose abortion as an alternative to carrying a fetus to term.

Legal restrictions have been reinforced by the direct actions of right-to-life groups. Freestanding women's health centers that provide a wide range of health services to women, including abortion services, have been the focal point of demonstrations and violence. Physicians who provide abortion services have become the targets of militant activists; some providers have been attacked and killed. The result of this intimidation and terror is palpable. In 1975, 93 percent of U.S. medical schools offered training in abortion techniques to obstetrics residents and 26 percent of the programs required this training. In 1992, one third of these schools were not providing any abortion training, even when residents requested it, and only 12 percent required this training. By 1992, only 18 percent of obstetricians performed abortions and only 7 percent of rural counties had abortion providers. Unlike the Medicaid restrictions, these obstacles affect all women. However, their impact is especially severe on poor women, who often lack the resources to seek out a physician who will provide abortion services. Like minors, women living in rural areas, and women who passed the first trimester of pregnancy, economically disadvantaged women have great difficulty exercising their constitutional right to choice. On paper, *Roe v. Wade* granted all women the right to choose abortion; in reality, free choice is restricted to women older than 18 who live in urban areas where clinics have resisted pressure from anti-choice protestors and who have health insurance plans that fund elective abortions.

SEE *Beal v. Doe* et al.; Class and Reproductive Rights; *Harris v. McRae*; Hyde Amendment; *Planned Parenthood of Southeastern Pennsylvania v. Casey;* Violence Against Abortion Providers; *Webster v. Reproductive Health Services.*

Further References. Amy Goldstein, "Abortions: Still Legal but Less Available," *Washington Post Weekly Edition* (30 Jan.–5 Feb. 1995): 32. Mira Weinstein, "On 25th Anniversary of *Roe v. Wade*, NOW Asks 'Who Still Has a Choice?'" *NOW Times* (Jan. 1998), http://www.now.org.

MARIAN LIEF PALLEY

ABORTION AND PUBLIC OPINION. Access to legal abortion has been recognized as a constitutionally guaranteed right since *Roe v. Wade* was decided in 1973. In theory, therefore, abortion should be like all constitutional rights: people should be able to make the choice no matter what other people think about it. In reality, however, distribution of public opinion on the issue is perhaps the most important predictor of the availability of abortion services in particular states. Moreover, attitudes toward abortion have become increasingly important in determining the vote choices and partisan identifications of U.S. voters since the Reagan administration.

The distribution of abortion attitudes has been relatively stable since 1973, albeit with some slight movement in the "pro-life" direction among whites since the mid-1980s. Approximately 25 percent of the U.S. population can be characterized as "pro-choice;" they favor virtually no restrictions on a woman's right to terminate a pregnancy intentionally. Conversely, about 10 percent of Americans can be described as "pro-life." They believe that abortion should never be legal under any circumstances, or that abortion should be used only to save the life of the mother. The balance of the population might be described as a "situationalist majority;" they favor legal abortion in some situations, but not others. About 80 percent of Americans favor legal abortion for "physical" or "traumatic" reasons (for example, rape, incest, fetal defect, or threat to the mother's health) while about half favor legal abortion for "elective" or "non-medical" reasons, such as economics or marital status.

Abortion attitudes cut across most demographic characteristics in the United States. Thus, there exist only very small differences defined by gender, race, region, or level of education. One exception seems to be age, which exhibits a curvilinear relationship with abortion attitudes. In general, younger citizens are more permissive of legal abortion than are older ones, although the youngest cohorts in the U.S. population (those who came of voting age during or after the Reagan administration) are somewhat more "pro-life" than their immediate elders. The reasons for this age difference are not clear at this point.

Religion is by far the strongest predictor of abortion attitudes. This relationship holds for both religious affiliation and intensity of religious commitment. Evangelical Protestants and Roman Catholics are somewhat more pro-life than the rest of the U.S. population, while Jews and those without religious affiliation are the most pro-choice. Across all religious groups, frequent church attenders hold more restrictive abortion attitudes than less religiously observant Americans.

Some interesting contextual effects exist with respect to the relationship between Roman Catholicism and abortion attitudes. In general, Catholics are slightly more pro-life than the average U.S. citizen. However, non-Catholics appear to be more pro-choice in states in which Roman Catholics are quite numerous. Apparently, a strong Catholic presence at the state level occasions a pro-choice counter-mobilization. There appears to be no equivalent effect for evangelical Protestants.

Somewhat surprisingly, at the level of mass opinion, attitudes about feminism and the social roles of women appear to make no independent contribution to attitudes about abortion. While there exist moderately strong bivariate relationships between abortion attitudes and feminism, these patterns virtually disappear when controls for intensity of religious commitment are imposed. Thus, although elite-level discourse makes a connection between abortion rights and gender roles very explicit, any such relationship at the mass level appears to be spurious.

SEE Abortion and Political Conflict; Abortion and Political Rhetoric; Religion and Reproductive Rights.

Further References. Greg D. Adams, "Abortion: Evidence of Issue Evolution," *American Journal of Political Science*, 41 (July 1997): 718-737. Elizabeth Adell Cook, Ted G. Jelen, and Clyde Wilcox, *Between Two Absolutes: Public Opinion and the Politics of Abortion* (Boulder, Colo., 1992). Robert E. O' Connor and Michael B. Berkman, "Religious Determinants of State Abortion Policy," *Social*

Science Quarterly, 76 (June 1995): 447-459. Matthew E. Wetstein, *Abortion Rates in the United States: The Influence of Opinion and Policy* (Albany, N.Y., 1996).

TED G. JELEN

ABORTION AS A REPRODUCTIVE RIGHT. *Roe v. Wade* (1973) established a constitutional right to abortion. The Supreme Court ruled that the Fourteenth Amendment's Due Process right to privacy was "broad enough to encompass a woman's decision whether or not to terminate her pregnancy" without interference from the state. This ruling struck down at least 46 state laws. However, *Roe* also established that a woman's privacy right to choose an abortion "is not unqualified and must be considered against . . . [the state's] important and legitimate interest in protecting the potentiality of human life." This state interest is present throughout pregnancy, "grows in substantiality as the woman approaches term," and becomes 'compelling'" at viability (the end of the second trimester). After viability, the state might protect the fetus by prohibiting abortions, unless a woman's health or life is in danger.

Most abortion decisions since *Roe* have significantly narrowed the scope of the right. In 1977 and 1980, the Court made it clear that the right to an abortion did not entail the right of access to the procedure. *Beal v. Doe* and *Harris v. McRae* upheld state and federal laws prohibiting the use of public funds and facilities for abortions. Although a woman has a constitutional right to an abortion for any reason prior to fetal viability, in effect the state may protect the fetus from the moment of conception by prohibiting the use of public resources for abortion services, even when a medically abnormal pregnancy threatens an indigent woman with severe health damage. Later rulings, culminating in *Planned Parenthood v. Casey* (1992), have upheld numerous restrictive regulations, including mandatory 24-hour waiting periods, informed consent requirements, and parental consent regulations. The plurality opinion in *Casey* rejected *Roe*'s trimester framework and "compelling interest" standard in favor of "accommodating . . . the State's profound interest in potential life" *throughout pregnancy*. *Casey* held in effect that discouraging abortion is a legitimate governmental purpose; restrictions are legitimate unless they place an undue burden on a woman's right to choose an abortion.

Although the Court has upheld *Roe*'s guarantee of a constitutional right to choose an abortion, rulings like these, sustaining restrictions on access to abortion services, severely limit women's ability to exercise these rights. Women who are young or poor (or both) are especially vulnerable to these restrictions—and racial minorities are disproportionately numbered among the poor. Many critics find the *Roe* framework, as refined in later decisions, an inadequate doctrinal basis for women's reproductive rights. Scholars and activists have sought to fashion better defenses of abortion rights.

Pro-choice advocates have relied on equal protection and suspect classification analysis to refute the arguments of *McRae* and *Casey*. The Equal Protection Clause of the Fourteenth Amendment, as interpreted, requires courts to apply strict scrutiny to legislation that invokes a suspect classification, such as race, and intermediate scrutiny to legislation that invokes a quasi-suspect classification, such as sex. Proponents of the equal protection approach to abortion rights maintain that the failure of state policies to provide abortions is a form of unconstitutional sex discrimination against pregnant women.

However, this creative effort to use the Supreme Court's own general doctrine against its particular conclusions has run up against another established constitutional principle. *Geduldig v. Aiello* (1974) declared that discrimination on the basis of pregnancy is *not* necessarily sex discrimination. The Court reasoned there that pregnancy classifies people not into two groups distinguished by sex, namely, men and women, but rather into two groups distinguished by pregnancy, pregnant and nonpregnant persons. While the first category contains only women, the second category contains both men and women. Therefore, the state does not necessarily engage in sex discrimination when it treats pregnant women differently from other people. Discrimination on the basis of pregnancy does not necessarily involve even quasi-suspect classification. As a result, the Court does not apply even intermediate scrutiny, let alone strict scrutiny, to prohibitions against the public funding of abortions. These prohibitions survive as long as they bear a rational relationship to some legitimate governmental purpose.

The foregoing approach does not exhaust the equal protection arguments for abortion rights. Another promising avenue of equal protection analysis has yet to be applied to abortion rights and has not been tested in court, but has real potential as an innovative doctrine. This approach invokes fundamental rights analysis in relation to a woman's right to state protection of her bodily integrity and liberty to the same extent that the state provides such protection to others. This analysis focuses on a woman's right to consent to what happens to her body during pregnancy. Building upon the path-breaking work of moral philosopher Judith Jarvis Thomson and legal scholar Donald Regan, this thesis claims that a woman who does not consent to pregnancy is seriously harmed by it, even when a pregnancy is medically normal. Not only does a woman have a right to protect herself from the harm of a nonconsensual pregnancy, but that harm situates her with others who suffer harm to their bodily integrity and liberty. Although the Due Process Clause does not obligate the state to act to stop harm, the Equal Protection Clause does obligate the state to treat similarly situated people in a similar way when their fundamental rights, such as bodily integrity and liberty, are involved. The state does act to protect people from harm to their bodily integrity and liberty, by making violence criminal and allowing people to recover civil damages for physical harm. Therefore, according to this argument, a woman suffering the harm of a nonconsensual pregnancy has a right to state assistance to aid her in terminating the nonconsensual pregnancy. Failure to provide this assistance violates the Equal Protection Clause.

The fundamental rights approach is designed to fortify *Roe* by securing for women not only the constitutional right to choose an abortion, but also the constitutional right to state assistance in obtaining one. While it has little chance of finding favor with the present Supreme Court or the federal judiciary, the undergraduates and law students who are learning it now will become the judges of the future.

SEE Abortion and Public Assistance; *Beal v. Doe* et al.; Class and Reproductive Rights; *Geduldig v. Aiello*; *Harris v. McRae*; Hyde Amendment; Abortion and Parental Consent and Notification; *Planned Parenthood of Central Missouri v. Danforth*; *Planned Parenthood of Southeastern Pennsylvania v. Casey*; *Roe v. Wade*.

Further References. David H. Gans, "Stereotyping and Difference: *Planned Parenthood v. Casey* and the Future of Sex Discrimination Law," *Yale Law Journal*, 104 (May 1995): 1875-1906. Eileen L. McDonagh, "My Body, My Consent: Securing the Constitutional Right to Abortion Funding," *Albany Law Review*, 62, #3 (1999): 1057-1118. Dorothy E. Roberts, *Killing the Black Body: Race, Reproduction, and the Meaning of Liberty* (New York, 1999). Robin West, *Progressive Constitutionalism: Reconstructing the Fourteenth Amendment* (Durham, N.C., 1994).

EILEEN L. McDONAGH

ABORTION AND SPOUSAL CONSENT. "Spousal consent" laws require that a married woman receive her husband's consent before obtaining an abortion. Supporters of these laws argue that a husband has a right, independent of a woman, to procreate. Therefore, any decision to terminate the pregnancy should be jointly made. Spousal consent advocates cite Supreme Court cases such as *Stanley v. Illinois* (1972) and *Skinner v. Oklahoma* (1942), which have recognized a man's constitutional right to father children and associate with his offspring, and *Griswold v. Connecticut* (1965), which recognizes the importance of the marital relationship. Opponents, however, view these laws as a means of depriving married women of their independent right of privacy by giving husbands an absolute veto. They regard spousal consent laws as a throwback to early patriarchal legislation that made women subject to their husbands and deprived wives of independent rights to own property, work outside the home, or enter into contracts.

Spousal consent became an issue after the Supreme Court legalized abortion in *Roe v. Wade* (1973). In *Planned Parenthood v. Danforth* (1976) the Court held unconstitutional a Missouri law mandating spousal consent for a first trimester abortion. The Court ruled that. since the government had no power to prohibit early abortions, it could not delegate that power to a third party. While the Court recognized the parental rights of fathers and the legitimate concerns of husbands in their wives' pregnancies, it was the woman who bore the burden of carrying and delivering the child; therefore, the decision must be hers. The Court has never retreated from this position. In fact, *Planned Parenthood v. Casey* (1992) went even further, striking down a Pennsylvania law requiring spousal notification.

SEE Abortion and Parental Consent and Notification; *Griswold v. Connecticut*; *Planned Parenthood of Central Missouri v. Danforth*; *Planned Parenthood of Southeastern Pennsylvania v. Casey*; *Roe v. Wade; Skinner v. Oklahoma*.

Further References. Barbara Hinkson Craig and David M. O'Brien, *Abortion and American Politics* (Chatham, N.J., 1993). Charles A. Johnson and Jon R. Bond, "Coercive and Noncoercive Abortion Deterrence Policies: A Comparative State Analysis," *Law and Policy Quarterly* 2 (January 1980): 106-128.

MICHAEL W. BOWERS

ABORTION PROVIDERS AND VIOLENCE. Violence against abortion providers is a tactic used by abortion foes to inhibit access to safe and legal abortions. After efforts to pass a constitutional amendment to overrule *Roe v. Wade* failed, the National Right to Life Committee held a seminar at its 1976 annual meeting entitled "How to Disrupt an Abortion Clinic." This seminar quickly produced results and instigated the adoption of a wide variety of tactics to disrupt the day-to-day business of abortion clinics through sit-ins, picketing, bomb threats, stink bombs, and lock tampering. It was but a short jump from these tactics to outright violence directed both at the clinics themselves and providers. Pro-life extremists hoped that fear of violence would keep potential clients from seeking abortions and discourage providers from performing them.

The first clinic bombing occurred in 1977. By 1980, the Pro-Life Action League, headed by Joseph Scheidler, was advocating violence against abortion providers as part of its strategy to stop abortions. Eight clinics were bombed between 1977 and 1983. The following year, after the right-to life movement's defeat in *Akron v. Akron Center for Reproductive Health* (1983), the number of reported clinic bombings skyrocketed to 18, beginning a cycle of violence against abortion providers. Negative court reactions seemed to fuel frustration on the far right, and more clinics were bombed. However, partial victories for the anti-choice movement like *Webster v. Reproductive Health Services* (1989) and *Planned Parenthood v. Casey* (1992) did not reduce the incidence of violence. The federal government did little to stop clinic violence throughout the Republican, anti-abortion Reagan and Bush administrations (1981-1993). Since the federal government was not helping women and providers exercise their constitutional rights, the Fund for the Feminist Majority created the National Clinic Defense Project to help keep open clinics threatened by anti-abortion blockades and violence.

Anti-choice extremists redoubled their efforts after the right-to-life community's next major political defeat: the election of the first pro-choice president, Bill Clinton, in 1992. All forms of violence and harassment against clinics increased as groups became more desperate. A rash of fire bombings in February 1993 prompted pro-choice advocates in Congress to urge consideration of legislation to deter clinic violence. In March, violence escalated into murder for the first time. The fatal shooting of Dr. David Gunn outside a clinic in Pensacola, Florida caused the Clinton administration to throw its support behind federal legislation to end clinic violence. Another provider was killed in August, while Congress was debating this legislation. The assailants in both cases were well-known right-to-life activists. In response to this continued violence against abortion providers and clinics, Congress passed the Freedom of Access to Clinic Entrances

Act (FACE) in May 1994. FACE forbids the use of "force, threat of force or physical obstruction" by anyone attempting to prevent someone from providing or receiving any kind of reproductive health services. It also gives federal courts the power to order injunctive relief and damages.

Since passage of this law, buttressed by court decisions and several jury awards against right-to-life groups, clinic blockades and some other types of violence have been decreasing. But this legislation has not prevented several clinic bombings and the killing of yet another provider, Dr. Barnett Slepian, in 1998. The slow but steady decline in the number of abortion providers in the United States in the past several years indicates that clinic violence may continue to be an effective means of thwarting women in the exercise of their constitutional rights.

SEE Abortion and Political Conflict; Abortion and Public Opinion; Human Life Bill/Human Life Amendment; *Madsen v. Women's Heath Center, Inc.*; Operation Rescue; *Roe v. Wade.*

Further References. Dallas A. Blanchard, *The Anti-Abortion Movement and the Rise of the Religious Right: From Polite to Fiery Protest* (New York, 1994). Feminist Majority Foundation, *1997 Clinic Violence Survey Report: A Five Year Analysis of Anti-Abortion Violence Trends.* Karen O'Connor, *No Neutral Ground: Abortion Politics in an Age of Absolutes* (Boulder, Colo., 1996).

KAREN O'CONNOR

ABORTION SELF-HELP is as old as unwanted pregnancy and folk medicine. Common methods of self-induced abortion have included the ingestion of substances such as drugs and herbs and the introduction of foreign bodies into the uterus—in other words, versions of the procedures used in medical abortions to make the uterus contract and expel the fetus. When medical abortion is illegal or inaccessible, self-induced abortion is an attractive alternative to underground abortion. It is less expensive and more difficult to police. Nonprofessionals can learn to perform abortions if someone teaches them, just as they can learn to carry out other clinical procedures. As far as safety is concerned, self-abortion has been used effectively and without the complications, such as hemorrhaging or infection, that can follow. However, the historical record of death and injury to women from self-induced abortion proves that it is less safe than medical abortion—though not necessarily less safe than an illegal abortion performed by another person. Safe, legal and available clinical abortion reduces the demand for amateur abortion.

An abortion self-help movement began in the United States in the early 1960s as a political strategy to circumvent the laws prohibiting elective abortion. In California, Patricia Maginnis, later joined by Rowena Gurner and Lana Clarke Phelan, openly challenged the state's anti-abortion laws by distributing abortion information. By 1968, their civil disobedience extended to inviting police officers to classes teaching women how to induce abortion using the "digital method" (that is, their fingers). In Chicago, the Jane project, realizing that underground abortionists had no more skill or training than they, learned how to do abortions themselves.

Carol Downer, who met Phelan through a local chapter of the National Organization for Women, incorporated self-help abortion into general concern for women's health and ultimately the founding of women's health clinics. Downer taught women menstrual extraction using the Karman cannula, then Lorraine Rothman's improvement, the Del-Em. This simple bottle and tubing device empties the uterus, shortening menstrual cycles or ending an early pregnancy. In 1971, Downer and Rothman toured the country demonstrating gynecological self-exams, selling speculums, and showing a film in which a pregnant woman aborted herself by performing menstrual extraction. They left behind covert groups of women planning self-help projects and learning menstrual extraction.

By that time, momentum was building for the liberalization of abortion laws. Several states legalized abortion in the early 1970s. With *Roe v. Wade* (1973), self-help groups turned their attention to establishing clinics to provide abortions and other health services. Self-help gynecology became a tool for women's general health and well-being, and a part of the consciousness-raising activities that fueled the women's movement in the 1970s. While self-help abortion never saw wide implementation, the idea of women controlling their own medical care, and the organizing tool of self-help demonstrations, contributed to ending the ban on abortion in the United States and breaking the stranglehold of the medical establishment on women's health.

SEE Artificial Insemination; Birth Control and African-American Women; Jane (collective).

Further References. Ninia Baehr, *Abortion without Apology: A Radical History for the 1990s* (Boston, 1990). Jo Freeman, *The Politics of Women's Liberation: A Case Study of an Emerging Women's Movement* (New York, 1975). Judith Hole and Ellen Levine, *Rebirth of Feminism* (New York, 1971). Linda Yanney, "The Practical Revolution: An Oral History of the Iowa City Feminist Community, 1965-1975" (Iowa City, 1991).

LINDA J. YANNEY

A.C. SEE *In re* (A.C.)

ADOPTION. As a reproductive rights issue, child adoption presents a paradox. It extends the definition of reproduction beyond biology, encompassing social means of acquiring children and challenging the view that blood is thicker than water. Yet the matching paradigm that has governed adoption throughout most of the twentieth century stipulates that adults who raise children born to others should look, feel, and behave as if they were the children's biological parents. By making similarity the most salient predictor of love and belonging, matching adoptive parents with their adopted children reinforces the cultural superiority of biogenetic kinship over purely social ties and denies one of the most obvious and important things about adoption: it is a different way to make a family.

Adoption is a kind of pre- or non-technological reproductive technology. Since ancient times and in all cultures, exchange mechanisms have transferred children from adults who would not or could not be parents to adults who wanted them for love, labor, and property. The close association of adoption with humanitarian rescue during the nineteenth century and infertility during the twentieth century are, however, uniquely modern phenomena. Only since the middle of the nineteenth century have widespread notions of childhood innocence and malleability made it possible for adopters to feel both virtuous and lucky when taking in the children of impoverished, socially marginalized parents. Only during this century has adoption been so inextricably linked to infertility that it has become a solution for childless heterosexuals seeking to approximate, emotionally and legally, the family they cannot produce themselves. The myth that adoption could actually cure infertility by facilitating pregnancy lasted for decades in spite of empirical evidence to the contrary. It was sustained by desperation, anecdote, and Freudian theories that held "psychogenic" resistance responsible for physiologically inexplicable reproductive failures.

In the United States, state legislatures began passing adoption laws in the mid-nineteenth century, considerably earlier than other western, industrial nations. (England, for example, did not pass adoption legislation until 1926). Over the past century, the number of adoptions and the extent of legal regulation have both increased dramatically. In 1900, formalizing adoptive kinship in a court was still rare. By 1970, the numerical peak of twentieth-century adoption, 175,000 adoptions were finalized annually. "Stranger" or "non-relative" adoptions have predominated over time, but today growing numbers of children are adopted by natal relatives and stepparents. Since World War II, adoption has been globalized. The familiar rhetoric of rescue that pervaded the late-nineteenth-century evangelical phase of domestic adoption echoes in more recent international placements. From Korea in the 1950s to China in the 1990s, countries that export the most children for adoption have been devastated by poverty and violence. These disasters are compounded by policies (China's one-child policy, for instance) that make it difficult or impossible for birth families to keep their children. United States citizens who adopt foreign children have followed a global trail of misery, war, and genocide.

A campaign to modernize adoption by surrounding it with legal and scientific safeguards accompanied adoption's growing popularity and resulted in the secrecy that has been under attack in recent decades. In 1917, Minnesota passed the first state law sealing adoption records. By midcentury, most states in the United States had revised their statutes so that even adoptees were forbidden access to original birth records. Well-intentioned parents and professionals hoped that engineering wholesale kinship replacement would lessen adoption's disgraceful association with illegitimacy. Ironically, this determination to make adoption as real as the real thing by severing children's ties to natal kin cemented adoption's reputation as a last resort. By reinforcing the view that biogenetic ties were the most authentic and desirable, secrecy intensified desires for pregnancy along with sus-

picions that adoption was inherently defective. The benevolent project of engineering ideal families encompassed all sorts of social and economic biases. It narrowed the definition of an acceptable family to married couples with emotional
profiles as healthy as their bank accounts. Adoption could make normal families,
but only after the normal (and preferred) method of biogenetic reproduction
failed.

The effort to mask adoption's distinctiveness has been uniquely problematic
for women. Adoption shows that motherhood is a *social* status, separable from
conception and pregnancy, and that reproductive autonomy is implicated in achieving *or* escaping motherhood. Yet making the deliberate construction of adoptive
kinship invisible has made women's decisions to reject or embrace the labor of
mothering invisible as well. Adoption, an institution premised on voluntarism, has
often served to tighten the strictures of mandatory maternity. Instead of enhancing the independence of women who have children (and cannot care for them)
and women who want children (but do not have them), surreptitious acts of child
exchange have merely added to women's guilt and reinforced the biased view that
they cannot be complete human beings without being mothers both biogenetically
and socially, an impossibility in adoption. For the birth mothers who give children and the adoptive mothers who take them, the choices involved in adoption
have rarely been free.

Curiously, this unfree, "second-best" choice has been a privilege rather than a
right. Adoption involves upward mobility, with children moving from poorer
individuals (and groups and countries) to wealthier individuals (and groups and
countries). Parental tastes comprise a definite hierarchy: infants are desired over
older children; whiter children are desired over browner and blacker ones; girls
are desired over boys. Beginning with nineteenth-century baby farms, children
commanded significant prices just as they became "priceless," with their value
supposedly residing in the love that middle-class parents invested rather than the
labor that working-class parents extracted. The insistent refrain, "adoption for children who need homes, not homes who need children," has never concealed the
fact that a market in children endures, that adult consumers call the shots, and
that "demand" has long exceeded "supply" for its most desirable commodities.

Since *Griswold v. Connecticut* (1965), reproductive rights have been concep-
tually tied to the personal privacy that making decisions about contraception, abortion, and sterilization requires. Some proponents of new reproductive technologies
have suggested that the hunger for biogenetic continuity is so primal that it should
constitute a new basis for procreative freedom. Adoption, which turns biological
strangers into kin, obviously cannot depend on the theory that genes make parents and children. Whatever freedoms adoption involves are those conferred by
the market rather than the Constitution: birth parents with desirable infants are
free to decide when and with whom they are placed; adopters with money are
free to specify the sort of children they want; intermediaries with good contacts
are free to manage the process for humanitarian reasons, profit, or both. Adults
without such resources are as powerless as children. There is no legal right to

adopt and the laws that exist to protect children cannot effectively extract decent parental care from adults who abandon the obligations that accompany reproductive liberty.

Nevertheless, government has intervened in adoption in order to prevent unnecessary and unacceptable risks, such as the risk of buying and selling human beings. But non-relative placements have been closely regulated largely for the same reason they have been highly stigmatized: the idea that kinship without blood is so flimsy a bond that managerial expertise is considered necessary to avoid disaster. This premise is what distinguishes adoption from newer, unregulated reproductive technologies. Regulatory rationales vary by state and have changed dramatically over time. During the formative Progressive era, the first two decades of the twentieth century, fiscal worries about the future costs of crime and dependency motivated governments to start certifying child-placers, conducting social investigations to ensure all parties were qualified, and supervising the post-placement period. Eugenic fears and beliefs about the permanence of maternal duty made many Progressives the original advocates of family preservation. Some were so hostile to adoption that they called it "abortion after birth."

As the demography of unmarried motherhood shifted and the nature/nurture debate swung decisively toward nurture in the post-Nazi era, resistance to separating birth mothers and babies softened. After 1945, with unmarried mothers more likely to be white, middle-class adolescents, adoption seemed positively desirable. Immature birth mothers would get a second chance at normal (i.e., married) life. Virtuous adopters would get the children they deserved. Lucky children would get good homes. As the shame of illegitimacy decreased and women secured abortion rights, the availability of healthy white infants dwindled. This decrease in supply fueled enthusiasm for international placements and new, high-tech reproduction.

Since 1950, adoption has changed so dramatically that some observers suggest an "adoption revolution" has occurred. The concept of "adoptability" has expanded to include older, disabled, and nonwhite children. Some families have been formed across racial and cultural chasms formerly regarded as unbridgeable. Since 1970, secrecy has been seriously questioned and at least some children have found permanence without sacrificing all possibilities of natal connection. "Open adoption" today describes a remarkably varied set of kinship arrangements, from those where children grow up knowing birth parents' identities to those in which natal relatives play an active part in children's lives. Perhaps these changes are revolutionary. But many adults are still considered undesirable parents, because they are single, too poor, too old, gay, or lesbian. If allowed to adopt at all, they must take the children that young, affluent, heterosexual couples do not want. Transracial placements have had more symbolic significance than social or statistical impact. They remain controversial and rare. Most Americans have always supported race-matching, and they continue to do so today. The foster care crisis of the past two decades, during which a ballooning population of older and special needs children have been temporarily but not legally separated from their birth families, means that tens of thousands of children who need permanent parents will never have them. "Family preservation" policies have too often preserved only the ideal of family life, leaving children without reliable care or the sense that they belong to anyone or anywhere in particular.

Adoption is a valuable social institution whose potential for children has never been realized because of persistent prejudice linking blood and belonging. Rights talk may be the most potent language in American political life, but at the dawn of the twenty-first century, it is woefully inadequate. Individual and community choices about family formation are still mediated by the perpetual economic interests and social inequalities endemic to a society where stratification seems only to be sharpening. Adoption, like other reproductive issues, shows that private and public matters are inseparable. Culture and commerce have profoundly shaped personal desires and legal rules about defining families and deciding who belongs in them. Why is a pluralistic conception of reproductive freedom—acknowledging the diversity of ways that Americans acquire and care for children—any less fundamental than a pluralistic conception of religious freedom? In the meantime, there is no right to family life.

SEE Birth Mothers and Reproductive Rights; Child Custody; Eugenics; Fathers' Rights Movement; *Griswold v. Connecticut.*

Further References. *Adoption Quarterly*, published by the Haworth Press since 1997, edited by Renee Garfinkel, President, Adoption Studies Institute, Washington, D.C. Elizabeth Bartholet, *Family Bonds: Adoption and the Politics of Parenting* (Boston, 1993). E. Wayne Carp, *Family Matters: Secrecy and Disclosure in the History of Adoption* (Cambridge, Mass., 1998).

ELLEN HERMAN

AFRICAN-AMERICAN WOMEN AND REPRODUCTIVE RIGHTS. The history of Black women and reproductive rights is best described as a chronicle of reproductive wrongs, ranging from the exploitation of enslaved women to increase the slave population in the eighteenth and nineteenth centuries to present day efforts to control Black women's fertility through welfare policy and criminal prosecution. For women with race and class privilege, the struggle for reproductive autonomy in the United States historically has meant emancipation from stereotypical assumptions that motherhood is both their destiny and their primary societal mission. Black women endure a more complex set of burdens. These burdens are rooted in the lasting belief that the reproductive choices of Black women, including motherhood, warrant neither legal protections nor social respect. Therefore, the struggle for the reproductive rights of Black women has focused on liberation from government policies that at various points either compelled or punished childbearing.

The story of Black women and reproduction originates with the legal system of slavery, which legitimated both racial and gender subordination by permitting slave masters to coerce slave women's childbearing to replenish the masters' labor force. One of the first American slavery laws, a 1662 Virginia statute, accorded the legal status of slave to the children of slave mothers and white fathers. The institution of slavery was dependent upon rape, slave-breeding and other forms of terroristic control of Black women's reproductive capacities. The law, in cases such as *Banks' Administrator v. Marksberry* (1823), sanctioned slave masters' ownership of Black women, their offspring, *and* their future descendants; slave mothers had no legal claim to their own progeny. This situation led in some circumstances to self-induced abortion and even infanticide, through which slave women rebelled against forced childbearing and the inevitable bondage of their children.

With the rise of the U.S. birth control movement in the early twentieth century, Black women again faced the onus of racism in their quest for reproductive autonomy. The efforts of white feminists such as Margaret Sanger, who founded the American Birth Control League in 1921, benefitted all women by defending their right to practice contraception. However, the birth control crusade gained momentum through alliances with the eugenics movement, which sought to curtail the birth rates of groups, including Blacks, that it deemed genetically inferior and therefore "unfit." In political as well as academic discourse, eugenicists such as University of Chicago professor Charles Davenport ascribed behavioral traits (for example, eroticism, pauperism, and criminality) to particular races and ethnic groups, and advocated reproduction control through anti-miscegenation laws, stringent immigration policies, and state-sponsored sterilization. Thus, the compulsory childbearing suffered by Black women of the slave era had metamorphosed by the 1920s into eugenicist birth control programs targeted at reducing the birth rate of the Black community. Although Black women continued to make autonomous choices about their own reproductive capacities by using various forms of contraception and abortion, the debate about birth control in the Black community was heavily influenced by the genocidal implications of the eugenics movement.

Throughout the 1920s and 1930s, Black women suffered disproportionately from the implementation of mandatory sterilization laws. Typical of such statutes was a Virginia law enacted in 1924 to ban reproduction by "potential parents of socially inadequate offspring." The U.S. Supreme Court upheld this law in *Buck v. Bell* (1927). More than 70,000 individuals were involuntarily sterilized under such statutes; more than 2,000 eugenic sterilizations were performed each year between 1929 and 1940. Even as these laws were repealed, sterilization abuse against Black women continued in hospitals and mental institutions at the hands of government-paid doctors. Of the 8,000 people deemed "mentally deficient" and sterilized by order of the North Carolina Eugenics Commission in the 1930s and 1940s, five thousand were Blacks. All 23 persons sterilized at the State Hospital in South Carolina in 1954 were Black women. By the 1970s, sterilization had become the fastest-growing form of birth control in the United States, increasing from 200,000 cases in 1970 to more than 700,000 in 1980. A disproportionate number of these sterilizations were performed on Black women.

As in the slave era, the grossest injustice of the rampant sterilizations performed on Black women during these decades was the exploitation of their bodies to promote government agendas. At times, teaching hospitals coerced women into unnecessary tubal ligations and hysterectomies in order to provide "practice" for their medical students and doctors; legal consent for the procedures was often nonexistent or fraudulently obtained. So prevalent were these abuses in the South that they were nicknamed "Mississippi appendectomies." In the landmark case of *Relf v. Weinberger* (1974), two Black teenage girls led a class action lawsuit demanding a ban on the use of federal funds for sterilizations. The girls, ages 12 and 14, had been sterilized unbeknownst to them and their parents. They had been coerced into participating in federally funded experimental trials of the contraceptive Depo-Provera. The trial judge in the case found that the challenged programs had resulted in approximately 100,000 to 150,000 sterilizations of poor women annually; a later study found that approximately half of these were Black women. The case resulted in the adoption of federal guidelines regulating government-subsidized sterilizations.

From the 1970s to the present, pervasive government control of Black women's reproductive capacities continues in several legal and public policy arenas. Although *Roe v. Wade* and its progeny in principle uphold a woman's right to choose abortion, several rulings upheld the denial of public funding of abortion services. Thus, the Court has denied a fundamental constitutional right to millions of poor, including Black, women. At the same time, public assistance and other government funding policies encourage long-acting and permanent contraceptive options such as sterilization, the insertion of Norplant capsules, and the injection of Depo-Provera. Black women who are welfare recipients continue to confront restrictions on their fertility decisions through welfare "family caps" legislation, which bars additional payments for children born to women who are already receiving Aid to Families with Dependent Children (AFDC). Debates about welfare reform are often infused with vicious stereotypes about Black "welfare queens" who have multiple children in order to stay on public assistance.

Finally, the most drastic recent examples of government intervention from the 1990s to the present involve the racially disproportionate prosecution of drug-addicted, Black pregnant women and the assertion of control over their fetuses and children. During their pregnancies, these women are prosecuted and often convicted and incarcerated for endangering their fetuses in the womb; they are then coerced with the imposition of birth control (including abortion) as a condition of probation. If the women have given birth to babies who test positive for drugs, they may lose their children to foster care.

Feminist activism and leadership in law, public policy, and academia have begun to address the above problems, but the full measure of Black women's reproductive rights remains an unrealized goal.

SEE Abortion and Public Assistance; *Beal v. Doe* et al; Birth Control and - African-American Women; Birth Control Movement; *Buck v. Bell*; Class and Reproductive Rights; Eugenics; Federal Sterilization Guidelines (1979); Fetal

Protection; *Harris v. McRae*; Native American Women and Reproductive Rights; *Roe v. Wade*; Sterilization Abuse; Substance Abuse and Pregnancy.

Further References. *Banks' Administrator v. Marksberry,* 3 Littell's Rep. 275 (1823). Stanlie M. James and Abena P. A. Busia, eds., *Theorizing Black Feminisms: The Visionary Pragmatism of Black Women* (London, 1993). Angela Davis, "Racism, Birth Control, and Reproductive Rights," in Marlene Gerber Fried, ed., *From Abortion to Reproductive Freedom: Transforming a Movement* (Boston, 1990): 15-26. *Relf v. Weinberger,* 372 F. Supp. 1196 (D.D.C. 1974), 565 F. 2d 722 (D.C. Cir. 1977). Dorothy Roberts, *Killing the Black Body: Race, Reproduction, and the Meaning of Liberty* (New York, 1997). Jessie M. Rodrique, "The Black Community and the Birth Control Movement," in Ellen Carol DuBois and Vicki L. Ruiz, eds., *Unequal Sisters: A Multicultural Reader in U.S. Women's History* (New York, 1990): 333-344.

MARGARET M. RUSSELL

AKRON. SEE *City of Akron v. Akron Center for Reproductive Health.*

AKRON II. SEE *Ohio v. Akron Center for Reproductive Health.*

AMERICAN CYANAMID. SEE *Secretary of Labor v. American Cyanamid.*

ARTIFICIAL INSEMINATION (AI) is the technique whereby semen is deposited in the vagina or uterus by a means other than sexual intercourse. Originally developed for use in animal husbandry, AI is now used by women seeking to overcome infertility, as well as by those wishing to become mothers without a male partner (for example, lesbians and single women). Whether the sperm is from the woman's husband (AIH) or a donor (AID), insemination is available through a wide range of methods. Basic home self-insemination, using no technology more complex than the human hand and a turkey baster, has been practiced since the late nineteenth century. Today, sperm banks buy semen from donors and sell it to recipients. At the hi-tech end of the spectrum, new options such as IUI (Intra Uterine Insemination) and IVF (*InVitro* Fertilization) are available. The method a woman chooses will usually depend on her reasons for using AI. The latest research in AI involves attempts to manipulate the sperm to select the sex of the child.

Artificial insemination clearly increases women's reproductive freedom, as well as men's. The procedure enables women to bear children who would otherwise not be able to do so, whether because they are not heterosexually active or because they or their male partners have fertility problems. However, AI raises some complex moral, economic, and legal issues. First, the separation of pregnancy from sexual intercourse and the ability of recipients to choose among donors with different characteristics disturbs those who distrust high-tech reproduction. Second, professionalized AI is not equally available to all women. Cost is a major factor in determining who has access to it. Studies of AI as an infertility treatment have tended to concentrate on white women having children later in life, past the age of 35. While these are not the women with the highest incidence of infertility, they are the women who can afford treatment. Those most likely to suffer from infertility, but least likely to be able to afford treatment, are young women of color. Half of all women seeking infertility treatments have either no insurance at all or insurance that does not cover AI. Even when health insurance does cover AI, the coverage is often incomplete, leaving the woman to pay a significant part of the cost. Self-insemination may be a less expensive option, but some costs are still involved in purchasing semen from a sperm bank.

A third problem with AI is that the laws regulating it were framed with medical providers and married women in mind. Their meaning is often ambiguous when applied to single women and/or self-insemination, especially with regard to the legal status of the donor. In *Jhordan C. v. Mary K.* (1986), the California Court of Appeals awarded visitation rights to a sperm donor because the self-insemination had been arranged without medical intervention. Existing statutes would not regard the donor as the natural father if he had provided the semen to a licensed physician. Since this donor had given the semen directly to the mother, without a physician being involved, the statutes did not apply. Regarding non-medical AI as equivalent to sexual intercourse, the court gave paternity rights to the donor.

Twenty-one states now have laws explicitly requiring that AI be performed with the involvement of a licensed physician. The level of involvement required ranges from provisions that only physicians can provide donor semen to a recipient (who may then use it for self-insemination) to requirements that a physician perform the entire procedure. The ostensible purpose of these requirements is to protect the health of the mother and potential child and the anonymity of the donor, but the rules also serve the financial self-interest of physicians. (Typically, doctors and clinics buy semen from donors and sell it to recipients, but there are cases of doctors using their own semen for AI—a practice these statutes do not exactly discourage). In Georgia, non-medical AI is a felony.

SEE *In Vitro* Fertilization; Surrogate Motherhood.

Further References. Maria Gil de Lamadrid, *Lesbians Choosing Motherhood: Legal Implications of Donor Insemination and Co-Parenting* (San Francisco, 1991). *Jhordan C. v. Mary K.*, 179 Cal. App. 3d 386, 224 Cal. Rptr. 530 (1986). Michelle Stanworth, "Birth Pangs," in Marianne Hirsch and Evelyn Fox Keller, eds., *Conflicts in Feminism* (New York, 1990): 288-304. J. J. Tate, *Artificial Insemination and Legal Reality* (Chicago, 1992).

FIONA M. YOUNG

ASHCROFT. SEE *Planned Parenthood of Kansas City v. Ashcroft.*

B

BABY M. *In the Matter of Baby M*, (537 A. 2d 1227 N.J., 1988), was the first dispute resulting from a surrogacy contract to receive national media attention. In 1985, William Stern and his wife Elizabeth, a pediatrician, decided not to incur the risks of pregnancy (Dr. Stern had diagnosed herself with multiple sclerosis). The Sterns wanted a child genetically related to them, so William Stern entered into a contractual arrangement with Mary Beth Whitehead, a working-class mother of two. Married to an alcoholic, she was struggling to support her family. The surrogacy contract bound only Whitehead and William Stern and was explicitly designed to avoid breaking laws that prohibited "baby-selling," or the exchange of money for placement of a child for adoption. Instead, the explicit purpose of the contract was "giving a child to William Stern, its natural and biological father." Whitehead was required to surrender the child to the Sterns and to terminate her parental rights so that Elizabeth Stern could adopt the baby. For "completion of [these] duties and obligations," Whitehead would be paid $10,000.

Whitehead was inseminated with Stern's sperm and became pregnant. She gave birth to a daughter on March 27, 1986. She bonded with her baby, and decided that she could not complete the terms of the surrogacy contract. She cared for the baby for four and a half months. The Sterns sought enforcement of the contract and were granted temporary custody of the child, named Sara Elizabeth by Whitehead but known officially as "Baby M." The trial court's ruling, issued on March 31, 1987, declared the surrogacy contract valid and enforceable, granted custody to the Sterns, approved Elizabeth Stern's petition to adopt, and terminated Whitehead's parental rights. Judge Harvey Sorkow concluded that the best interests of Baby M could be met by the Sterns.

Sorkow's decision accorded with public opinion, which characterized White-head as a bad mother and a bad woman. Proponents of women's reproductive rights were divided on the issue. Whitehead received little help from established feminist groups, some of which joined libertarians in worrying that endorsing her custody bid would threaten women's general freedom of contract. But some prominent feminists did support Whitehead, on the grounds that surrogacy contracts exploited vulnerable women and ignored the interests of natural mothers.

The Whiteheads appealed, and the New Jersey Supreme Court issued its decision on February 3, 1988. Chief Justice Wilentz announced the Court's conclusion that surrogacy contracts are illegal and unenforceable. The Stern-Whitehead contract was held to violate state adoption regulations designed to prevent the commodification of infants, as well as public policy considerations respecting the status of women. Wilentz wrote: "While we recognize the depth of yearning of infertile couples to have their own children, we find the payment of money to a 'surrogate' mother illegal, perhaps criminal, and potentially degrading to women." The Court declared that state enforcement of surrogacy contracts was inappropriate because a woman's choice to participate can never be "a totally voluntary, informed decision." But even the alternative is unacceptable: "her consent is irrelevant. There are, in a civilized society, some things that money cannot buy." The Court chose to "void both the termination of the surrogate mother's parental rights and the adoption of the child by the wife/stepparent. We thus restore the 'surrogate' as the mother of the child . . . " Nevertheless, the Court upheld that the Sterns' custody of Baby M and found it to be in the child's best interests. Whitehead was granted visitation rights. Surrogacy remains illegal in New Jersey, although elsewhere such contracts have been declared legal.

SEE Surrogate Motherhood.

Further References. *In the Matter of Baby M*, (217 N.J. Super. 313 1987). Larry Gostin, ed., *Surrogate Motherhood: Politics and Privacy* (Bloomington, Ind., 1988). Katha Pollitt, "Contracts and Apple Pie: The Strange Case of Baby M," in *Reasonable Creatures* (New York, 1994): 63-80.

                                                    BETH KIYOKO JAMIESON

BEAL v. DOE, (432 U.S. 438, 1977) was one of three Supreme Court decisions that upheld state laws limiting public assistance for abortions. *Beal* its two companion cases, *Maher v. Roe* and *Poelker v. Doe*, were decided on June 20, 1977. The Court held, six to three, that neither Title XIX of the Social Security Act (which established Medicaid) not the Constitution required states to use Medicaid funds or public facilities for elective abortions. *Beal* rejected a claim by Medicaid-eligible women in Pennsylvania that the state's requirement that two physicians, in addition to the attending physician, certify in writing that any abortion paid for by Medicaid funds was medically necessary conflicted with, and was pre-empted by, Title XIX. Speaking through Justice Lewis Powell, the Court ruled that nothing in the original language of Title XIX required a participating state to fund any and all medical procedures. Instead, each state has broad discretion to determine the extent of medical assistance under the Medicaid program. The Court further noted that non-therapeutic abortions were illegal in most states at the time Title XIX was passed. Therefore, Congress could not have intended that such procedures be covered.

The next two cases involved constitutional rather than statutory questions. *Maher* sustained a Connecticut law prohibiting the use of Medicaid funds for "unnecessary" abortions, while *Poelker* upheld a St. Louis, Missouri ordinance prohibiting the performance of elective abortions in publicly funded hospitals. The Court distinguished these cases from rulings like *Planned Parenthood v. Danforth* (1976) which struck down spousal consent and parental consent provisions. Justice Powell held that "the Connecticut regulation places no obstacle—absolute of otherwise—in the pregnant woman's path to an abortion." Such a woman "continues, as before, to be dependent on private sources for the service she desires." The Court also rejected the plaintiffs' argument that the statue violated the Equal Protection Clause of the Fourteenth Amendment. A state's decision to use public funds and facilities to subsidize childbirth but not abortion was not irrational—even though childbirth is more expensive than abortion. Nor did poor women constitute a "suspect class" for which a state would have to demonstrate a compelling interest to justify and policy that would affect that group adversely. Neither the Constitution nor Medicaid's organic act precluded a state from adopting a policy of favoring normal childbirth over abortion and using its public funds to further that policy.

The court insisted that its decision signaled no retreat from its holding in *Roe v. Wade* four years previously. The majority held that *Roe* did not provide an unqualified constitutional right to an abortion; it merely protected a woman from unacceptably burdensome interference in the exercise of that right. Justices William Brennan, Thurgood Marshall, and Harry Blackmun disagreed, dissenting in all three cases. For "too many" pregnant women, wrote Brennan, "indigency makes access to competent licensed physicians not merely difficult, but impossible." Blackmun admonished his colleagues that "there is another world 'out there,' the existence of which the Court either chooses to ignore or fears to recognize."

Beal and its companion cases clarified the meaning of *Roe*, while obfuscating the constitutional status of abortion. Once the Court had refused to recognize poor women as a suspect class, the only remaining basis for concluding that the Equal Protection Clause had been violated was a decision that the laws infringed on a fundamental right protected by the Constitution. Although the Court has ruled that government must provide the indigent with certain constitutional rights (like the Sixth Amendment right to counsel), it did not apply this principle to abortion. While the state could not place limits on a woman's right to an abortion, neither was it obliged to facilitate her exercise of that right.

These three cases represented a major turning point in the debate over the use of public funds for abortions. At the time, several cases on the use of public funds for abortions were moving through the legal system, and legislative efforts to restrict funding were moving through Congress and the state legislatures. *Beal, Maher*, and *Poelker* strengthened the position of lawmakers who advocated eliminating or strictly limiting the use of public funds for abortions. After the Court's decisions, the restraining order that prevented enforcement of the Hyde Amendment (the provision prohibiting the use of federal Medicaid funds for abortions) was lifted. Within a month, over half of the states had eliminated Medicaid funding of abortions except as was specifically allowed by that year's version of the amendment. The use of federal funds was temporarily resumed until the Court upheld the Hyde Amendment in *Harris v. McRae* (1980).

SEE Abortion and Public Assistance; *Harris v. McRae*; Hyde Amendment; *Planned Parenthood v. Danforth; Roe v. Wade.*

MARY YOUNG

BELLOTTI v. BAIRD I, (428 U.S. 132, 1976) raises the question of parental consent for minors' abortions, but the decisive issue in the case was when a federal district court could rightfully determine that a state statute conflicted with the constitutional right to obtain an abortion. A 1974 Massachusetts law required a single woman younger than 18 years of age to obtain the consent of both her parents or guardians before undergoing an abortion (except in an emergency). In the absence of parental consent, a minor could seek such consent from a judge of the superior court if she was able to subsequently show "good cause." In 1975, the federal court held sections of the statute unconstitutional. It found that "a substantial number of females under the age of 18 are capable of forming valid consent" and that, in part, the statute failed because it required that "parents must not only must be consulted, they are given a veto."

The Supreme Court decided this case along with *Planned Parenthood of Central Missouri v. Danforth*, which struck down an absolute parental consent requirement. In *Bellotti*, however, Massachusetts made the additional argument that the district court had acted prematurely in deciding the constitutional issue before the state courts could review the statute. Under the well-established legal doctrine of abstention, the state argued that the federal court should have abstained from ruling until the state courts had offered their own interpretation of the statute, a decision which might have removed the constitutional issues the district court had decided.

The Supreme Court accepted this argument and vacated the lower court's decision voiding the Massachusetts statute. The justices directed the district court to seek an interpretation of the statute from the Supreme Judicial Court of Massachusetts as quickly as possible, in a process known as certification. The Supreme Court also ruled that the state court must recognize the limitations upon a parental veto created in *Danforth*. After receiving certification from the state supreme court, the federal court once again invalidated the law. Three years later, the Supreme Court upheld the statute in *Bellotti v. Baird II* (1979).

SEE Abortion and Parental Consent and Notification; *Akron v. Akron Center for Reproductive Health*; *Bellotti v. Baird II*; *H.L. v. Matheson*; *Hodgson v. Minnesota*; *Planned Parenthood of Kansas City v. Ashcroft*; *Planned Parenthood of Central Missouri v. Danforth*; *Planned Parenthood of Southeastern Pennsylvania v. Casey*.

SCOTT BARCLAY

BELLOTTI v. BAIRD II, (443 U.S. 622, 1979) invalidated a 1974 Massachusetts law regulating access to abortion for women younger than 18. The law required that minors seeking abortions receive the consent of both parents. If this consent was not forthcoming, the woman could obtain a court order allowing the abortion, but the judge had the discretion to grant or deny this request. Justice Lewis Powell, writing for a plurality of four, held that the law placed an undue burden on minors' privacy rights because it required parental consent in every case, without allowing the minor to show that she was mature enough to make the decision on her own or that the abortion would be in her best interests. Three other justices concurred, but wanted to go further and rule that the two-parent requirement violated the woman's abortion rights. Justice William Rehnquist concurred, but called for a reconsideration of *Planned Parenthood Association v. Danforth*, which he believed had been wrongly decided.

While the Court overturned this particular law, it did not ban all parental consent or notification requirements outright. Subsequently, it has upheld such laws when judicial bypass provisions exist. State legislatures have responded to these rulings. As of 2000, a majority of states had enacted such requirements.

SEE Abortion and Parental Consent and Notification; *Akron v. Akron Center for Reproductive Health*; *Bellotti v. Baird I*; *H.L. v. Matheson*; *Hodgson v. Minnesota*; *Planned Parenthood of Kansas City v. Ashcroft*; *Planned Parenthood of Central Missouri v. Danforth*; *Planned Parenthood of Southeastern Pennsylvania v. Casey*.

Further References. Mark Graber, *Rethinking Abortion: Equal Choice, the Constitution, and Reproductive Politics* (Princeton, N.J., 1996). Rosalind Pollack Petchesky, *Abortion and Woman's Choice: The State, Sexuality, and Reproductive Freedom*, rev. ed. (Boston, Mass., 1990).

ELLIOT TENOFSKY

BIRTH CONTROL AND AFRICAN-AMERICAN WOMEN. Historical accounts demonstrate that African-American women have been denied their right to reproductive freedom at various times and in various ways. Societal attempts at fertility control have been shrouded in arguments that claim a humanitarian approach to improving the quality of life for unborn children. However, these efforts have often denied African-American women the fundamental right of control over their reproduction. The history of birth control in the United States illustrates the factors that have shaped the reproductive rights struggle among African-American women and illuminates the effects of race, class and/or gender politics on their reproductive rights.

African-American women have struggled to preserve their reproductive autonomy ever since the forced migration of Africans to the shores of America began in the early seventeenth century. Slave women sought to control their fertility despite attempts by white men to control it for them. The peculiar institution of slavery mandated that African-American women's bodies were the property of their masters. The continuation of the plantation system depended upon the reproduction of slave labor. Producing baby slaves became a "responsibility" of enslaved African women. Slave breeding became a common practice among slave owners, whether they impregnated their slaves themselves or paired male and female slaves. "Breeding wenches" got rewards such as special privileges during pregnancy and sometimes even their freedom. Conversely, barren slave women commanded comparatively low prices at the auction block.

The attempts of African-American women to control their fertility under the harsh conditions of slavery constituted a quiet, deliberate rebellion against the dominant society and an effort to subvert the institution of slavery. Records of fertility control among African-American women can be found as early as the mid-nineteenth century. Medical journals document entire plantations of slave women who had no children. (Ingesting camphor was a common and effective method of preventing pregnancy.) Several social historians have documented active co-operation between slave men and women to limit the number of children born into slavery. One man wrote of his only child, "She was the first and last slave that I will ever father for chains and slavery on this earth" (Weisbord, 1975: 28).

As emancipation approached, African-American women believed that they would now get opportunities in all aspects of their lives, including reproductive freedom. They were quickly disillusioned. The social constructs of race, class and gender prevented full racial equality from being actualized. Though African-American women were legally granted their freedom and equal rights with white women, tactics by the dominant society such as "Jim Crow" laws enforced racial segregation and limited opportunities. However, Reconstruction did improve the lot of African-American women. Now legally allowed to attend school and work for wages, they were able to increase their involvement in informal and formal efforts to establish racial equality.

African-American women also supported the women's rights movement, but their reception was less than friendly. Although the first nineteenth-century feminists had been anti-slavery and anti-racist, by the end of the century the women's movement was sharply divided along race and class lines. This differentiation of women made it increasingly difficult to find unity on any issue, including fertility control. During the second half of the nineteenth century, both black women and white women recognized the need for reproductive freedom. But the motives for seeking this freedom and the methods chosen to achieve it were very different for each group. Black women wanted to exercise their fundamental right to control giving birth to children in a racially divided society. By the 1900s, black women were marrying later and having fewer children than in years prior to Reconstruction. White women were primarily concerned with establishing the right to control their fertility through abstinence and/or voluntary motherhood. These women embraced the Victorian ideal of "true womanhood," which valued chastity and monogamy and regarded sexual intercourse for women as a duty, not a pleasure.

The dominant white racist ideology in American society extended to the movement for fertility control. The view of African-American women developed during slavery and maintained ever since is a hostile one, often portraying African-American women as jezebels and sexually insatiable. This view, held by white men and women, excluded black women from the cult of true womanhood and has provided justification for reproductive control up to the present. Popular images of African-American women portrayed them as not "worthy" of the right to control their reproductive behavior. Consequently, white feminists perceived no need to develop alliances across racial lines in the struggle to gain reproductive control and evinced virtually no support for African-American women, despite their clear need and desire to control their fertility. African-American women were excluded from this movement from its inception.

The social reform movement for birth control initially emerged among white women in the second half of the nineteenth century as a campaign for voluntary motherhood, achieved through long periods of abstinence within marriage. Supporters of voluntary motherhood rejected contraceptive devices as unnatural and likely to encourage promiscuity among women. Between 1910 and 1920, the term "birth control" came into common usage and the emphasis shifted from abstinence to artificial contraception. The advocates of birth control were largely from professional families who subscribed to the belief that the white race in America was under the threat of extinction. They feared that immigrants and African-Americans would have large numbers of children and increase the non-white population. Thus, birth control was seen as necessary to limit the number of non-white children born.

The 1920s and 1930s saw the development of a liberal reform movement initiated by Margaret Sanger. During this stage, the term "planned parenthood" was coined, and family planning services were developed and implemented. Sanger shared the racism of her predecessors in the movement. She adhered to the ideology of eugenicism, which advocated the preservation of the European race through the prevention of the birth of non-white babies. This ideology largely defined the purpose of birth control and the boundaries of reproductive freedom. Birth control became a method of population control rather than a means of developing and nurturing reproductive autonomy. In conjunction with this new definition of birth control, there was an extreme fear among whites that their declining fertility rate posed a threat to maintaining the existing power structure. In reality, however, the fertility rate of African-Americans steadily decreased during the first three decades of this century.

The efforts of African-American women to take control of their own reproductive lives met both with discrimination from white women because of their
race and with racist and sexist oppression from white men. They could not always
count on the co-operation of African-American men, either. While some leaders
of the Black community supported the women's struggles, there were prominent
activists who resisted birth control. Marcus Garvey, for example, stressed the
importance of maintaining high birth rates and warned that Blacks "might be exter-
minated if they allowed themselves to be weakened by a reduction in population
size." These attitudes persisted for decades. In the late 1960s, the Black Women's
Liberation Group of Mount Vernon, New York, criticized "militant black broth-
ers" who asked women "not to practice birth control because it's a form of
Whitey's committing genocide on black people." The group insisted that "birth
control is the freedom to *fight* genocide of black women and children."

The debate over the fertility of African-American women continues to the present day, most notoriously around the issues of teenage pregnancy and single
motherhood. The consistent themes in this debate are a perception that the reproductive needs of African-American women are insignificant and a presumption
that white society may control their behavior for its own interests. While the denial
of their reproductive rights has been consistent, it has taken different forms. In
slavery, African-American women were forced to have children to serve their masters; in the twentieth century, they have been forced (often through sterilization
abuse) to limit their childbearing to serve what white America thinks are its
needs. In addition to specific efforts to control fertility, the use of opposing
images of white and African-American women (for example, true womanhood
versus jezebel) served as barriers for the latter group. These views continue to be
perpetuated in present-day debates around reproductive rights and freedom for
African-American women of childbearing age. But African-American women
have never assented to this treatment. From the days of slavery onward, they have
asserted their right to control their reproductive choices.

SEE African-American Women and Reproductive Rights; Birth Control Movement; Class and Reproductive Rights; Eugenics; Sterilization Abuse; Teenage
Pregnancy.

Further References. Angela Y. Davis, *Women, Race, and Class* (New York,
1981). Paula Giddings, *When and Where I Enter: The Impact of Black Women on
Race and Sex in America* (New York, 1984). Linda Gordon, *Woman's Body,
Woman's Right: A Social History of Birth Control in America* (New York, rev.
ed., 1990). Robin Morgan, ed., *Sisterhood is Powerful* (New York, 1970). Robert
Weisbord, *Genocide? Birth Control and the Black American* (Westport, Conn.,
1975).

VENA CRICHLOW-SCALES

BIRTH CONTROL MOVEMENT. The term "birth control" was first popular-
ized by Margaret Sanger during a campaign for the legalization of contraception

that began about 1914 in the U.S. Birth control in its generic sense—referring to any method of controlling reproduction, including abstinence and abortion—is as old as civilization. Few ancient societies were without some reproduction-control practices; these arose both from women's desire for control over reproduction and from community interests in controlling population size. But birth control was also socially regulated, and in most agricultural and early-industrial societies, prohibitions on reproduction control served also to control women's sexuality.

In modern times, birth control became associated with women's emancipation, individualism, personal rights, privacy, and smaller families. Thus, birth control has been a politicized and hotly contested battleground for almost two centuries. The first political campaigns for birth control arose from early nineteenth-century British neo-Malthusianism, a theory that the poor could improve their life's chances by reducing their birthrates, and that encouraging them to do so would control impulses toward social radicalism. Soon, American utopian communitarians, such as Robert Dale Owen and John Humphrey Noyes, began to preach and put into practice childbearing by choice. Opposed to "artificial" contraception, they recommended "male continence," a discipline by which men refrained from ejaculation. (The fact that this method sounds so bizarre today suggests how much our culture has internalized the notion that the male climax is an irrepressible urge).

By the 1870s, the organized American women's rights movement had begun to endorse birth control, albeit in euphemistic terms, using the slogan "Voluntary Motherhood." Suspicious of contraception and worried that removing the fear of conception would relieve men of any disincentives to exploit women sexually, feminists recommended abstinence except when conception was desired. Their prudery becomes a bit more understandable when we remember that they sought for women not only control over reproduction but also over sexual activity, rejecting an ancient marital tradition that required women's sexual submission to their husbands.

Since the methods recommended by these radicals—abstinence and male continence—were not generally practicable, women often relied on abortion as their first-line birth control method. New prohibitions on abortion enacted by the states during the mid-nineteenth century did not stop this traditional practice. But by the early twentieth century, women's need for reproductive control had outstripped the methods generally available to them. Their discontent gave rise to a grassroots birth-control movement in the World War I era. American feminists active in the then-strong socialist movement became aware of the availability of vaginal diaphragms in European clinics; they challenged the double standard by which many prosperous women had access to birth control while working-class women and families suffered terribly from unwanted reproduction. Activists such as Emma Goldman and, especially, Margaret Sanger began a civil disobedience campaign to resist the anti-obscenity laws which made it illegal even to discuss contraception, defying the law by distributing birth-control leaflets and opening clinics which fitted women with diaphragms. Several activists served jail time for their convictions, but women flocked to the clinics. Soon a national movement arose, composed of birth-control leagues in many towns and cities, and in the 1920s the state legislatures began to reform their anti-birth control legislation.

As the decentralized movement united into a national organization led by Margaret Sanger, its victorious strategy rested on two alliances. The first was with physicians, who had become increasingly favorable toward reproduction control. Although male-controlled contraceptives, i.e. condoms, were sold openly in drugstores, diaphragms were available only by doctors' prescription, initiating a new era in which physicians became the arbiters of women's morality and family strategies. This alliance stopped short, then, of making birth control a woman's right or an individual right. Moreover, the compromise created an unprecedented moral distinction between contraception and abortion, legalizing the former while the latter remained criminal.

Sanger's band of birth controllers also developed a subsidiary alliance with eugenics, a movement popular through the first half of the twentieth century which proposed to limit the reproduction of those of "inferior stock." A form of hereditarian genetics, eugenics was popular across the political spectrum in the late nineteenth and early twentieth centuries. But given American political culture, formed in the context of slavery, the Indian wars, and military conquest of Mexican territory, it is hardly surprising that notions of genetic superiority and inferiority soon became mapped onto racial categories. The eugenics movement gave rise to programs of coercive sterilization (which continued well into the 1970s) and to arguments for birth control as a policy that ought to be promoted primarily among the poor and the nonwhite. Thus, the birth control/eugenics alliance alienated people of color from the whole reproductive rights project, and de-legitimized women's freedom in favor of their duty to the race.

With the second wave of feminism in the late 1960s and 1970s, activists reclaimed birth control as a fundamental part of the women's rights agenda. These activists focused on assuring safer and more accessible birth control, banning coercive sterilization, and especially securing legal abortion. Women who had experienced illegal abortions spoke out in public, rejecting the guilt and shame that had been attached to abortion. States began repealing anti-abortion laws in the 1960s; 18 states had done so by the time *Roe v. Wade* was decided in 1973. Meanwhile, women's demand had stimulated the development of a hormonal contraceptive pill, first marketed in 1960. Soon afterwards, a woman's health movement began protesting the Pill's inadequate testing and exposed the health dangers of what was then a very high dosage of hormones; its pressure hastened the development of lower-dose pills. The women's movement also forced change in the double standard that governed sterilization policy up through the 1970s, a policy which made it difficult for young, middle-class, white women to get access to voluntary sterilization while imposing coercive, sometimes even undisclosed sterilizations on poor women of color. This last campaign was extremely effective in restricting coercive sterilization while ensuring access to sterilization as a freely chosen form of birth control.

A well-funded, anti-abortion movement started by the Catholic hierarchy in the 1970s drew conservative Protestant support in the 1980s. This movement has succeeded not only in limiting women's access to abortion, but also in hindering contraceptive developments. Anti-abortion forces successfully frustrated access to both the "morning after" pill, a high hormonal dose which prevents uterine implantation, and RU-486, which causes shedding of the uterine lining. At the end of the twentieth century, birth control advocates are clearly on the defensive.

SEE Abortion as A Reproductive Right; Birth Control Movement and African-American Women; Class and Reproductive Rights; Eugenics; *Griswold v. Connecticut*; Planned Parenthood; RU-486; *Roe v. Wade*; Sanger, Margaret; Sterilization Abuse

Further References. Janet Farrell Brodie, *Contraception and Abortion in Nineteenth-Century America* (Ithaca, N.Y., 1994). Linda Gordon, *Woman's Body, Woman's Right: The History of Birth Control in America* (New York, rev. ed., 1990). Carole R. McCann, *Birth Control Politics in the United States, 1916-45* (Ithaca, N.Y., 1994).

LINDA GORDON

BIRTH MOTHERS AND REPRODUCTIVE RIGHTS. The legal rights of birth mothers in Anglo-American law are never absolute and rarely exclusive. Mothers' rights are limited by children's reciprocal rights to care and support and by many legal regulations (for example, those requiring school attendance and prohibiting child labor). When the birth mother is married to the child's biological father, the two always share parental rights. Traditionally, mothers who were not married to their children's fathers had exclusive parental rights—but court cases initiated by natural fathers have limited these rights. The rights of birth mothers come into question in the following situations: when a mother gives up her children (temporarily or permanently); when a natural father tries to prevent adoption; when the state seeks to terminate a mother's parental rights; and when married parents divorce.

In the case of adoption, the birth mother relinquishes all her parental rights to the adoptive parents. Subsequently, the birth mother has no legal claim to the child and cannot expect to have ongoing contact with the child. Nor can the birth mother make major decisions, such as those involving medical treatment and religious participation, on the child's behalf. In a traditional, closed-record adoption, when the birth mother does not meet or know the identity of the adoptive parents (and vice versa), these issues rarely, if ever, arise. But, with the increasing popularity of open adoptions, the familial designation dividing birth mother and adoptive parent may become blurred.

There are several types of open adoption. In restricted open adoption, the adoptive family provides the birth parents with information about the child for a short period of time, using the adoption agency as intermediary. Semi-open adoption allows the biological parents to meet with the adoptive parents, but there is no ongoing exchange of information after the birth. Fully open adoption allows birth parents to meet with the adoptive family and receive information about the child for a limited time. In continuing open adoption, the biological and adoptive parents plan to stay in contact while the child is growing up; both sets of parents are permitted contact with the child. Each of these arrangements allows for varying degrees of contact between the birth parents and adoptive parents, but in no case does the birth mother retain any kind of true legal "right" to the status of parent. Even continuing open adoption cannot and should not be understood as legal co-parenting. The birth mother and the adoptive parents have agreed to conduct the adoption process in a certain manner, but enforcing contact beyond the initial meeting may be extremely difficult. Because of the complicated nature of the relationship between birth parents and adoptive parents, it is always possible that the adoptive parents will choose to limit or discontinue contact with the birth parents. Open adoption also raises issues of birth mothers' rights to privacy that have yet to be fully resolved. The limited contact in most forms of open adoption implies that the relationship between the child and the birth mother will not be continued over time. However, there are many activist groups in the United States and Canada for both birth mothers and adoptive children who wish to find one another. The Internet has become an important source for birth mothers seeking adopted children and vice-versa. Either party may begin the process and initiate contact.

The adoption process becomes more complicated when the birth father does not wish to give up parental rights, or when the birth father is not notified of the pregnancy and subsequent adoption plans. Birth mothers do not have sole decision making rights regarding adoption. Unlike birth mothers, birth fathers can choose to be uninvolved in the pregnancy and birth process and thereby show a lack of interest in parenting. The critical distinction for purposes of custody is whether or not the biological father legally fits the determination of the "presumed father" through providing emotional and financial support to the child and by publicly recognizing the child as his own. A man who is married to a woman who becomes pregnant during the marriage automatically is designated the presumed father; an unmarried biological father does not have this same protection. In most cases, unmarried biological fathers' parental rights can be terminated so that a child can be placed for adoption or adopted by the mother's new spouse if the biological father has not been involved in the child's life. A birth father has the right to maintain parental ties so long as he is the presumed father. If the birth father shows the commitment and involvement required for presumed father status, his parental rights are not terminated for the purposes of adoption unless he is deemed an unfit parent.

Fathers who are not told that they have a child have a strong basis for contesting termination of rights because they have not been given adequate opportunity to become involved as the presumed father. A father who intends to establish himself as the presumed father must also do so in a loosely defined "timely manner." The lack of specifically outlined fathers' rights statutes opens the adoption process to serious consequences for all involved parties. Recent cases include the legal battle over Baby Girl M., whose father was not informed that his former girlfriend had become pregnant, and Michael H., whose father decided to contest the adoption process but did not tell his girlfriend during her pregnancy. The birth father of Baby Girl M. was told of her birth after the prospective adoptive parents had temporary custody, and was unable to establish himself as the presumed father as a result. He was not allowed to veto the adoption in the original decision. This decision was later overturned on appeal, and the child was placed in her father's custody when she was four years old. She had been living with her adoptive family since shortly after birth. Michael H. also was placed with an adoptive family over the protests of his biological father. In this case, however, the fact that the father did not contest the adoption during the pregnancy was taken as evidence that he was not fully committed to parenthood.

After several highly publicized cases in the 1990s involving unwed fathers who sought to interfere with adoptions, several states changed their consent provisions to limit these fathers' rights. A 1995 Utah law went even further, limiting notice of an adoption proceeding to fathers who have taken prior affirmative steps to establish paternity. This law established a presumption that any man who has a sexual relationship with a woman is on notice that a child may be born and the woman may arrange an adoption.

The state has the power to remove a child from a parent's home and even to terminate parental rights. However, a birth mother whose child is taken away and placed in foster care does not automatically forfeit her rights. The federal Adoption and Safe Families Act of 1997 provides that children in foster care are eligible for adoption only if they have spent 15 of the previous 22 months in foster care, and if reasonable efforts to help the birth parent(s) rectify the problems that caused the child originally to be taken from the home have been unsuccessful. The term "reasonable" is somewhat problematic and vague; it can be difficult to determine on a case-by-case basis how much effort is sufficient and reasonable. The law is much clearer regarding situations in which parents are not entitled to expect that efforts will be made to return their children to them. Birth mothers (and fathers) who have had a child removed from the home due to physical or sexual abuse or abandonment, who have had parental rights regarding another child terminated, or who have committed or contributed to the murder or voluntary manslaughter of another of their children, will have their parental rights terminated as a matter of course.

Mothers' rights regarding child custody in divorce cases also vary according to the familial situation. Matters that directly affect children, such as child support, custody, and visitation, are not left for parents to decide. Instead, the court exercises *parens patriae* power (the state as parent) and rules in "the best interests of the child." In actuality, the courts generally do not intervene in uncontested cases where both parents agree on the custody arrangement. Conflicting custody requests result in fathers taking custody about half of the time. When both parents seek sole legal or physical custody of children, the court often awards custody to the parent who is living with the child at the time of the hearing. This practice helps ensure continuity for the child. One study of contested custody requests in the years 1920, 1960, 1990, and 1995 shows that the critical factor in custody awards seems to be the determination of which parent is the "friendly parent," or the parent more likely to allow the child ongoing interaction with the ex-spouse.

Financial matters are not supposed to play a role in the decision of who receives child custody. According to guidelines enacted in the Family Support Act of 1988, formal guidelines for the determination of child support have been established in all states. Most states consider the total income of both parents, and the relative amount of income each earns, in determining how to meet the financial obligation of childrearing fairly. Thirty-two states use some version of a proportion framework to allocate financial responsibility. To provide an oversimplified example, if the noncustodial parent makes 65 percent of the former pre-divorce income, then he or she will be required to meet 65 percent of the calculated average costs of raising the child for the year. Ideally, the best interests of the child are met by granting custody to whichever parent is deemed to have better parenting skills, and any financial lack is made up by child support payments from the noncustodial parent. However, in some cases the ability to provide a more affluent lifestyle for the children may become a proxy for the child's "best interests." And mothers who are awarded child support may still suffer economic deprivation. Recent data suggests that just under half of mothers who are awarded child support will receive less than the full amount, and a quarter will receive nothing at all.

SEE Adoption; Child Custody; Fathers' Rights Movement.

Further References. Marianne Berry, "The Effects of Open Adoption on Biological and Adoptive Parents and the Children: The Arguments and the Evidence," *Child Welfare* 70, 6 (1991): 637-651. Diane Eyer, *Motherguilt: How Our Culture Blames Mothers for What's Wrong with Society* (New York, 1996). Lois Gilman, *The Adoption Resource Book,* 3rd ed. (New York, 1992). Carol A. Gorenberg, "Fathers' Rights vs. Children's Best Interests: Establishing a Predictable Standard for California Adoption Disputes," *Family Law Quarterly*, 31, 2 (1997): 169-214. Eleanor E. Maccoby and Robert H. Mnookin, *Dividing the Child: Social and Legal Dilemmas of Custody* (Cambridge, Mass., 1992). Karen R. March, *The Stranger Who Bore Me: Adoptee-Birth Mother Relationships* (Toronto, 1995). Mary Ann Mason and Ann Quirk, "Are Mothers Losing Custody?: Read My Lips: Trends in Judicial Decision-Making in Custody Disputes—1920, 1960, 1990, and 1995," *Family Law Quarterly*, 31, 2 (1997): 215-236. Public Law 105-89, the Adoption and Safe Families Act of 1997. Jerome Smith, *The Realities of Adoption* (Lanham, Md., 1997).

ERICA A. OWENS

BREAST-FEEDING AND THE LAW. Breast-feeding is becoming more popular in the United States as current research emphasizes what an important health choice this is. The idea that breast-feeding is a value-neutral lifestyle choice is giving way to greater awareness of its significant health benefits. Over the past 10 years, there has been much publicity regarding breast-feeding issues such as whether a woman has the right to breast-feed in public. Nearly half of the states in the U.S. have enacted some form of breast-feeding legislation, in an attempt to encourage more mothers to make this healthy choice.

There are many legal theories on which a right to breast-feed can be based. One is the idea of a constitutional right to breast-feed. This principle was established by a federal appeals court decision in 1981. However, the constitutional right does not apply in all situations. For example, courts have ruled that the right to breast-feed does not apply in divorce cases or criminal cases. It may not apply in private businesses or social agencies. Even when the right does apply, it is not absolute; the right to breast-feed is balanced against competing interests. Given that our society is not very baby-friendly, it is not surprising that the competing interests often outweigh the right to breast-feed.

Over the last 10 years, breast-feeding issues have received considerable publicity. Most media attention has focused on the right to breast-feed in public. Breast-feeding legislation has its roots in the early 1980's, when a handful of women who were told to stop breast-feeding in public refused to accept that mandate. However, not much was accomplished until 1992, when a reporter for the Miami Herald was told by a security guard that she could be "cited" if she refused to stop breast-feeding in a mall. The humorous, informative article that the reporter subsequently wrote caught the attention of a Florida legislator, who was outraged to learn that any mother would be told to stop breast-feeding in public. The resulting legislation encouraged other states to enact laws that would clarify a woman's right to breast-feed in public. By 2001, one-third of the states had some form of legislation addressing breast-feeding in public. Remember that if there is no legislation, women still can breast-feed in public. After all, no one has the right to tell a mother how to feed her baby, or where to do it.

Breast-feeding in public does not represent the only legal battle that nursing mothers have had to wage. Legislative attention now focuses on the employment setting. Policies which accommodate a mother's desire to breast-feed while working are beneficial not only to mother and baby, but also to the employer and to society at large. Less maternal absenteeism and lower health care costs for both mother and baby are two of these benefits. At present, Minnesota, Tennessee and Hawaii have laws that either prevent discrimination against breast-feeding mothers or require employers to accommodate breast-feeding mothers by providing them with a place to express breast milk and allowing them time to do so. Several other states are considering legislation either encouraging or requiring employers to support breast-feeding women when they return to work. In the states that do not have any legislation, an employer may have no obligation to accommodate a breast-feeding mother. Federal legislation that would help has been introduced but not yet enacted. The proposed bills include a measure that would amend the Pregnancy Discrimination Act of 1978 to include breast-feeding.

Currently, most employers (except in Minnesota, Tennessee, and Hawaii) are not required to accommodate the breast-feeding mother. However, discrimination against women is prohibited by law. A breast-feeding employee who is treated less favorably than other employees may be able to argue that she is being subjected to sex discrimination. Thus, an employer might be within its legal rights to refuse to give a woman extra time to express breast milk, but an employer should not be able to tell her that she cannot express milk on her regular break. If other employees can do errands or smoke cigarettes on their break, why shouldn't the breast-feeding mother be allowed to do what she wants to on her break—especially something so important for the health of her baby? Any mother who believes that she is being discriminated against at work should seek legal advice.

The majority of court cases on breast-feeding involve family law matters such as divorce, separation, custody, and visitation. Women may have a difficult time protecting the breast-feeding relationship when custody and visitation decisions must be made. These decisions should balance two important goals. Breast-feeding is best for a baby, but so is a close, loving relationship with the father. Courts do not want to pick one parent over the other. The laws of many states require courts to look for ways to help every child have a close, loving relationship with both parents after they separate. Courts generally will not give breast-feeding priority over the father's bond with his child. Courts can and do order mothers to pump their milk or even wean their children in divorce cases, especially if judges believe they are being asked to pick breast-feeding over the father's bond.

The key to protecting the breast-feeding relationship is to show how the father can have a significant relationship with his child while breast-feeding continues. The best approach is to work these issues out through some form of settlement or mediation, rather than letting the issue go to trial. If that is not possible, it may be helpful to show the court how the father can have a significant bond while the baby continues to breast-feed. A plan is often the most helpful tool a parent can have in a divorce case, whether the case is settled out of court or goes to trial. Concrete, specific and feasible parenting time plans that promote the father's bond and protect the breast-feeding relationship are often a necessity in family law cases.

Parents are the best people to determine what is optimal and what is feasible for their child. Courts look with disfavor on restrictive visitation plans. They can even result in an adverse custody ruling, as more courts are looking at which parent will promote the other parent's bond in deciding custody. Keep in mind that standard visitation can be anywhere from 27 to 40 hours per week. If a parent is seeking to avoid lengthy separations—such as a ruling that gives the father every other weekend with the child—it may be necessary to fashion a plan that provides for almost daily contact with extra time on most weekends. With young babies, it may be difficult or impossible for a mother to avoid long separations if short, frequent visits are not feasible for any reason. These long separations can destroy the breast-feeding relationship. Therefore, it probably is not in a breast-fed baby's best interests for the parents to live far apart from each other.

The law sometimes requires a nursing mother to be in a place which may not be baby-friendly. Jury duty is a common situation which raises this problem. Children are generally not allowed in courtrooms. Although this rule is not aimed at breast-feeding mothers in particular, they might face sanctions (including contempt and even jail) if they bring the baby into the courtroom to feed. Oregon, Idaho, and Iowa are the only states that currently exempt breast-feeding mothers from jury duty. However, other states may have exemptions that breast-feeding mothers can use, such as exemptions for people who are responsible for the daily care of a child, or who have a hardship that prevents them from serving as a juror. Mothers who are called for jury duty should first determine if there are any exemptions that could apply to their situation. If not, they should look to see if they can qualify for a general hardship situation. A letter from the baby's doctor specifying current medical recommendations about breast-feeding, addressing the relevant medical risks that can be reduced by breast-feeding, and recommending that the mother not be separated from the baby may convince the court to exempt the prospective juror. The mother herself, or her doctor, can provide information about the pumping procedures that would be required if the mother is apart from the baby, or the physical problems, including leakage, engorgement, pain, mastitis, and fever, that the mother might suffer if she is unable to breast-feed or pump her breasts. If a mother must appear for jury duty, one solution is to leave the baby in the hallway with a friend or relative, letting the judge know what the situation is.

Police stations, jails, and prisons welcome children even less than courtrooms do. Mothers who are incarcerated, charged with a crime, or reported to a social service agency for abuse or neglect may not have a right to breast-feed. Incarceration is not consistent with the right to rear children, and, temporarily at least, nullifies this right.

A mother who is separated from her baby because of a criminal matter may not have the right to breast-feed her baby, but her breast-feeding may be a factor in deciding her sentence, or when she will begin serving it. While a mother might have a legal right to breast-feed her baby during visitation times, she does not have a right to express milk and have the jail store and deliver the milk to the baby. Mothers are more successful in resolving these issues in a calm, informative manner than by demanding it as their right.

On the rare occasions when breast-feeding becomes an issue in a criminal case, issue, information and education must be provided to everyone concerned. The case of Tabitha Walrond, the young woman who was convicted of manslaughter in New York in 1999 after her baby died of malnutrition, is a powerful example of the harm done by ignorance. Apparently, Walrond was never told that the breast reduction surgery she underwent several years earlier could interfere with milk production. Clearly, there is not much anyone can do to help a breast-feeding mother who is charged with manslaughter when her baby dies after she ingests illegal substances. However, experts do not recommend that all mothers with a substance abuse problem wean. Each case must be evaluated separately. Society should avoid these tragedies through substance abuse programs that closely monitor the mother and allow her to continue providing her baby with this healthy form of nurturance.

Occasionally, breast-feeding becomes an issue in social service agency cases. A few mothers have been reported to public agencies when it appeared that their babies were failing to thrive. The standard "knee-jerk" reaction in this country is to immediately place the baby in foster care instead of trying to discover why the baby is failing to thrive or if that is even truly the case. More than likely, misinformation and mismanagement of breast-feeding has resulted in the dire situation. Remember that no court in the United States has found extended breast-feeding to be abuse or neglect, regardless of the age of the child. While many experts are unaccustomed to children nursing past infancy, and discourage the practice, it is currently recommended that children wean naturally. The American Association of Pediatrics recommends that children be breast-fed for a minimum of 12 months or as long as is mutually desirable, even through ages five or six. Growing numbers of Americans are convinced that extended breast-feeding is beneficial to children, and that nature intended children to wean themselves when they are ready.

In conclusion, our legal system is a reflection of society's standards. As our society becomes more baby-friendly, we will see these changes reflected in the courts. Until that time, it is important to provide accurate information so that legal decisions can truly look at the best interests of our children.

SEE Child Custody; Midwifery as a Reproductive Right; Prisoners, Reproductive Rights of; Pregnancy Discrimination Act of 1978; Title VII, Civil Rights Act of 1964.

Further References. Elizabeth N. Baldwin, Esq., "Breast-feeding and the Law," http://www.lalecheleague.org/LawMain.html; http://breastfeeding.com.

ELIZABETH N. BALDWIN, ESQ.

BUCK v. BELL (274 U.S. 200, 1927) is an 8-1 Supreme Court decision which upheld the constitutionality of a Virginia law permitting compulsory sterilization of the "mentally defective," defined in many states at the time as the mentally ill or deficient, epileptics, sexual perverts, and habitual criminals. Carrie Buck, a rape victim, had been institutionalized because of her foster parents' embarrassment of the resulting pregnancy. Bell, the superintendent of the institution where Carrie was confined, alleged that she, her mother, and her daughter were "feeble-minded." Questions continue today about whether Buck was seriously retarded or "anti-social." Scholars have found unethical collusion between Carrie's lawyer, hospital officials, and legislators. All of them were eugenicists who advocated race improvement through sterilization, were obsessed with controlling the sexual behavior and propagation of "moral delinquents," and, in an economic recession, sought ways to enable inmates to leave institutions and become self-supporting without risking pregnancy and the production of more "mental defectives."

In the majority opinion, Justice Oliver Wendell Holmes, Jr. likened compulsory sterilization to compulsory vaccination, viewed sterilization as a "lesser sacrifice" than those imposed on citizens in wartime, and made the famous comment,

"Three generations of imbeciles are enough." Holmes saw no violations to citizens' liberty interests under the Fourteenth Amendment Due Process Clause; nor did he see an Equal Protection Clause violation even though this law reached only citizens who were institutionalized by the state. *Buck* gave a "green light" for more than 4,000 sterilizations in Virginia until the practice was stopped in 1972, and more than 50,000 sterilizations nationwide.

Although *Buck* has never been reversed, subsequent cases have limited its authority. Since *Skinner v. Oklahoma* (1942), lower courts have held that judges cannot order sterilization without clear statutory authorization. While compulsory sterilization is no longer allowed as a punitive measure, it may be ordered today as a condition of probation. Courts still wrestle with such issues as the adequacy of the procedural protections for those whom sterilization is requested, and who, other than the person to be sterilized, should have power to consent to the procedure.

SEE Eugenics; Federal sterilization guidelines (1979); *Skinner v. Oklahoma*; Sterilization Abuse; *Stump v. Sparkman*.

Further References. Paul A. Lombardo, "Three Generations, No Imbeciles: New Light on *Buck v. Bell*," *New York University Law Review,* 60 (April 1985): 30-62.

RONALD KAHN

C

_____

CALIFORNIA FEDERAL SAVINGS AND LOAN ASSOCIATION v. GUERRA
(479 U.S. 272, 1987) upheld a state law requiring employers to provide unpaid
maternity leave (up to four months) and to reinstate employees upon their return to
work. The law did not mandate leave or reinstatement for any other reason. The
legal issue in the case was whether this law conflicted with the Pregnancy Discrimination Act (PDA) of 1978. The PDA directs that employers treat employees
unable to work due to pregnancy and childbirth in the same way that they treat those
disabled by other temporary conditions. When a federal law and a state law conflict, the former pre-empts the latter, and the state law is void. The case also raised
broad questions about the nature of sexual equality. Specifically, is identical treatment truly equal when men and women fulfill different biological functions? When
California said "no," the U.S. Supreme Court let that determination stand.

Lillian Garland, a receptionist in a Los Angeles branch of "Cal Fed," got caught
between state and federal notions of equality. When she tried to return to work
after her daughter was born, the bank told her she had no job. When she sued,
the bank argued that the PDA pre-empted the state law. Feminists split, sometimes heatedly, over Garland's case. Some supported California's position that sexual differences must be taken into account to insure equal results. Others, citing
the legacy of protective labor legislation in the early twentieth century, argued
that the dangers of departing from strict equality were too great, even if strict
equality imposed disproportionate burdens on women. The National Organization of Women, for instance, expressed fears that employers might refuse to hire
women of childbearing age if the California law survived.

The Supreme Court ruled, six to three, that the statutes did not conflict. Both
sides relied extensively on the legislative history of the PDA. The majority

concluded that the PDA prohibited employers from treating pregnant workers worse than others, but left room for states to require additional protections for them. Moreover, the Court reasoned that employers could eliminate any potential for conflict by extending the leave and reinstatement provisions to all temporarily disabled workers.

At any rate, Congress limited the long-term impact of this ruling by passing the Family and Medical Leave (FMLA) of 1993. The FMLA returned to the gender-neutral standard by requiring that all employees be accorded up to 12 weeks of unpaid leave for the birth or adoption of a child, the serious illness of a family member, or the employee's own serious illness.

SEE Family and Medical Leave Act of 1993; Pregnancy Discrimination Act of 1978; Protective Labor Legislation and Reproductive Rights; Title VII and Reproductive Rights.

Further References. Doug Gutherie and Louise Marie Roth, "The States, Courts, and Maternity Policies in U.S. Organizations: Specifying Institutional Mechanisms," *American Sociological Review*, 64 (1999): 41-63. Herma Hill Kay and Martha S. West, *Sex-Based Discrimination: Text, Cases and Materials*, 4th ed. (Minneapolis, 1996).

JILDA M. ALIOTTA

CARDER, ANGELA. SEE *In re* (A.C.)

CAREY v. POPULATION SERVICES INTERNATIONAL (432 U.S. 678, 1977) involved a New York law that made it a crime to advertise, display, sell, or distribute contraceptives to minors younger than 16, and allowed only licensed pharmacists to sell or distribute contraceptives to people 16 or older. A three-judge federal district court unanimously found those portions of the law applying to nonprescription contraceptives unconstitutional under the First and Fourteenth Amendments. On appeal, the U.S. Supreme Court struck down all provisions relating to nonprescription contraceptives, including the ban on advertising and display, by a 7-2 vote. Justice William Brennan's opinion cited the holding in *Roe v. Wade* (1973) that the liberty protected by the Fourteenth Amendment Due Process Clause includes "a right of personal privacy." Restrictions on the availability of contraceptives, which limit the freedom to make these decisions, must be "justified by compelling state interests" and "narrowly drawn to express only those interests." New York failed to present an interest.

The Court also struck down the prohibition on distributing nonprescription contraceptives to minors. However, there was no majority opinion. Justice Brennan, writing for himself and three others, stated that the right to privacy extends to minors as well as adults. When a state burdens this right, it must present evidence to support its assertion that the burden is connected to a legitimate and compelling interest. In response to New York's argument that the law was constitutional because it did not totally prohibit access to contraceptives through physicians, Brennan concluded that even partial restrictions on access to contraceptives "must also pass constitutional scrutiny," whether they apply to adults or to minors.

Justices Lewis Powell, John Paul Stevens, and Byron White each wrote separate concurring opinions on this issue. Powell suggested that the state might design a law that "encouraged" adolescents to seek the advice and guidance of their parents before deciding whether to engage in sexual intercourse" by requiring prior parental consultation for the distribution of contraceptives to minors. Stevens accepted the state's assertion of a legitimate interest in discouraging sexual activity among unmarried minors, but insisted that persuading minors to abstain by subjecting them to increased risk of unwanted pregnancy and venereal disease was not; "it is as though a State decided to dramatize its disapproval of motorcycles by forbidding the use of safety helmets." White agreed with Stevens that the state might have a significant interest in discouraging sexual activity by minors, but insisted that the state had not demonstrated that its prohibition on contraceptives actually accomplished this.

Carey has been cited primarily in support of two positions: that a state-created obstacle to exercising the right to privacy need not be absolute to be constitutionally impermissible, and that the constitutional significance of state interests may differ for adults and minors.

SEE Abortion and Parental Involvement; *Eisenstadt v. Baird*; *Griswold v. Connecticut*; *New York v. Schweiker; Roe v. Wade*; Youth and Reproductive Rights.

BARBARA HAYLER

CASEY. SEE *Planned Parenthood of Southeastern Pennsylvania v. Casey.*

CHILD CUSTODY. American women's rights to custody of their children have depended on the interaction of many complex historical, social and cultural factors. The American colonies followed English common law. Before the American Revolution, therefore, free children were legally the property of their fathers. A father who died while his children were minors could deprive the mother of custody through his will by assigning custody of the children as he wished. Divorce (which was rare) did not weaken the father's control; he retained custody unless he was proven unfit. Courts determined the fate of children born to unmarried women. Most unmarried mothers probably lost custody once the children were weaned. The ancient common law rule that assigned custody of these children to the "parish" never took hold in the religiously diverse colonies. The common law did not apply to slaves. Any child born to a female slave was the property of the mother's owner, and remained so even if the mother was sold or freed. Slave mothers had no right to custody. Mulatto children born to free or servant white women became indentured servants until they were 30.

By the end of the nineteenth century, slavery was gone. "Illegitimate" children remained with their mothers. Divorce, though still rare, occurred often enough to afford judges and legislators the opportunity to rethink the paternal preference doctrine. Early in the century, courts began to recognize that it was appropriate for infant children to be placed with their mothers, who bore primary responsibility for their care. However, divorcing mothers had to petition the courts for custody; they did not automatically get it. By 1900, the "tender years doctrine" had been extended to apply to any young or female children. This doctrine essentially established an automatic maternal preference. Mothers were awarded custody unless they were proven unfit.

Maternal preference did not fit well with the norms of a male supremacist society. The tender years doctrine came to mean, in practice, that the mother got custody as long as she met the social expectations of appropriate motherhood. The concept of "unfitness" took on a wide definition in the nineteenth and twentieth centuries. For example, women who gave birth to mixed-race children risked loss of custody. Factors which made a mother "unfit" included poverty, adultery (before or after marital separation), or leaving one's husband without just cause. An "unfit" mother could lose visitation rights as well as custody. Fathers were not held to the same moral standards.

The replacement of the paternal preference with the tender years doctrine represented the rejection of a doctrine which ranked the fathers' interests supreme in favor of one which emphasized children's interests. The next step, which accompanied a steady rise in the divorce rate, was to sever the nexus between childrens' interests and maternal preference. This development ultimately proved fatal to the tender years doctrine. As early as 1881, a Kansas court declared that "Above all things, the paramount consideration is, what will promote the welfare of the child?" By the 1980s, every state had discarded maternal preference in favor of "best interests of the child"—often abbreviated "BIC."

On its face, BIC is a gender-neutral policy. Its application has resulted in some clear benefits for mothers and children. Applied to financial settlements, for example, BIC has led to decisions requiring fathers to support their non-custodial children and these children's mothers. Traditional assumptions about family roles—for example, the idea that mothers are "naturally" more nurturing than fathers—often led to decisions in which mothers retained custody. But the divorce reform, feminist, and fathers' rights movements of the late twentieth century challenged these stereotypes. What has not changed much is the mother's role within the family or the relative socioeconomic positions of men and women.

Today, most child development experts maintain that the child's best interests are served by placement with the "psychological parent," the parent to whom the child has a primary attachment. This parent is usually the primary caretaker, who, in most cases, is the mother. (This is why fathers' rights groups oppose the use of the primary/psychological parent criterion). Either sole maternal custody or joint custody, which was common by 2001, can protect this mother-child bond. Approximately 84 percent of biological mothers retain physical custody of their children through one of these arrangements, usually by agreement between the parents. However, courts have not identified the best interests of the child with the psychological parent criterion. When fathers demand custody, they have an excellent chance of winning—even when the mother has been the primary caretaker.

Several factors privilege fathers in custody cases. Fathers usually have an economic advantage, reinforced by the fact that their working is not regarded as incompatible with their parental role. Fathers' greater resources enable them to obtain better legal counsel than mothers. Another reason fathers win is that the BIC standard is vague; the determination of contested custody cases is left up to a judge's discretion. Because the standard is vague, economic factors, social expectations and sex-role stereotypes inevitably influence custody decisions. These considerations often work in favor of fathers. Women are evaluated by traditional standards of motherhood, and fathers by traditional standards of fatherhood. Both sets of standards are tied to traditional gender roles.

When the father's financial situation is better than the mother's, he may argue that the children are better off with him because he can provide a more financially secure home. It is easy to identify a child's interests with a parent's resources. A mother who stays home with the children may risk loss of custody because of her economic disadvantage, especially if the father has a new stay-at-home wife. But a woman may also risk losing custody if she tries too hard or succeeds too well in the working world. Women who work or attend school have lost custody. For example, Sharon Prost, chief counsel for the Republicans on the Senate Judiciary Committee, lost custody of her two children to her husband because he convinced the court that she failed to make the children her first priority. WNBA (Women's National Basketball Association) player Pamela McGee lost custody of her children due to the time commitments of professional basketball. All too often, mothers are damned if they do and damned if they don't.

Women have lost custody of their children regardless of the nature, quality, or success of their parenting. Their sexuality may be used as a basis for custody decisions. Both heterosexual and lesbian relationships have been used as bases for denying custody to mothers. Even battered mothers may be labeled deviant mothers. Some courts have seen an abused woman's decision to leave a relationship as indicative of unstable behavior that makes them less fit for custody. Most states have passed laws requiring that domestic violence be considered as a criterion in child custody cases. Ironically, women who are trying to leave a violent environment may lose custody because they "fail to protect" their children by exposing them to a violent environment.

Some fathers who do not want custody of their children use the threat of custody challenges to punish or coerce mothers. Fathers may do this in order to decrease a divorce settlement or to discourage the mother from seeking an increase in child support. Fathers may also use violence and other threats to coerce concessions from mothers.

American women have won the right to make the ultimate decision whether or not to bear a child. But once the child is born, women's custody rights have historically been and continue to be at a disadvantage relative to those of fathers. Women's reproductive rights do not always include the right to raise the children

they bear. Legal doctrine has progressed from an emphasis on the interests of fathers to an emphasis on the interests of children. Even the tender years doctrine—the rule most favorable to mothers—was often bent to serve the interests of the father. Custody law has consistently reflected and reinforced the sexism of American society.

SEE Adoption; Birth Mothers and Reproductive Rights; Breast-Feeding and the Law; Fathers' Rights Movement (FRM); Lesbians and Reproductive Rights.

Further References. Phyllis Chesler, *Mothers on Trial* (New York, 1986). Failure to Protect Working Group, "Charging Battered Mothers with 'Failure to Protect:' Still Blaming the Victim," *Fordham Urban Law Journal*, 27 (February 2000): 849-872. Susan Jacobs, "Note & Comment: The Hidden Gender Bias Behind 'The Best Interest of the Child' Standard in Custody Decisions," *Georgia State University Law Review*, 13 (June 1997): 845-898. Mary Ann Mason, *From Fathers' Property to Children's Rights: The History of Child Custody in the United States* (New York, 1994). Patricia Murphy and Elaine Cleeton, *In the Best Interests of the Child: Good Mothers, Bad Mothers, and the Law* (Philadelphia, 2000).

PATRICIA MURPHY

CITY OF AKRON v. AKRON CENTER FOR REPRODUCTIVE HEALTH (462 U.S. 416, 1983) dealt with several abortion regulations in Akron, Ohio. These included hospitalization for all second trimester abortions and a 24-hour waiting period between the first clinic visit and the abortion appointment. In addition, "informed consent" regulations required doctors to describe the physical attributes of the fetus, to tell the patient that life begins at conception, and to explain all possible negative consequences of, and alternatives to, abortion.

The Supreme Court heard *Akron* two years after Ronald Reagan had won the presidency and Republicans had taken control of the Senate. However, six of the seven justices in the *Roe v. Wade* majority remained on the Court. By a 6-3 vote, the Supreme Court invalidated the regulations as either vague or unreasonable. The majority opinion, written by Justice Lewis Powell, reaffirmed the "essential element of personal liberty" recognized in *Roe v. Wade* and "respected the doctrine of stare decisis" (adherence to precedent). But this adherence to *Roe* was accompanied by hints that change might be coming.

On the same day, the Court upheld laws from Missouri and Virginia requiring pathology reports, hospitalization for late abortions, and parental or judicial consent for minors. Another indication of change was a dissent by Justice Sandra Day O'Connor, Ronald Reagan's first appointee to the Court. Although she had opposed abortion regulations as a member of the Arizona Senate, she refused to hold them unconstitutional here. She asserted that the Akron regulations did not hinder a woman's access to abortion but provided medical care and a "period of reflection." Because medical advances since *Roe* had reduced the age of fetal viability, she rejected *Roe*'s trimester framework as "unworkable" and proposed

instead a constitutional rule that would invalidate only those regulations that imposed an "undue burden" on women at all stages of pregnancy. *Planned Parenthood of Southeastern Pennsylvania v. Casey* (1992), authored in part by Justice O'Connor, accepted the undue burden rule and upheld informed consent requirements and a 24-hour waiting period.

SEE *Ohio v. Akron Center for Public Health; Planned Parenthood of Kansas City v. Ashcroft; Planned Parenthood of Southeastern Pennsylvania v. Casey; Roe v. Wade;* Undue Burden.

Further References. David J. Garrow, *Liberty and Sexuality: the Right to Privacy and the Making of* Roe v. Wade (New York, 1994). Cynthia Gorney, *Articles of Faith* (New York, 1998).

MELISSA HAUSSMAN

CLASS AND REPRODUCTIVE RIGHTS are intimately linked in the United States, as women's economic position profoundly affects all aspects of reproductive freedom. The meaning of reproductive rights embraces both the right to have and rear children and the right not to do so. Reproductive rights are protected by the U.S. Constitution. The Supreme Court has determined that what it calls "the right to procreate"—the decision whether to become a parent—is so central to a person's identity and well-being that it is protected by the Fourteenth Amendment's guarantee of individual liberty. Two factors, however, limit this promise of protection. First, the Court has ruled that poverty does not trigger special consideration under the Constitution. The second, and related, limiting factor is that the Court understands reproductive rights as matters of privacy and not as matters of gender equality. This conception of reproductive rights throws women back on their own private resources to carry out their reproductive decisions.

The gap between rich and poor in the United States is the widest it has been since World War II. In a society where people have to purchase basic services like health care and child care, this stratification jeopardizes the reproductive rights of poorer women. Some 43 million Americans lack health insurance, including approximately 14 percent of women nationwide. Because the distribution of wealth is not neutral with respect to gender or race, women of all races and men of color are more likely than white men to be poor and lack access to medical care, job security, and work flexibility, all of which facilitate reproductive self-determination.

Access to safe, effective contraception and abortion is fundamental to individual women's control of their fertility, and both are all too dependent on a woman's financial resources. The right to use contraceptives was first upheld, for married couples only, in the 1965 Supreme Court decision *Griswold v. Connecticut.* Subsequent decisions extended this right to unmarried persons and to minors. The rulings ended a century of struggle that began in 1873 when the Comstock laws prohibited the distribution of "obscene" materials through the mail—including birth control information and devices—and encompassed

Margaret Sanger's 30-year campaign to get contraceptives into the hands of American women and onto the public health agenda. Today, a variety of government programs like Medicaid and Title X subsidize birth control for poor and young women. However, young women may fear that their parents will be notified if they seek contraceptive care, a "squeal rule" that many lawmakers continue to advocate.

Birth control is one area where the benefits of higher class status do not always translate into superior access. Many private insurance plans do not pay for prescription birth control, such as the Pill or diaphragm. Consequently, women with insurance wind up paying directly for these expenses, and have higher out-of-pocket health care costs than men. Federal employees and residents of six states are guaranteed equity, and Congress and many legislatures are debating measures to ensure that all insurance plans cover contraceptives on the same basis as other prescriptions. Many advocates contrast women's inadequate coverage with the way that companies have rushed to cover the impotence drug Viagra for men. But research on new contraceptives, especially for men, is not a priority for pharmaceutical companies. This is partly due to fears of liability; many recent female contraceptives, such as the Dalkon Shield intra-uterine device, have harmed women and costs manufacturers money in lawsuits and settlements.

Access to abortion is very closely related to class status. Only seven years after the Supreme Court legalized abortion in *Roe v. Wade,* the Court upheld the Hyde Amendment, which prevents Congress from funding abortions for Medicaid recipients except in such dire circumstances as when the woman's life is endangered (*Harris v. McRae*, 1980). Most states stopped paying for Medicaid abortions as a result. In 1998, less than one-third of the states fully funded abortions for Medicaid recipients. Feminists have started grass-roots organizations like the Abortion Rights Fund of Western Massachusetts to lend poor women money to obtain abortions they cannot otherwise afford. The *Webster* and *Casey* decisions (1989 and 1992) gave states the green light to enact new barriers to abortion. Since then, many states have implemented laws like 24- or 48-hour waiting periods that make it more difficult to obtain abortions, especially for poor women and women who live in rural areas and must travel long distances to abortion facilities. A variety of local, state, and federal policies impede access to abortion for minors and for incarcerated women (both of whom usually lack financial resources). Military personnel and members of their families are denied abortion services at military hospitals even if they are willing to pay for the procedure themselves.

Laws are not the only factors which limit access to abortion. Escalating violence against abortion providers means that fewer doctors are willing to provide this vital service, and anti-abortion attitudes mean that fewer medical schools require—or even offer—abortion training to their students. The drug RU-486, which might diffuse the violence by shifting early abortion services to the relative anonymity of private physicians' offices, did not get final marketing approval from the Food and Drug Administration until September 2000, and is still not available to most women in the United States. These conditions do not bode well for access to abortion in the twenty-first century. The situation increasingly resembles that of the time when abortion was illegal, and money and connections were the crucial determinants of who could get a safe abortion and who could not.

Class position affects a woman's right to become a mother at least as strongly as it does her right not to do so. As I mentioned earlier, the right to bear children is a recognized constitutional right. Yet, to put that right into practice, poor women may require an array of social rights that enable them to exercise rights equally with wealthier women. Instead of facilitating this social equality, public policy more often actively discourages poor and lower-income women from becoming mothers. Many features of U.S. social welfare policy make the right to motherhood problematic for poor women. Fertility and health, the foundation of any right to reproduce, are compromised by poor enforcement of occupational safety and health laws and by the lack of universal health coverage. When sexually transmitted diseases (STDs) go undiagnosed and untreated, for instance, this neglect can permanently damage a woman's ability to conceive. Since the United States has the highest rate of STDs in the industrialized world, this is no small problem.

In addition to neglecting women's needs, government policies take away poor women's power to make their own decisions. The federal government will not reimburse states for Medicaid abortions, but it will pay for permanent sterilization. Rather than allow women to decide whether and when to have children, this policy means that poor women must carry each pregnancy to term or lose the opportunity to become pregnant altogether. This policy recalls a long history of sterilization abuse in this country, starting with the "race suicide" panic and eugenics movement at the beginning of the 1900s and continuing throughout this century with government sterilization of Native American, African-American, and Puerto Rican women, often against their will or without their knowledge.

Poor women experience many other assaults on their fertility. Unsafe workplaces pose a threat to women with few occupational choices, like farm workers who are exposed to pesticides known to cause birth defects. Judges' attempts to forbid pregnancy as a condition of sentencing in criminal cases present women with coercively structured choices. Although sentences with these kinds of conditions will almost certainly be struck down on appeal because they violate the constitutional right to procreate, appeals take time and cost money.

The impact of new "fetal protection" policies, which undermine women's civil and reproductive rights, has often had powerful race and class biases. While some women of all classes and races drink alcohol and take drugs during pregnancy, it is overwhelmingly poor women—most often, poor African-American women—who are prosecuted for alleged violations of fetal rights and who lose custody of their newborns because of their conduct during pregnancy.

Perhaps the most striking current illustration of how public policy dissuades poor women from bearing children is welfare policy. The 1996 Personal Responsibility and Work Ethic Act not only put strict lifetime limits on the number of years a poor woman may receive assistance, but also approved of "family caps" that end the longstanding practice of increasing a woman's aid if she has another child while receiving welfare payments. Although more white women receive welfare than do women of color, the dominant image of the "welfare mother" (or "welfare queen") is of an African-American woman; poor African-American single mothers bear the symbolic brunt of policy-makers' disapproval of women parenting alone, outside of patriarchal family structures. A look at other public policies shows that congressional repeal of the welfare entitlement is an indictment of poor single mothers and not just a cost-cutting measure. Widows relying on Social Security, for instance, receive payments that are four times higher and last until their children are grown, because they were proper married mothers. The negative consequences of losing welfare support are compounded when women and their children lose eligibility for Medicaid.

If women who depend on welfare are scorned, that does not mean that women who work for wages are always rewarded with protection of their reproductive health and decisions. Discrimination against pregnant women in the workplace violates federal civil rights laws (see Title VII of the 1964 Civil Rights Act). Discrimination, however, is understood as treating pregnant women differently from their co-workers. Hence, pregnant workers have no right any job modification, such as help lifting heavy objects. If a pregnant woman loses her job and her health insurance, she is unlikely to be able to buy new coverage, because pregnancy is a "pre-existing" condition that most insurers will not pay for. Furthermore, the United States has only a meager parental leave policy compared with other industrialized nations. This policy affects employed women of many classes, for few can afford to take unpaid leaves. Finally, the scarcity of affordable, high-quality child care is particularly severe for low-income women.

Poor women face pressures and constraints outside the realm of official public policy that may compromise their reproductive rights, such as economic incentives to bear children for other people. Not surprisingly, lower-income women comprise the majority of those who have become "surrogate mothers." Ten thousand dollars, long the going rate for this "service," may represent a lot of money to a financially insecure woman. A surrogate mother's economic position disadvantages her if she changes her mind and wants to keep the baby. Not only will she have difficulty retaining a good attorney, but (as was true in the lower court decision in *Baby M*) the middle-class status of the parties contracting for the baby may convince a court that they can better meet a child's needs.

Because there is virtually no reproductive rights issue on which class does not bear, this essay can only illustrate that relationship, not exhaust the topic. Class issues are basic to both the right to reproduce and the right not to reproduce. The intersections between class, race, and gender mean that singling out any one dimension is to some extent artificial, compared to the way people actually experience their lives. Class status, along with race and gender, powerfully affect women's ability to plan their reproductive lives as they would like to.

SEE Abortion and Public Assistance; Abortion Providers and Violence; African-American Women and Reproductive Rights; *Baby M*; *Carey v. Population Services International*; *Eisenstadt v. Baird*; Eugenics; Fetal Protection; *Griswold v. Connecticut*; *Harris v. McRae*; Hyde Amendment; Lifestyle Restrictions and Pregnancy; *Planned Parenthood of Southeastern Pennsylvania v. Casey*; Privacy and Reproductive Rights; *Roe v. Wade*; Sanger, Margaret (1879–1966); Sterilization Abuse; Surrogate Motherhood; *Webster v. Reproductive Health Services*.

Further References. Elaine Tyler May, *Barren in the Promised Land: Childless Americans and the Pursuit of Happiness* (Cambridge, Mass., 1995). Gwendolyn Mink, *Welfare's End* (Ithaca, N.Y., 1997). Rachel Roth, *Making Women Pay: The Hidden Costs of Fetal Rights* (Ithaca, N.Y., 1999).

RACHEL ROTH

CLEVELAND BOARD OF EDUCATION v. LAFLEUR (414 U.S. 631, 1974) was a constitutional case involving long, mandatory, and unpaid maternity leaves. Jo Carol LaFleur and Susan Cohen, public schoolteachers in Cleveland, Ohio and Chesterfield County, Virginia, challenged regulations that forced them to begin their leaves in the fourth or fifth month of pregnancy. The school boards argued that the rules were reasonably related to two important public interests: the protection of expectant mothers and their babies, and the continuity of education. The U.S. Supreme Court ruled seven to two that these policies violated the Fourteenth Amendment.

Interestingly, the majority did not base its decision on the sex discrimination component of the equal protection guarantee, but on the Due Process Clause. Justice Potter Stewart relied on the "rational basis" test to conclude that the state interests, while legitimate, did not support the fixed limits. The policies created an "irrebuttable presumption" that linked pregnancy and unfitness to teach; earlier decisions had ruled that such presumptions were constitutionally dubious. Requiring the teacher to begin her leave at a fixed point so early in the pregnancy had no reasonable relationship to maternal or fetal health and might even frustrate the desire to ensure continuity of education. If the real reason for such laws was to "save pregnant teachers from embarrassment at the hands of giggling schoolchildren," as one school official had testified, such logic was an "outmoded taboo." The justices were also concerned by the effects of these regulations on the constitutional right of privacy. Past decisions like *Griswold v. Connecticut* and *Eisenstadt v. Baird* had held that intimate decisions relating to marriage and the family were protected from state intrusion. The "irrebuttable presumption" of pregnant teachers' unfitness unduly interfered with the teachers' rights to decide "whether to bear or beget a child."

LaFleur linked its ruling to established precedents on privacy and the minimal scrutiny of the rational basis test. Other decisions at about the same time, in which the Court refused to recognize any sex discrimination in employer maternity policies, reinforce the impression that the Court did not view *LaFleur* in the context of women's reproductive rights.

SEE *Eisenstadt v. Baird*; Family and Medical Leave Act of 1993; *Geduldig v. Aiello*; *General Electric v. Gilbert*; *Griswold v. Connecticut*; Pregnancy Discrimination Act of 1978.

MARY THORNBERRY

COMMON GROUND is a grassroots social movement headed by prominent pro-life and pro-choice activists that facilitates dialogues between opponents and proponents of abortion rights in order to change the dynamic of the conflict over abortion. Common Ground does not attempt to resolve the differences between the two sides, and never asks dialogue participants to change their beliefs. Instead, participants promise to enter into an honest dialogue with those present in order to understand the position and motivations of their opponents and to find areas of common conviction and concern.

Common Ground dialogues between pro-choice and pro-life activists began as early as 1990 in Missouri. The establishment in 1993 of the Washington, D.C.-based Common Ground Network for Life and Choice further strengthened the movement. The network's mission is to facilitate dialogues as requested by activists in local communities and to help communities initiate action projects. The network also sponsors national conferences and publishes papers coauthored by pro-life and pro-choice activists on areas of common concern such as adoption, teenage pregnancy, and clinic activism. Both sides agree that impediments to adoption should be removed, teenage pregnancy reduced, and clinic violence eliminated.

Participants in Common Ground are often targets of heavy criticism from their own camps. The most common charge is that the willingness to engage in dialogue with the "enemy" lends credibility to the opposition. Common Ground has been most successful at increasing understanding and developing friendships between supporters and opponents of abortion, and least successful at sustaining action projects. The failure to sustain action has multiple causes. These include the inability to find concrete actions which both sides can agree on, and the immense complexity of the causes of unwanted pregnancies. The eventual failure of one Missouri project resulting from Common Ground dialogues may well indicate that the greatest barrier to actions is the unwillingness of most activists to recognize any common ground. In 1990, the Missouri abortion clinic which had challenged governmental restrictions in *Webster v. Reproductive Health Services* opened an on-site adoption agency and was highly successful in placing African-American infants. However, the agency ran into financial problems when too few minority families were able to pay the adoption fees needed to sustain the agency. Even though the adoption agency clearly increased the choices available to women facing unplanned pregnancies and probably helped prevent some abortions, both pro-life and pro-choice groups refused appeals for support. The agency was forced to close.

SEE Abortion and Political Conflict; Abortion and Political Rhetoric; National Abortion and Reproductive Rights Action League; Operation Rescue; *Webster v. Reproductive Health Services.*

Further References. Jean Cavender, Marilyn Dickstein Kopp, Amelia McCracken, Mel Taylor, Loretto Wagner and Harry Webne-Behrman, *Common Ground on Teen Pregnancy: A Pro-Choice, Pro-Life Conversation*, http://www.cpn.org/common_ground/abortion (Washington, D.C., 1996). Frederica Mathewes-Green, "Pro-Life, Pro-Choice: Can We Talk?" *Christian Century*, 113 (January 3-10,1996): 12-15. Andrew F. Puzder and B. J. Isaacson-Jones. *Adoption As Common Ground* (Washington, D.C., 1995). Todd David Whitmore, "Common Ground, Not Middle Ground: Crossing the Pro-Life, Pro-Choice Divide," *Christian Century*, 113 (January 3-10 1996): 10.

NELIA BETH SCOVILL

D

DANFORTH. SEE *Planned Parenthood of Central Missouri v. Danforth.*

DILATION AND EXTRACTION (D&X) is an abortion procedure in which the fetus is partially delivered and then destroyed. It is a rare procedure known as dilate and extract (D&X or D&E) to professionals and partial-birth abortion (PBA) to right-to-life activists. In popular discourse, D&X has become largely synonymous with "late-term abortion." This general term is used to describe any induced abortion taking place after the 20th or 21st week of gestation. Since the fetus attains viability between the 20th and 24th week, late-term abortions are generally prohibited either by law or medical societies unless required to save the life of the woman or avoid serious health consequences to her. According to the Alan Guttmacher Institute, approximately 1 percent of medical terminations of pregnancies occur at 21 weeks or later.

It is worth reinforcing the distinction between late-term abortions and D&X abortions. A late term abortion refers to *any* type of abortion that occurs during the late second or third trimester of pregnancy. "D&X" and "partial-birth abortion" refer to a *specific* procedure which can be done at any time during the second and third term. It is almost never done unless the mother is in grave danger or the fetus has developed abnormalities incompatible with life. Banning D&Xs would not eliminate late-term abortions. It would merely ban one procedure used for them. This fact often gets lost in the rhetoric surrounding the issue. Opponents of legalized abortion use the phrase "partial-birth abortion" to stigmatize the procedure. This rhetorical tactic has met with considerable success as politicians and much of the mass media have adopted the term.

Debate on D&X leapt to the national scene in 1995, when H.R. 1833, the "Partial-Birth Abortion Ban of 1995," was introduced in Congress and passed by both House and Senate. The bill allowed imprisonment and fines for any doctor who "knowingly performs a *partial-birth abortion* and thereby *kills* a human fetus or infant" (emphasis added) unless it was "necessary to save the life of the woman upon whom it was performed, and no other form of abortion would suffice for that purpose." Legislative hearings produced conflicting testimony regarding the number of D&Xs performed annually in the United States, with figures ranging from 450 to 5,000. A Senate amendment allowing the procedure if necessary to "avert serious adverse health consequences" was defeated. President Clinton vetoed the 1995 bill and a subsequent 1997 bill, citing the lack of a clause allowing D&X where a woman's health would be "grievously damaged."

Following the second veto, the debate moved to the states. Twenty-three legislatures passed laws outlawing "partial-birth abortions." Most of these were modeled on the congressional version. The federal courts, however, have consistently struck down these laws, on the grounds that they are unconstitutionally vague or that they impose an undue burden on a woman's exercise of her right to abortion. In *Stenberg v. Carhart* (2000), the Supreme Court struck down a Nebraska law on similar grounds.

The irony of the "partial-birth abortion" debate is the widespread consensus—among mothers, doctors, activists, lawmakers, and the American public—that the procedure should not be performed in most cases. The issue hinges on making an exception for abortions that protect the health, not just the life, of the woman. Proponents of the bills argue that a health clause would be interpreted broadly to include problems such as suicidal tendencies and depression. President Clinton's reference to "grievous damage," however, implies a more stringent criterion. This controversy is exacerbated by a lack of concrete and verifiable information on the frequency and motivation for D&Xs. While pro-life groups claim that most D&Xs are elective and take place during the second trimester, pro-choice groups claim just the opposite. Without accurate reporting, both sides continue to rely on circumstantial evidence to make their case.

SEE Abortion and Political Rhetoric; *Planned Parenthood of Southeastern Pennsylvania v. Casey.*

Further References. Abortion Law Homepage, http://hometown.aol.com/abtrbng/index.html. James Bopp, Jr., and Curtis R. Cook, "Partial-Birth Abortion: The Final Frontier of Abortion Jurisprudence," *Issues in Law and Medicine*, 14 (Summer 1998): 3-58. Janet E. Gans Epner, Harry S. Jonas, and Daniel L. Seckinger, "Late Term Abortions," *Journal of the American Medical Association* (26 August 1998): 724-729.

EVAN GERSTMANN AND CHRISTOPHER SHORTELL

DISABILITY AND REPRODUCTIVE RIGHTS. The words of this title rarely coexist in the public's ideology about motherhood. In a world where one of women's key roles is that of "mother," the woman with a disability has been considered incapable of bearing or raising children who would contribute to society. Social expectations that disabled women will not be sexual and cannot or should not be mothers persist, and continue to affect public policy and societal practice. Girls with disabilities are still denied sex education classes; many parents still fail to discuss sexuality and reproduction with their disabled daughters. Gynecological services are often unavailable to disabled women because clinics, physicians' offices, and examining tables have not been designed to be used by women with mobility impairments. Disabled women often lack access to safe, reliable birth control because their physical conditions may contra-indicate the use of the Pill or make diaphragms difficult to insert. Some women who cannot use print books because of visual, learning, or other disabilities lack access to reproductive health information because it is not available in Braille or recorded formats. Mothers with disabilities have lost custody of their children because of the perception that a mother's condition rendered her incapable of caring for her child, even in the face of evidence to the contrary. The involuntary sterilization of women with cognitive or emotional impairments is much less frequent than it once was, and is forbidden by federal regulations. Nevertheless, the practice continues.

Despite these barriers, many women with disabilities become mothers. Some of these women have their children after the disability occurs; others acquire their disabilities after they become mothers and persist in raising their children. The fact that the incidence of disability increases as people age means that most women become disabled after they have become mothers.

Disabled women are typically thought of as childlike, dependent, and helpless: unable to work and to care for their own needs, and to need others to care for them. Thus, these women are thought to be incapable of assuming the adult responsibility of raising a child. For people whose impairments occur before typical ages for childbearing and child raising, the first obstacle to motherhood can stem from limited social opportunities for forming romantic heterosexual or lesbian relationships in which to consider becoming a mother. Women with disabilities typically marry later than nondisabled women; they also become divorced or separated more frequently than their nondisabled counterparts.

Disabled women who are prepared to become mothers, in relationships or alone, face opposition from family, the medical profession, and society. Objections stem from the following fears: that the pregnancy, labor, and delivery may worsen a woman's physical impairments; that women with disabilities cannot properly care for children; and that disabled women will give birth to children who will also have impairments. None of these statements is true in general, but some disabled women may face one or more of these situations. Pregnancy, labor, and delivery may have adverse affects on some physical conditions. However, disabled women's desires to nurture children lead many of them to undertake pregnancies, to seek out reproductive alternatives such as surrogate mothering, or to pursue adoption. Unfortunately, many obstetricians, infertility clinics, and adoption agencies reject disabled women as clients. The decision to deny services to disabled women reflects the common belief that children will be harmed by growing up with a less-than-whole parent.

The presumption that disabled women are inadequate parents springs from the widespread social belief that a "good-enough mother" must manage to do everything without support from anyone else. But a mother who cannot physically cuddle or diaper her infant can insure that her infant is physically cared for under her supervision, while she touches, strokes, sings to, and smiles at the baby. The woman with mild or moderate cognitive impairments is often viewed as incapable of disciplining or stimulating the child after infancy, but she can arrange for others to help her. A mother who is blind cannot drive her 10-year-old son to his baseball games, but she can arrange for someone else to drive him, just as any working parent might recruit volunteer or paid help with some facet of childcare.

For the small percentage of women whose impairments are genetically transmissible, social hostility to reproduction flows from the belief that it is immoral and irresponsible to bear a child who will have a "less than perfect" mind and body, face any physical pain or psychological problems, or drain society's resources. In the late 1800s and early 1900s, it was widely assumed that human mental temperamental and moral traits were determined by heredity. Shiftlessness, religiosity, courage, patriotism, a sense of humor, a love of beauty, a taste for philosophy, a trustful nature, and a tendency to wander were only a few of the traits once ascribed to good or bad "blood." Although modern genetics and social science discredit these ideas when applied to members of racial and ethnic minorities, the idea that disability is automatically bad and should not be passed on still holds considerable appeal. These ideas surface in the form of pressures on women with disabilities to avoid giving children their conditions. In the Western world, and increasingly worldwide, all women are being urged to use prenatal diagnostic tests and have abortions if they learn that their fetus carries a disabling trait. Some scientists are reviving claims about the genetic bases for complex behavioral and personality characteristics such as sexual orientation, shyness, or risk-taking. If public support for such beliefs increases, there may be a call for more testing of fetuses and selecting of the characteristics of future generations.

Some women with disabilities reject the notion that their conditions prevent them from having a rewarding life. They believe that they and others should be willing to consider having children even if their children might have impairments. Those who assert the essential dignity and autonomy of people with disabilities decry efforts to prevent women with disabilities from becoming mothers. At the same time, they fight for better counseling for all women trying to decide whether they can mother children who will have disabling conditions. True reproductive freedom for women with and without disabilities can occur only when all women can decide whether or not to raise children and can count on affirmation and tangible supports from the community in which they and their children will live.

SEE African-American Women and Reproductive Rights; *Buck v. Bell*; Child Custody; Eugenics; Federal Sterilization Guidelines; Hispanic/Latina Women and Reproductive Rights; Native American Women and Reproductive Rights; Sterilization Abuse; *Stump v. Sparkman*.

Further References. Michelle Fine and Adrienne Asch, eds., *Women with Disabilities: Essays in Psychology, Culture, and Politics* (Philadelphia, 1988). Danuta Krotoski, Margaret Nosek, & Margaret Turk, eds., *Women with Physical Disabilities Achieving and Maintaining Health and Well-Being* (Baltimore, 1996). E. Parens & Adrienne Asch, eds., *Prenatal Testing and Disability Rights* (Washington, D.C., forthcoming). Diane B. Paul, *Controlling Human Heredity: 1965 to the Present* (Atlantic Highlands, N.J., 1995). Philip R. Reilly, *The Surgical Solution: A History of Involuntary Sterilization in the United States* (Baltimore, 1991). Michele Wates and Rowen Jade, eds., *Bigger than the Sky: Disabled Women Talk About Parenting* (London, 1999).

ADRIENNE ASCH

E

ECTOGENESIS is a term meaning "the extra-uterine gestation of human beings." "Partial ectogenesis" can refer either to the development of an embryo or fetus outside of the uterus for part of gestation, before implantation or in a neonatal intensive care unit (NICU), or to the development of organs or other parts of embryos externally during stages of development that would normally take place inside the uterus. The complete external gestation of humans would require the utilization of artificial placentas that allow for the entire growth and development of the fetus outside of the uterine environment in the laboratory. The term "ectogenesis" was first used by J.B.S. Haldane in his 1923 address "Daedalus or Science and the Future," which addressed the possibility of invention and widespread societal adoption of the ultimate reproductive technology of ectogenesis or complete extra-uterine gestation.

At present (2001 C.E.), complete ectogenesis remains hypothetical, existing only in science fiction (for example, Aldous Huxley's *Brave New World* or Marge Piercy's *Woman on the Edge of Time*). There is considerable disagreement among scientists as to whether complete ectogenesis will ever become feasible. Biologists Mark Ferguson and Anne McLaren, for example, believe that ectogenesis will remain impossible for the foreseeable future. Ferguson argues that the environment of fetal development within the pregnant woman is highly complex in terms of nutrition, growth factors, endocrinological control, and so forth. Therefore, it would be extraordinarily difficult to replicate these conditions externally. The creation of an artificial placenta would require finding replacements for a complex series of biochemical processes performed by women's bodies during pregnancy: egg maturation, fertilization, implantation, temperature control, waste removal, and transport of blood, nourishment and oxygen to the fetus. "Even if vast resources were to be devoted to it," McLaren asserts, "the chances of achieving a successful result before the end of the twenty-first century would be slim" (1980: 90). Although great strides have been made in neonatal intensive care over the past several decades, there is substantial evidence that many problems persist even in relatively well-developed low birth weight infants. Furthermore, the long-term problems facing graduates of neonatal units demonstrates the futility of pushing the boundaries back beyond the halfway point in gestation.

Other experts, however, contend that complete ectogenesis is possible. The biologist William Walters argues that it is not as far-fetched as it sounds because very small premature babies are already kept alive in NICU incubators. "Although an artificial placenta has not yet been successfully designed to support fetal life in the first half of pregnancy, the time is not far off when an embryo may be encouraged to grow and develop through fetal life to gestational maturity" (1982: 116). Likewise, ethicists Peter Singer and Deane Wells point out that the period in which it is essential for the human fetus to be in its mother's womb is shrinking from both ends. Therefore, they predict, it is only a matter of time before the present gap of five months is eliminated altogether, "not . . . by researchers deliberately seeking to make ectogenesis possible but rather by doctors attempting to save the lives of premature babies" (1985: 118).

It might be noted that a variety of Internet sites contend that ectogenesis is a reality. They note many reports of alien abductees who have witnessed gestational nurseries on board alien spacecraft. Interestingly, one of the first applications of ectogenesis seriously discussed in the 1960s was the technique's potential use for intergenerational space travel where large numbers of frozen embryos would be transported and at destination would be matured by ectogenesis.

Ectogenesis has implications for three reproductive rights issues: the right to have children; the right not to have children; and the right to control the characteristics of one's progeny. First, artificial placentas (AP) could be used as a form of surrogacy for women who are unable or unwilling to carry a pregnancy to term or for whom the risk might be too high. In this scenario, *in vitro* fertilization of the woman's ovum could be followed by transfer to the artificial womb for external gestation. Through this process, ectogenesis could allow women who would otherwise be unable to exercise a right to have their own genetic progeny to do so. Some have argued that this procedure would also free a woman from the risks of pregnancy and thus extend her control over the means by which gestation proceeds.

Second, complete separation of the fetus from a woman's body could reinforce the right not to have a child by allowing for termination of an unwanted pregnancy and transfer to an artificial placenta. Once complete ectogenesis is perfected, such a transfer might be possible, particularly in the first trimester of pregnancy. This possibility, of course, raises grave issues concerning the decision to make the transfer. For instance, removal of the fetus from the uterine environment could be utilized in cases where the behavior of the pregnant woman might threaten the life or health of the fetus. Instead of incarcerating the pregnant drug or alcohol user or forcing her into treatment, as some fetal protection advocates have proposed, authorities could take the fetus into "protective custody" by placing it in an artificial womb.

Third, AP would likely provide a highly controlled environment for fetal development. Presumably, there would be easy access to the fetus for genetic diagnosis and monitoring and for potential gene therapy and fetal surgery. From this standpoint, it is likely that women using this technology would be able to exert considerable control over the characteristics of their child prenatally.

The idea of ectogenesis has provoked strong reactions from many quarters. So far, the opponents are in the majority. Not surprisingly, right to life groups and ethicists concerned with fetal welfare have attacked the procedure. One World Wide Web site devoted to rights of the unborn declares: "A human embryo has the right to natural development within a human womb and not by forms of ectogenesis, or implantation in the uterus of another animal." Many critics invoke "Brave New World" scenarios of oppression, manipulation, and inhumanity with regard to ectogenesis. Those commentators who oppose assisted reproductive technologies in general, or surrogate motherhood in particular, often use ectogenesis as a worst case scenario of what might follow in the slide down the slippery slope. Ectogenesis, they argue, represents experimentation with human life, would severely weaken the intimate mother-child relationship which is crucial for bonding, and would make it technically possible to mass produce babies or farm human beings for spare parts.

Most feminist commentators share Dion Farquhar's view that the "desire for ectogenesis can 'only' be about the gender domination of women by men" (1992: 27). Farquhar argues that, although ectogenesis appears to extend women's rights to control reproduction, in effect it will result in the full surrender to a patriarchal medical community. Shulamith Firestone stands virtually alone among feminists in her call for ending compulsory motherhood by developing ectogenesis technologies. Writing in the 1970s, Firestone contended that the "freeing of women from the tyranny of reproduction" would come about only by freeing women from the onus of their own biology through extra-uterine gestation (1971: 11).

In contrast to the opposition, support for ectogenesis in the literature has been sparse. Singer, Wells, and Joseph Fletcher, the founder of situation ethics, are among the few defenders of ectogenesis. Arguing from a utilitarian standpoint, they contend that the benefits of ectogenesis to society, women, and even the children outweigh any objections to development of the artificial womb. Ectogenesis offers an alternative to surrogate motherhood to enable women who are incapable of pregnancy or have diseases that might threaten their lives during pregnancy to produce a child of their own. While ectogenesis will carry serious risks in its early, experimental stages, it will improve a fetus's chance of survival when used to rescue it from abortion. If medical science could keep a fetus alive outside the body, abortion would no longer mean terminating the life of the fetus. Instead, the fetus could be carried to term *ex utero* and adopted.

Citing Firestone (*ibid.*), Singer and Wells also argue that ectogenesis will promote reproductive equality between the sexes and free children "from the burden of possessive mothering."

Despite the fact that complete ectogenesis is but a fantasy, the reaction of many commentators and analysts has largely been one of revulsion and alarm. In Great Britain, for instance, the Warnock Committee recommended that the procedure be outlawed while refusing to speculate on whether it would in fact ever be possible. Similarly, the Council of Europe in 1986 recommended prohibition of ectogenesis and related techniques such as transfer of human fetuses to other species for gestation. Germany and Spain have legislation that specifically bans ectogenesis, while Australia, Canada Denmark, Sweden, Switzerland and United Kingdom would presumably ban such attempts under existing laws regarding reproductive technologies.

At present, the United States has no legislation or regulation on ectogenesis. The model legislation proposed by the American Bioethics Advisory Committee would bar the use of cloning techniques to replicate human beings, but does not address the development of an artificial placenta. Although current U.S. policy would appear to preempt public funding of ectogenesis research *per se*, it does not apply to privately funded initiatives, nor does it bar medical research that pushes back viability in neonatal intensive care units.

The author of this article finds the arguments for any future development of ectogenesis unpersuasive, and would strongly reject any public policy to do so. Despite all the potential dangers for a fetus in the womb, it is most unlikely that an artificial environment can ever come close to replacing what in most cases is a natural process that works remarkably well. As noted earlier, recent evidence on the developmental delays and problems of neonatal unit graduates, even those who were born with birth weights more than 1500 grams and viewed as successes, demonstrates that we are far from even marginally approximating the uterine environment. Moreover, from a public policy standpoint, money would be better spent to ensure that pregnant women have access to the resources necessary to provide a healthy environment than to invest scarce resources in yet another technological fix fantasy. Ectogenesis is likely to be an expensive technology. The escalation of NICU costs as applied to extremely low birth weight infants suggests the per case cost of ectogenesis will be prohibitive and if routinely used would divert resources from more appropriate strategies of producing healthy babies.

SEE *In Vitro* Fertilization; Fetal Protection; Surrogate Motherhood.

Further References. Robert H. Blank, *Regulating Reproduction* (New York, 1990). Dion Farquhar, *Machine: Discourse and Reproductive Technologies* (New York, 1996). Mark W.J. Ferguson, "Contemporary and Future Possibilities for Human Embryonic Manipulation," in Anthony Dyson and John Harris, eds., *Experiments on Embryos* (London, 1990): 6-26. Shulamith Firestone, *The Dialectic of Sex: The Case for Feminist Revolution* (London, 1971). J.B.S. Haldane, "Daedalus or Science and the Future," unpublished paper read to the Heretics, Cambridge University, England, 4 February, 1923. Anne McLaren, "Reproductive

Options: Present and Future," in C.R. Austin and R.V. Short, eds., *Manipulating Reproduction* (Cambridge, England, 1980):176-192. Peter Singer and Deane Wells, *Making Babies: The New Science and Ethics of Conception* (New York, 1985). Susan Merrill Squier, *Babies in Bottles: Twentieth-Century Visions of Reproductive Technology* (New Brunswick, N.J., 1994). Martin Thomason, "A Very Wise Child: Ectogenesis and the Biological Family, "in Carole Ulanowsky, ed., *The Family in the Age of Biotechnology* (Brookfield, Vt., 1995): 79-89. William A.W. Walters, "Cloning, Ectogenesis, and Hybrids: Things to Come?" in William A.W. Walters and Peter Singer, eds., *Test-Tube Babies* (Melbourne, Australia, 1982):110-118.

ROBERT H. BLANK

EISENSTADT v. BAIRD, (405 U.S. 438, 1972) is significant for its recognition of the reasoning of *Griswold v. Connecticut* to the reproductive rights of individuals. The Supreme Court's articulation of the principle that reproductive autonomy is part of the constitutional privacy rights of individuals extended the reasoning of *Griswold v. Connecticut* (1965) beyond its recognition of rights inherent in the marriage relationship. In *Eisenstadt*, Bill Baird, a longtime birth control educator and activist, was charged with violating a Massachusetts statute that, among other things, forbade the prescription or distribution of any contraceptive medication or device to anyone other than a married person. Baird displayed various contraceptive devices during an address at Boston University and gave a container of contraceptive foam to a young woman at the end of his talk.

By a vote of six to one, the Court overturned the law. Justice William Brennan wrote the Court's opinion. Brennan argued that the right to make decisions about reproduction is an individual right. This right begins in an individual (something *Griswold* missed) and remains with that individual—whether married or not. According to Justice Brennan,"[T]he marital couple is not an independent entity with a mind and heart of its own, but an association of two individuals each with a separate intellectual and emotional makeup. If the right of privacy means anything, it is the right of the individual, married or single, to be free from unwarranted governmental intrusion into matters so fundamentally affecting a person as the decision whether to bear or beget a child."

SEE Birth Control Movement; *Carey v. Population Services International*; *Griswold v. Connecticut*; Privacy and Reproductive Rights; *Roe v. Wade*.

SUSAN E. GROGAN

EMPLOYMENT AND REPRODUCTIVE RIGHTS. In the United States, employment rights and reproductive rights have often been at odds, largely because the concept of equality underlying each set of rights has been different. The law of employment discrimination aims at ensuring equality of opportunity, and is premised on the understanding that individuals who are similarly situated with regard to their skills, experience, education and training should have the same opportunities for advancement in the workplace, regardless of their sex. Employment policy is gender-neutral on its face, but it incorporates the far from neutral expectation that workers can put their jobs before their private lives. In contrast, while reproductive rights are often phrased in gender-neutral terms, reproductive rights are derived from an appreciation of the different procreative functions of men and women.

Throughout American history, women's childbearing and childrearing functions have been placed in opposition to their workplace roles. Courts and legislatures have been called upon to reconcile these conflicts in the twentieth century. In the 1900s, public policy gave preference to women's reproductive role at the expense of their workforce participation. But, since the passage of Title VII of the Civil Rights Act of 1964, courts and legislatures have emphasized women's workplace role and given less weight to their reproductive role. As a society, we have been unable to reconcile women's employment and reproductive roles largely because we have placed them in opposition to each other, instead of trying to accommodate procreative function while ensuring equality of opportunity.

Protective Labor Laws. In the early part of the twentieth century, state legislatures adopted legislation that regulated the workforce participation of women, ostensibly to protect them from overwork and exploitation. In 1908, the U.S. Supreme Court upheld a state law that limited women's employment to 10 hours a day and six days a week, despite the fact that it had, three years earlier, struck down maximum hours legislation for men. *Muller v. Oregon* justified its differing treatment of men and women by arguing that women's "physical structure and the performance of maternal functions" necessitated state protection.

The Court's decision in *Muller* encouraged the widespread adoption of what was called protective labor legislation for women. By 1920, nearly all states had laws limiting women's hours, working conditions, and the occupations in which they could be employed. Protective labor legislation was part of the sex segregation of the working world which was accepted by most Americans as a fact of life well into the second half of the twentieth century, and which remains a fact of life as the century ends. *Muller v. Oregon* and its kin have never been declared unconstitutional. However, protective legislation is a dead letter now. Some policies, like mandatory maternity leaves for schoolteachers, were invalidated under the Due Process Clause of the Fourteenth Amendment. But most special rules were superseded by federal legislation.

Title VII. This portion of the Civil Rights Act of 1964 barred employment discrimination on the basis of race, color, national origin, sex and religion. On paper, Title VII abruptly changed the balance between employment and reproductive rights. To the extent that it was enforced, the statute compelled equality of employment opportunity by attempting to treat all employees similarly, regardless of their sex. Title VII adopted a gender-neutral approach and assumed that men and women could be made equal in the workplace, regardless of their procreative roles.

This approach has worked well when gender-based distinctions were the result of inaccurate stereotypes, but less well when the distinctions derived from the different reproductive functions of the two sexes.

Among the early targets of Title VII litigation were "sex plus" classifications, which employers used to treat married women or women with children differently than other workers. In 1971, the U.S. Supreme Court struck down an employer's policy of refusing to hire women with preschool age children (*Phillips v. Martin-Marietta Corporation*). The employer justified this policy by contending that it was discriminating against a class of employees based on their status as parents, not on the basis of sex, and that this discrimination was justified by the higher rates of absenteeism and greater familial responsibilities of female employees. It bears noting, however, that the Court did not hold that employers were barred from discriminating against workers because of their family responsibilities; instead, it held that the employer had to have the same policy in place for men and women, even if it was not family-friendly.

More recent cases have demonstrated the difficulty of establishing a "sex plus" violation, and have underlined the extent to which Title VII aims at ensuring equality of opportunity, as opposed to equality of result. While Martin-Marietta had an explicit policy of barring the employment of women with preschool age children, other employers have adopted more subtle policies that are more difficult to challenge. For example, in a 1995 case, a circuit court rejected the plaintiff's argument that her employer had denied her tenure as a college professor because she had taken eight years off to rear her children (*Fisher v. Vassar College*). The court held that plaintiffs alleging "sex plus" claims must prove that the employer's action was the result of a sex specific policy.

Employer policies that explicitly discriminate against an employee or group of employees because of their sex are Title VII violations in all cases except where an employer is able to demonstrate that the policy is a bona fide occupational qualification (BFOQ) reasonably necessary for its business. Employers have attempted to use the BFOQ exception to justify a broad range of discriminatory policies. But courts have construed this exception narrowly. Courts have held that employers relying on a BFOQ defense must demonstrate that the classification, like sex or pregnancy, is closely tied to the employee's ability to do the job in question. The BFOQ defense was not available to employers seeking to rely on state protective legislation (*Rosenfeld v. Southern Pacific Company*, 1971), nor to employers who excluded women from certain jobs out of a concern about harm to fetuses or potential fetuses (*UAW v. Johnson Controls*, 1991). The exception has, however, been available to employers justifying mandatory maternity leave for flight attendants. This ruling was based upon concerns that pregnant flight attendants might not be able to respond effectively in an emergency and that the safety of airline passengers might be compromised (*Leonard v. Pan American Airways, Inc.*, 1990).

Pregnancy Discrimination Act (PDA) of 1978. Until Congress passed the PDA, no federal law forbade discrimination against women because of pregnancy. This act formally amended Title VII to establish that pregnancy discrimination is discrimination on the basis of sex. The PDA was a direct response to two Supreme Court rulings that pregnancy classifications did not constitute gender discrimination. The Court held that an employer policy that excluded pregnancy from disability benefits did not constitute sex discrimination since women could be either pregnant or not pregnant. The PDA declared that the words "on the basis of sex" in Title VII "include, but are not limited to, because of or on the basis of pregnancy, childbirth, or related medical conditions." Women affected by pregnancy, childbirth or related conditions were to be treated similarly to others who were similar in their ability or inability to work, and this law established that employer policies that single out pregnancy for disadvantageous treatment constitute Title VII violations.

Unfortunately, the PDA has a number of shortcomings. First, it requires that women who are pregnant analogize their "disability" to other disabilities. This comparison is sometimes not easy, and places the burden of persuasion on the employee, who must demonstrate that she was treated differently solely because of her pregnant status. Second, this statute mandates only *equal* treatment of pregnant workers. It does not require that employers accommodate the needs of women who are pregnant, may not encompass pre- and post-pregnancy conditions, like infertility, abortion and breast-feeding, and leaves employers free to deny disability benefits to all workers.

The Court did rule in *Cal Fed v. Guerra* (1987) that state laws singling out pregnancy-related disabilities for preferential treatment are not pre-empted by the PDA. However, employers are not allowed to provide additional leave beyond the disability period. The emphasis of the PDA and Title VII is on achieving formal equality between the sexes, and little attention is given to the uniqueness of men and women's procreative functions. Moreover, women's reproductive role is seen as of secondary importance to their employment role, and employers are under no obligation to reconcile these roles or to facilitate fluidity between them. The statute's reliance on a simple anti-discrimination formula has placed these roles at odds, and required that women choose between employment and reproductive health. The Supreme Court's holding in *Johnson Controls* was a limited victory for women, because all it did was protect them from being excluded from lead-exposed jobs and establish that discrimination on the basis of capacity for pregnancy is sex discrimination. The decision did nothing to require, or even encourage, companies to mitigate the reproductive hazards that occasioned the exclusionary policy.

In its reliance on anti-discrimination principles and its requirement that men and women be treated the same, Title VII fails to fully accommodate the often different experiences of men and women. Title VII does nothing to ameliorate the indirect forms of discrimination faced by women who become pregnant or have children at risk of less overt forms of discrimination. For example, the interruptions in workforce participation that are the result of pregnancy, childbirth and adoption may interfere with women's ability to acquire those skills and experiences that will enable them to successfully compete in the workplace.

Family and Medical Leave Act (FMLA) of 1993. Like Title VII, the FMLA uses a gender-neutral approach to conveying benefits to workers. Under the

FMLA, employers with 50 or more workers must provide unpaid leave up to 12 weeks to any eligible employee to care for a child following birth, adoption or placement in a foster home. Either men or women may take unpaid leave, provided they can afford it. Once the employee returns to work, s/he must be offered either the same job or a job with equivalent pay, benefits and working conditions. This law aims at treating women and men equally, in terms of their child care obligations, but ignores the gender and class issues that limit its application.

Americans with Disabilities Act (ADA) of 1990. Title VII mandates that pregnant employees may not be granted more generous leave periods than other workers when such leave is granted in excess of the actual period of disability. While the ADA excludes pregnancy from its coverage, its requirement that employers accommodate the disabilities of all workers, and the PDA's mandate that pregnancy be treated the same as other temporary disabilities, means that pregnancy is effectively covered by this broad statute. Unlike the PDA, the ADA requires that employers take steps to accommodate the needs of disabled workers, and in this expanded role, pregnant workers may find more protection. Moreover, the ADA may mandate that the employer takes certain affirmative steps to accommodate employees seeking abortion or infertility treatments. This law may provide more protection for men and women's procreative roles, but it does so only by viewing pregnancy and its related conditions as disabilities.

American law is confounded by its attempts to place employment and reproductive rights within the mold of traditional equality analysis. Title VII, the PDA, the FMLA, and the ADA, and judicial interpretations of these laws have viewed equality as requiring the same result for male and female workers, but have ignored the real biological differences between men and women that often shape their workforce participation. The conflicts between women's reproductive freedom and their right to equal employment opportunities resist resolution.

SEE *Secretary of Labor v. American Cyanamid; California Federal Savings and Loan Association v. Guerra; Cleveland Board of Education v. LaFleur;* Family and Medical Leave Act of 1993; *Geduldig v. Aiello; General Electric v. Gilbert; International Union, United Auto Workers v. Johnson Controls; Muller v. Oregon; Newport News Shipbuilding v. EEOC;* Pregnancy Discrimination Act of 1978 (PDA); Protective Labor Legislation; Title VII and Reproductive Rights.

Further References. Ruth Colker, "Pregnancy, Parenting, and Capitalism, " *Ohio State Law Journal,* 58 (1997): 61-84. Jennifer Gottschalk, "Accommodating Pregnancy on the Job," *University of Kansas Law Review,* 45 (November 1996): 241-272. Suzanne U. Samuels, *Fetal Rights, Women's Rights: Gender Equality in the Workplace* (Madison, Wis., 1995).

SUZANNE UTTARO SAMUELS

EUGENICS is the scientific endeavor to improve the human race through the application of the study of heredity to human reproduction. A product of nineteenth- century social thought, eugenics was heavily influenced by Darwinism.

It was given its name (derived from the Greek words for "good" and "born") by Sir Francis Galton, who established a eugenics movement in England in the late 1800's. By the early 1900s, the eugenics movement had spread throughout Western Europe and the United States.

The U.S. eugenics movement can be divided into three stages. During the first stage, from 1870 to 1905, eugenicists were primarily concerned with negative eugenics: restricting reproduction of the "unfit" or "dangerous classes" of feeble-minded, criminals, insane, epileptics, and paupers. Positive eugenics encouraged the propagation of the "fit" classes, or those with supposedly superior genes.

The second stage, lasting from 1905 to 1930, marked the height of eugenics in the United States and the movement of eugenics into the universities where it was studied in psychology, sociology, and biology. Eugenicists increasingly directed their efforts toward blacks and immigrants. The movement campaigned for custodial care, marriage restrictions, and sterilization of "defectives." Sterilization was viewed by eugenicists as more cost-effective than permanent institutionalization. Along with sterilization, the eugenics movement advocated the legalization of contraception which led to an eventual alliance with Margaret Sanger and leaders of the birth control movement. The greatest legal triumph of the eugenics movement came in 1927, when the Supreme Court upheld the constitutionality of the practice in *Buck v. Bell*.

The third and final stage of the eugenics movement began after 1930. The eugenics movement began to disintegrate with new scientific evidence that heredity and genetics were more complicated than proposed by eugenicists and that environment interacted with heredity in terms of traits such as intelligence, character, and physique. After World War II, the horror felt at the discovery of the use of sterilization and euthanasia in Nazi Germany to eliminate thousands of mentally ill and disabled patients, as well as millions of Jews, led many Americans to question the motives of the eugenics movement and accelerated its decline.

Eugenics was closely connected with a conservative social outlook. Many conservatives argued that social reforms were useless because problems did not reside in the social system, but in the genes of the "unfit." Although eugenics is no longer an active movement in the United States, its underlying assumptions are illustrated in the 1990s by books like Roger Pearson's *Race, Intelligence, and Bias in Academe* and Richard J. Herrnstein and Charles Murray's *The Bell Curve: Intelligence and Class Structure in American Life*. Any theory that some people are genetically superior or inferior to others poses a powerful potential threat to reproductive rights.

SEE Birth Control and African-American Women; Birth Control Movement; *Buck v. Bell*; Sanger, Margaret; *Skinner v. Oklahoma*; Sterilization Abuse.

Further References. Francis Galton, *Inquiries Into Human Faculty* (London, 1883). Mark Haller, *Eugenics: Hereditarian Attitudes in American Thought* (New Brunswick, N.J., 1963). Stefan Kuhl, *The Nazi Connection: Eugenics, American Racism, and German National Socialism* (New York, 1994).

LARA FOLEY

F

_____

FAMILY AND MEDICAL LEAVE ACT (FMLA) OF 1993 allows workers to take up to 12 weeks a year of unpaid leave with benefits during any 12-month period for birth, adoption, or placement of a foster child, a serious personal illness, or the care of a child, spouse or parent with a serious health condition. Workers are guaranteed their old job or an equivalent position upon their return. The act only applies to private employers with more than 50 workers and full-time workers who have been with the same employer for over a year. Employers are allowed to deny leave to the highest-paid 10 percent of workers if such denial is necessary to prevent substantial and grievous economic injury to the business.

The impetus for FMLA was the changing role of women as workers and primary caregivers for children and aging relatives. Initially members of Congress wanted to restrict the bill to maternity leave and the politically more popular needs of mothers and babies. However, women's groups insisted on a gender-neutral parental leave so as to avoid differential (and possible discriminatory) treatment for women. Organized support for FMLA was led by the Women's Legal Defense Fund and other women's advocacy groups. As new versions of the bill added categories of leave, organized labor, health groups, and the American Association of Retired Persons joined in support. Prominent opponents included business groups such as the Chamber of Commerce and the National Association of Manufacturers.

Supporters argued that the FMLA was needed to resolve the family-work conflict and to establish uniform family benefits. They pointed to a survey of 118 nations by the International Labor Organization that found the United States was the only nation without parental leave and that other nations have longer leave, universal coverage, and usually paid leave. Opponents warned of regulatory expenses, job and wage reductions, disadvantages in international competition, and the specter of a mandate from a future Congress to provide paid leave.

The first version of FMLA was introduced in 1985. Successive versions were weakened as leave was shortened and the number of exempted employers expanded. FMLA passed Congress in 1990 and 1992, but was vetoed by President George Bush. Presidential candidate Bill Clinton (and the Democratic Party, in search of a "family values" issue) made family leave a top campaign issue in 1992. The bill was signed into law on February 5, 1993, in Clinton's first public bill-signing.

The law had bipartisan support. Some socially conservative Republicans defined FMLA as a family issue that protected the rights of men and women to procreate and raise a family without losing the income of the working wife. At worst, limiting leave time to 12 weeks may discourage parents from staying home with children for a longer time. Pro-life forces reasoned that parental leave might encourage pregnant workers to carry to term, an argument that drew Rep. Henry Hyde (R-Ill.). and the U.S. Catholic Conference into active support. Women workers who need time off to recover from an abortion are covered under provisions for a non-recurring condition for which treatment and recovery last no more than a few days; abortion, however, never appeared as a concrete example in congressional reports in deference to FMLA's pro-life supporters.

Evaluations of FMLA indicate that by June 1996, more than 12 million workers had used this leave (despite a very traditional definition of "family" that omits cohabiting adults, step family members, gays and lesbians, and siblings) and most businesses reported minimal problems. However, the limitations of an unpaid leave that exempts 95 percent of all employers (and thus covers only about 60 percent of all workers) are becoming evident. Because it is unpaid, only two to four percent of those eligible took family leave. Length of leave taken is directly related to income, and low-paid minority women were much less likely than other workers to take any leave. Mothers were more likely to take leave than fathers, even though women are concentrated in exempt small businesses and part-time jobs. Despite its gender-neutral language, the FMLA, in practice, reinforces rather than challenges traditional gender roles. However, it enhances women's reproductive freedom by helping them reconcile their family and work responsibilities.

In January 2000, the Supreme Court ruled in *Kimel v. Florida Board of Regents* that Congress lacked the power to override state retirement laws. This decision jeopardizes the FMLA, in so far as it applies to state employees.

SEE *California Federal Savings and Loan Association v. Guerra*; Pregnancy Discrimination Act of 1978.

Further References. Sonja Klueck Elison, "Policy Innovation in a Cold Climate: The Family and Medical Leave Act of 1993," *Journal of Family Issues*, 18 (January 1997): 30-54. Ronald D. Elving, *Conflict and Compromise: How Congress Makes The Law* (New York, 1995).

JANET K. BOLES

FATHERS' RIGHTS MOVEMENT (FRM). Fathers' rights activists often consider the organization of the Divorce Racket Busters in California in 1960 to be the birth of their movement. This group (which changed its name to United States Divorce Reform in 1961) sought to change California divorce laws, which they claimed discriminated against men. They protested alimony and child support settlements and the presumption in favor of maternal child custody. As chapters formed in other states, the leaders of the organization began to expand their views of sex discrimination beyond the area of family law. In 1968, Charlie Metz wrote, "Throughout the world, American men are held as prime victims of a female-dominated society." As the divorce rate increased in the 1960s and 1970s, more and more men formed local grass-roots organizations devoted to divorce reform.

Popular accounts indicate that these local groups were composed of men who shared the experience of bitter divorces and nasty custody disputes. These men gathered to offer one another support and to promote divorce reform. By 1977, fathers' rights groups were active in more than 30 states. By the early 1980s several associations existed in every state. These groups engaged in various political activities: lobbying state legislatures, picketing courthouses, filing class action suits, and setting up "court watches" to monitor judges' decisions. For the most part, these men were not interested in macro-social issues such as redefining masculinity or reconceiving gender roles. Rather, they concentrated on fighting what they perceived as sex discrimination in family law. They targeted the maternal preference in custody decisions and the ways in which courts calculated child support and alimony.

Although much of the rhetoric of fathers' rights advocates embraced equal rights and emphasized the discrimination suffered by fathers upon divorce, these views did not entail a commitment to feminism. In fact, many in the FRM sought a "return to patriarchy." Feminism, they argued, had destroyed the traditional nuclear family by encouraging women to leave their husbands in search of self-fulfillment. Only by restoring men to their proper place as the heads of their families (through revised custody and child support laws) would children's needs be served. Those subscribing to this anti-feminist ideology are often called the "conservative" branch of the FRM. The "liberal" branch of the movement shares with the conservative wing a desire to revamp family law and a sharp criticism of contemporary feminism. The "liberals," however, claim to be the true heirs to the feminism of the 1960s. They advocate formal equality with women and argue that contemporary feminists now want women to have privileges denied to men. Whereas the conservative branch wants a return to traditional gender roles, the liberal wing advocates pure gender neutrality.

Since the early 1980s, both liberal and conservative men's rights advocates have attempted to create national organizations in order to bring the disparate local groups together. The Men's Rights Association, Men's Equality Now (MEN) International, Men's Rights Incorporated, and Free Men (later the Coalition of Free Men) all sought to provide links for men's rights activists across the United States. MEN International held conventions from 1977 to 1980 in an attempt to create an "organization of organizations." Another effort was made in 1981, when a group of individuals organized a National Congress for Men (NCM) in Houston, again hoping to found a national organization to which local, independent, fathers' rights organizations could belong. The NCM still exists, although it changed its name to the National Congress for Men and Children in 1990 and more recently to the National Congress for Fathers and Children, and continued to hold annual conventions. However, it failed to become the sole national organization of fathers' rights activists. Further attempts to unify the FRM included a Unity Conference in Gaithersburg, Tennessee, in the mid-1980s, and conferences in the mid-1990s organized by the Missouri Center for Men's Studies in Kansas City. None of these meetings, however, has produced a lasting coalition of men's rights groups.

The inability of the FRM to form more cohesive national associations has long distressed many of its activists. Some attribute the disarray to large egos and parochial interests, while others point to philosophical differences (the liberal/conservative cleavage) as a primary cause of fractiousness. Other explanations include the inability of local groups facing a wide diversity of state statutes and case law to agree on a national political strategy, and the disagreement over whether men should concentrate on addressing fathers' rights in particular or broaden their horizons to attack all areas of bias against males. Thus, the FRM has not been able to create unified national organizations on the level of those of the feminist movement. It remains primarily a loose coalition of local groups with a few national organizations that are maintained by a few steadfast workers.

However, interest in fathers' rights issues has not waned. After the World Wide Web took off in the 1990s, FRM cites proliferated on the Internet. Web sites offer bulletin boards, advice on divorce and custody disputes, referrals for attorneys, and links to various state statutes and case law. Indeed, the Internet may have provided both an outlet for fathers' frustrations and a needed link to nationwide resources such that a national organization now seems superfluous.

Some fathers' rights activists have continually criticized the 1976 U.S. Supreme Court decision in *Planned Parenthood v. Danforth*, which invalidated a state requirement that a married woman must receive her husband's consent for an abortion. If a father is willing to care for a child, they argue, the mother should not be allowed to terminate the pregnancy. Most FRM advocates, however, recognize the political futility of this position. In recent years, activists have concentrated on securing the right of unwed fathers to prevent third-party adoption of their biological children. Their position is that if a single mother wishes to place a child up for adoption, the father should be allowed to have custody of the child unless proven unfit. Some states have passed statutes to protect unwed fathers' rights in the context of third-party adoptions, particularly when the father has been unaware of the mother's pregnancy. State courts' responses to these statutes and the cases which produced them have been mixed. At present, courts are giving increasingly more weight to the rights of unwed biological fathers. However, judges but often want some evidence that the father made an attempt to monitor the mother's health and offered financial or emotional support before the baby was born.

With the law on fathers' rights in a state of flux, future developments are difficult to predict. A public outcry over the damage done to children who are abruptly removed from adoptive parents makes it unlikely that courts and state legislatures will give unwed fathers an unlimited right to retroactively veto adoptions. Nonetheless, the rise in out-of-wedlock births, the growing acceptance of non-traditional families, and pressure from men's rights activists will probably influence lawmakers to expand the rights of unwed fathers with respect to third-party adoptions in the same way they have expanded the rights of divorced fathers in the area of custody law.

SEE Adoption; Birth Mothers and Reproductive Rights; Breast-Feeding and the Law; Child Custody; *Planned Parenthood of Central Missouri v. Danforth.*

Further References. Kenneth Clatterbaugh, *Contemporary Perspectives on Masculinity*, 2nd ed. (Boulder, Colo.: 1997). Richard F. Doyle, *The Rape of the Male* (St. Paul, Minn.: 1976). Charles Metz, *Divorce and Custody for Men* (Garden City, N.Y.: 1968). Mary L. Shanley, "Unwed Fathers' Rights, Adoption, and Sex Equality: Gender-Neutrality and the Perpetuation of Patriarchy," *Columbia Law Review*, 95 (January 1995): 60-103. Tom Williamson, "A History of the Men's Movement," in Francis Baumli, ed., *Men Freeing Men: Exploding the Myth of the Traditional Male* (Jersey City, N.J., 1989): 308-24.

GWYNETH I. WILLIAMS

FEDERAL STERILIZATION GUIDELINES (1979). These regulations (42 C.F.R. 500.201-210), issued by the Department of Health, Education, and Welfare (HEW) [now Health and Human Services (HHS)], ended a decade of controversy about where and how to draw the line between consensual and coerced sterilization. The 1970s brought a dramatic increase in female sterilization after passage of the Family Planning Services and Population Research Act of 1970. This law made sterilization available in federally funded clinics. Charges soon surfaced that at least some of these sterilizations were performed with less than full informed consent from the clients, especially among women of color and welfare recipients. The history of the use of sterilization for eugenic and other social control purposes in the U.S. lent credibility to these concerns.

In response, HEW issued regulations in 1974 that imposed some protections but still provided for sterilization of minors and those incapable of giving informed consent. A federal judge soon issued a permanent injunction against the use of federal funds to sterilize anyone under 21 or legally incompetent, on the grounds that these regulations did not give sufficient protection to these women. The injunction stayed in effect until 1977, when an appellate court ruled that HEW had statutory authority to define federal standards of voluntariness.

The department developed new regulations that went into effect early in 1979. No sterilizations could be performed on persons who were under 21, institutionalized, or legally incompetent. Hysterectomies for the purpose of sterilization were prohibited. The client, the person obtaining the consent, the physician performing the procedure, and the interpreter, if relevant, were required to sign an informed consent form in the client's language. The consent form would explain the risks, possible side effects, and irreversibility of the operation, and give information about alternative forms of contraception. Consent could not be obtained immediately before or after an abortion, during labor, or when the client was under the influence of drugs or alcohol. Threatening the client with the loss of welfare or Medicaid benefits was prohibited.

These regulations garnered two separate, and contradictory, types of criticism from political activists and social welfare and health care professionals. Some critics argued that, because of the loss of federal funding for elective abortions and the history of sterilization abuse, these regulations were inadequate to prevent coercion. On the other hand, some critics asserted that the guidelines increased the risk of involuntary pregnancy for mentally disabled women and restricted freedom of choice for women capable of giving consent.

The guidelines have changed only minimally since 1979. Some evidence exists of a reduction in the gap between the numbers of African-American and white women receiving sterilizations. However, the federal guidelines have not ended the controversy over sterilization. Since most sterilizations are funded by state rather than federal programs, the arena has shifted to the states.

SEE Abortion and Public Assistance; Eugenics; Hyde Amendment; Sterilization Abuse.

Further References. Robert Blank and Janna C. Merrick, *Human Reproduction, Emerging Technologies, and Conflicting Rights* (Washington, D.C., 1995). Susan E. Davis, ed., *Women under Attack: Victories, Backlash and the Fight for Reproductive Freedom* (Boston, 1988). Betsy Hartmann, *Reproductive Rights and Wrongs: The Global Politics of Population Control* (New York, 1987).

SUSAN M. OLSON

FETAL ABUSE is a term which has been applied in the 1990s to fetal harms or potential harms caused by maternal substance abuse during pregnancy. Although social and environmental factors—poverty, malnutrition and inadequate medical care—can adversely affect the physiological and mental development of fetuses, the recent "fetal abuse" policy debate has focused almost exclusively on the lifestyle choices of pregnant women. The disparity in how society regards different types of threats to fetal well-being can be most starkly seen in the different policy responses to prenatal drug exposure and third party fetal killings and battery. Problems caused by pregnant substance abusers have received enormous public attention, while fetal damage by third parties (such as abusive husbands) is virtually invisible. Since up to 15 percent of all pregnant women are at risk of being battered, it is hard to argue that prenatal drug exposure is a more egregious threat to fetal health than prenatal battering. Medical researchers have found that pregnant women are not only more likely to be battered than non-pregnant women, the severity of the violence is greater and it is more likely to be directed at the abdomen. Government officials and health care professionals have tried to focus the attention of the media and policymakers on the problem of prenatal battering but have been unable to generate concern.

Defenders of prosecution for fetal abuse usually rely on *Roe v. Wade* (1973) and subsequent abortion cases which held that the state may have a "compelling interest" in the fetus from the point of viability. This reasoning allowed prosecutors to charge substance abusing pregnant women with a range of criminal offenses related to their exposing their unborn child to narcotics: for example, child abuse, child neglect, child endangerment, delivery of drugs to a minor, or involuntary manslaughter. (These prosecutions would have been much easier to justify if the Supreme Court had reversed *Roe* or never decided it; virtually no limitations would then exist on the state's power to protect the fetus.) Although these criminal statutes were intended to only apply to human beings after birth, prosecutors have attempted to expand the legal definition of "child" to include fetuses. Between 1989 and 1999, more than 240 women in 34 states were charged with one of these offenses; most have been found guilty. Appellate courts in Florida, Kentucky, Nevada and Ohio have overturned these convictions on the grounds that the statutes to were not intended to apply to unborn human life. The South Carolina Supreme Court was the first appellate court to uphold a fetal abuse conviction. *Whitner v. State* (1996) ruled that a viable fetus is a "child" or "person" and is thereby entitled to full legal protection. Two years later, the U.S. Supreme Court refused to review the case. Cornelia Whitner, whose son tested positive for cocaine at birth, must serve her eight-year prison sentence.

Fetal rights proponents also have tried to get state legislatures to revise their civil commitment statutes to allow substance abusing pregnant women to be involuntarily committed until they give birth. In 1988, Minnesota became the first state to pass such a law. It allows involuntary commitment of pregnant women who abuse hard drugs. By 1998, nearly 100 women (about 10 per year) had been committed under this law. In 1997 and 1998, several legislatures considered adopting civil commitment laws, but only Wisconsin and South Dakota did so. These new laws are far more severe than the Minnesota one. South Dakota allows the involuntary commitment of pregnant women who use drugs or alcohol until the birth of the child. Wisconsin allows the state to commit drug and alcohol abusing pregnant women against their will and take legal custody of their fetuses. In addition to punishing a class of people for engaging in the otherwise legal consumption of alcohol, the Wisconsin law confers custody rights on the state as early as conception. Ironically, all three states with commitment laws have acute shortages in drug treatment slots for pregnant women.

Civil libertarians argue that fetal abuse prosecutions and civil detention laws violate a woman's constitutional right to equal protection. They point out that prosecutors and legislators have not aggressively acted against men who knife, stomp, beat or shoot pregnant women, thereby killing or injuring the fetus. Roughly half of the states which have prosecuted women for exposing their fetuses prenatally to drugs have no law that makes it a criminal offense for a third party to kill a fetus of any age. Additional equal protection concerns are raised by studies showing that poor and non-white women are far more likely than middle class white women to be screened for drug use, and among those testing positive, minority women are disproportionately singled out for prosecution.

SEE Fetal Protection; Forced Medical Treatment and Pregnancy; Lifestyle Restrictions and Pregnancy; Substance Abuse and Pregnancy.

Further References. Deborah Mathieu, "Mandating Treatment for Pregnant Substance Abusers: A Compromise." *Politics and the Life Sciences* 14 (August 1995): 199-208. Jean Reith Schroedel, *Is the Fetus a Person? A Comparison of Policies across the Fifty States.* (Ithaca, N.Y.: 2000). *Whitner v. State*, 492 S.E. 2d 777 (S.C. 1996).

PAMELA FIBER, CHARMAINE JACKSON,
AND JEAN REITH SCHROEDEL

FETAL PROTECTION refers to policies based on the premise that the fetus has rights and interests separate from that of the pregnant woman, and that the state has an obligation to protect these interests. While the idea of fetal rights has been the subject of legal controversy for more than 100 years, it was not until the 1980s and 1990s that a full-blown theory of fetal protection emerged in the United States. Unprecedented forms of fetal protectionism have surfaced in the last 20 years in efforts to regulate and control what has been conceptualized as the harmful behavior of pregnant women. Fetal protection policies have included banning pregnant or fertile women from certain forms of hazardous work, forcing pregnant women to submit to medical treatment against their will, criminally prosecuting drug or alcohol-using pregnant women for fetal harm, and a range of other coercive measures against pregnant women.

Reproductive rights advocates have vigorously opposed such efforts, arguing that these represent thinly veiled attempts to restrict the reproductive rights of women under the false guise of protecting fetal health. They also argue that such efforts have been racist, noting that the vast majority of women prosecuted for fetal harm have been African-American. Reproductive rights advocates argue that coercive measures are neither effective at protecting fetal health nor equitable under the law. Opponents of fetal protection regulations insist that alternative policies must respect the right to bodily integrity while simultaneously addressing the health needs of both the fetus and the pregnant woman.

The fetus had no separate legal status under common law, gaining no rights as an individual until it existed outside of the mother's body. The earliest disputes over fetal protection had nothing to do with the behavior of mothers. In the very first case, *Dietrich v. Northampton* (1884), the mother was the plaintiff. She sued for damages after she fell as a result of a defect in the town highway and subsequently miscarried a four to five-month-old fetus. The supreme court of

Massachusetts ruled for the defendant. Chief Justice Oliver Wendell Holmes, who was later appointed to the U.S. Supreme Court, wrote that the unborn child had been lost "before he became a person" and that the fetus was "a part of the mother at the time of the injury."

For the next 50 years, the law recognized only limited rights of the fetus and granted such rights only after the fetus "sees the light of day." The earliest deviation from this legal standard came in the form of inheritance cases, recognizing that a fetus could inherit property upon its birth even though the fetus did not technically "exist" as a person at the time of death of its benefactor. It was not until *Bonbrest v. Kotz* in 1946 that a court recognized any rights for the fetus before birth. *Bonbrest* allowed a father to recover for fetal harm caused by a doctor during delivery. Other cases recognized the rights of parents to compensation for prenatal injuries in cases involving physical assault on the pregnant woman or injuries from automobile accidents.

While these decisions differed from *Dietrich* (which was binding only in Massachusetts), courts still maintained that the fetus gained no separate recognition until it passed the point of viability, usually after the 28th week of pregnancy. In addition, rights were conferred upon the fetus only after it was "born alive." It was not until *Brennan v. Smith* (1960) that a court allowed parents to recover for injuries inflicted on the fetus before the point of viability in an automobile accident. *Brennan* also asserted that "the child has a legal right to begin life with a sound mind and body." While this statement cannot literally mean what it says—not all prenatal injuries or birth defects are preventable—*Brennan* was interpreted to affirm not only the right of the child to sue for damages, but also his or her right to be protected from negligence or harm in utero. The far-ranging implications of this holding would not emerge until the 1980s.

As precedent, *Brennan* provided pregnant women with a powerful legal tool for recovering damages from third parties (including abusive husbands) who threatened the health of their wanted child. The right of the child (and parents) to sue for compensation due to prenatal injuries is now recognized by law in almost every state, but this right is still generally contingent upon the live birth of the child. In the 1980's, conservative advocates seized on the legal opportunity to expand the grounds for fetal rights. For example, legal scholar Jeffrey Parness argued that the "born alive" rule was archaic and no longer served a useful purpose, given the ability of modern technology to "save" the fetus before birth. Pro-life advocates argued that the destruction of fetal life one moment before birth should not be viewed so differently from the murder of an infant one moment after.

A dramatic shift in opinion began to emerge in the courts during the 1980's as a result of pressures brought by pro-life advocates. Exactly 100 years after *Dietrich* denied independent rights to the fetus, the same state set precedent in precisely the opposite direction by affirming, for the first time in legal history, the "personhood" of the fetus before birth. *Commonwealth v. Cass* (1984) recognized the fetus as a "person" when a fetus died as a result of injuries caused by an automobile accident. Since then, many states have enacted or attempted to enact laws which allow the prosecution for homicide of those who "murder" a fetus. Many states have also attempted to enact "feticide" laws, giving the fetus legal status as a person under criminal and tort law, though these laws remain contested in the courts.

As technological advances made it possible to prove a causal link between injuries sustained in early fetal development and medical problems experienced by the child after birth, the impetus to hold those responsible for such injuries became more and more compelling. The idea of fetal protection was explicitly turned against pregnant women, who were cast as the gravest threats to fetal health through their ignorance, negligence, or malevolent behavior. Whereas early fetal protection advocates had relied on pro-life arguments, their successors often used pro-choice rhetoric—with questionable sincerity. Ironically, these activists turned *Roe v. Wade* (1973), one of the greatest victories for women's reproductive rights, into a weapon against those rights. *Roe*, the fetal protectionists argued, affirmed the state's "important and legitimate interest in protecting the potentiality of human life" after viability. Once a woman chose to continue a pregnancy, she was obligated by a "duty to care" for that fetus to insure its healthy birth.

Since the late 1970s, fetal protectionism has emerged in many forms. The most significant court cases have related to the exclusion of fertile women from work deemed potentially hazardous for fetal health; the forced medical treatment of pregnant women; and the criminal prosecution of women suspected of abusing drugs or alcohol during pregnancy. No state has successfully enacted a law that criminalizes prenatal conduct. Instead, prosecutors have attempted to use existing statutes to charge women with prenatal neglect or abuse of children. In cases of suspected drug or alcohol abuse, pregnant women have been charged with delivering drugs to a "minor" through the umbilical cord in the moments after birth, but before the cord has been cut. In some cases, a mother's or newborn's positive drug test has lead to charges of assault with a deadly weapon or, in cases of stillbirth or infant death shortly after birth, women have been charged with homicide or feticide. Courts attempted to civilly commit pregnant women suspected of using drugs or have given pregnant women harsher sentences for minor criminal violations. Women have faced loss of custody of their children or termination of parental rights after a single positive drug test during pregnancy, even when such tests might be unreliable.

At least 200 women have been criminally prosecuted for suspected drug use during pregnancy. Most convictions have been overturned on appeal. Nevertheless, the South Carolina Supreme Court has upheld the child abuse convictions and prison sentences of two women of who used cocaine during pregnancy: Cornelia Whitner in 1996, and Malissa Ann Crawley in 1998. More than a dozen states have attempted to pass laws allowing for the civil detention of women suspected of abusing drugs or alcohol during pregnancy, though most of these legislative efforts have failed.

Reproductive rights advocates insist that the degree of drug use by pregnant women has been grossly exaggerated and that punitive efforts are ineffective because they scare women away from health care providers. Most women accused of drug or alcohol abuse, they argue, give birth to healthy children and most also seek medical treatment for addiction where it is available. Although opponents of fetal protection policies recognize the need to safeguard the health of the woman and fetus during pregnancy, they argue that the punitive treatment of pregnant women violates their constitutional rights to equal treatment before the law and threatens the foundation of women's rights to reproductive autonomy. In addition, the exclusive focus on women's reproductive behavior fails to address the ways in which men's reproductive health may be damaged by risks, as well as the ways in which harm can be transmitted to the fetus through the male reproductive system. More equitable policies must address both the male and female contributions to fetal health as well as the effects of social conditions, like poverty, access to health care and nutrition, on reproductive health.

SEE Fetal Abuse; Forced Medical Treatment and Pregnancy; *In re* (A.C.); *International Union, United Auto Workers v. Johnson Controls*; Lifestyle Restrictions; Protective Labor Legislation; Substance Abuse and Pregnancy.

Further References. *Bonbrest v. Kotz*, 65 F. Supp. 135 (D.D.C. 1946). *Brennan v. Smith*, 392 Mass. 799 (1960). *Commonwealth v. Cass*, 467 N.E. 2d 1324 (Mass. 1984). Cynthia R. Daniels, *At Women's Expense: State Power and the Politics of Fetal Rights* (Cambridge, Mass., 1993). *Dietrich v. Northampton*, 138 Mass. 14 (1884). Laura E. Gomez, *Misconceiving Mothers: Legislators, Prosecutors, and the Politics of Prenatal Drug Exposure* (Philadelphia, 1997). Sally J. Kenney, *For Whose Protection? Reproductive Hazards and Exclusionary Policies in the United States and Britain* (Ann Arbor, Mich. 1992).

CYNTHIA R. DANIELS

FETAL RIGHTS. The concept of "fetal rights" entails the idea that fetuses are persons and therefore entitled to all of the rights and privileges afforded all other persons in the United States. Fetal rights claims are predicated on philosophical, moral, religious or medical convictions that understand fetal humanity as indistinguishable from the humanity of born persons. Under the influences of classical liberalism, the philosophy that underlies the political culture of the United States, this conviction translates into a demand that the moral status of personhood entails the commensurate legal status of rights bearer. In other words, once a fetus is recognized as human, it must be granted legal rights as well.

The public conceptualization of fetal rights had its birth with the 1973 decision in *Roe v. Wade*. There, the state of Texas declared the fetus a person from conception and claimed responsibility for protecting the fetus's right to life against any woman's constitutional abortion right. The Supreme Court agreed that declaring the fetus a person and thus entitled to a right to life would necessarily override a woman's abortion right. While the Court chose not to make such a ruling in *Roe*, it did signal some acquiescence by recognizing a state's interest in the "potential life" of the fetus. This half-assent to the principle of fetal personhood invited a variety of subsequent state experiments with fetal protection. In the context of the abortion debate, the result has been that although the Court continues to recognize the privacy right to abortion recognized in *Roe* (see *Planned Parenthood v. Casey*, 1992), it has simultaneously overlooked state encroachments on how abortion rights are exercised.

Moral status and legal status are closely related in the late twentieth century. Since *Roe*, public discussions of both fetal personhood and fetal rights have moved well beyond abortion. In spite of the Court's refusal to recognize *constitutional* status for fetuses, state supreme courts, members of Congress, state legislators, pro-life political lobbyists, family members and healthcare workers are pressing for formal recognition of fetal personhood. Missouri, for example, formally recognized the fetus as a person at conception. The California courts were first to recognize the fetus as a person six weeks following conception for the purpose of criminal prosecutions for fetal damage. Other states have followed California's lead. Proposed constitutional amendments declaring the fetus a person are introduced in Congress each session. Lower courts are increasingly entertaining civil and criminal claims against pregnant women made by third parties in the name of fetal rights.

Medicine may have a greater impact on the development of fetal rights than law, as physicians and hospitals increasingly argue that fetal healthcare is a right. Ultrasound and other medical technologies bring the public into the once obscure space of the uterus, familiarizing those outside the womb with the fetal being within it. In doing so, these procedures deprive the fetus of its anonymity and make it publicly accessible, much like a newborn child. Additional medical technologies now permit diagnosis and invasive treatments for fetal illnesses. The cultural impulse to see the fetus as a person is thus amplified by a medicalized world view that translates the *ability* to treat illness into an *imperative* to do so. The consequence is a growing movement to "protect" fetuses by insuring them the maximum possible healthcare and protecting them against environmental influences that might harm their development. At the century's close, there is thus both a greater public familiarity with fetal life and a corresponding and growing ethos to *care* for the fetus as a public entity. The inevitable result, particularly in a political culture that reduces all public issues to legal arguments, is a growing list of fetal rights claims. It is a list which includes such rights as the right to life, to general well being, to health care, to nurturing, to nutrition, to freedom from abuse and from exposure to drugs, alcohol and tobacco. Health care representatives invoke legal authorities to insure that pregnant women follow their doctors' orders. Such actions have included court-ordered medical treatments including suturing to close the cervix, blood transfusions and caesarian sections—all performed against the will of the pregnant woman involved. Such actions have also reached beyond the pregnant woman to include her friends and family members, medical personnel, and strangers, whose behaviors may have been claimed to infringe on fetal being as well.

The *political* problem that arises from claims for fetal rights originates with the *practical* problem imposed by the physical state of pregnancy. In order to satisfy a public demand to exercise fetal rights, the state must do so by going through the body of a pregnant woman. This means that, unlike with other clashes between individuals' rights, the rights of one person must *necessarily* be invaded to protect the rights of another. In their zeal to protect fetal rights, courts, prosecutors and physicians have been willing to ignore the rights of pregnant women. This is not surprising, given that women's entitlement to the personal rights granted by classical liberalism and American law has been limited and, to borrow Justice Blackmun's characterization of abortion laws in *Roe*, "of relatively recent vintage." Until *Roe* and *Casey*, women's claims to rights of bodily integrity had minimal legal and social recognition.

This rising conflict between pregnant women and the "rights" of their fetuses is underscored by those who demand extraction of "threatened" fetuses and transplantation into "more suitable" hosts. Once women are confronted with the technological possibility that fetuses can be gestated "more safely" elsewhere, the state's imperative to comply with particular standards of "appropriate" pregnancy behaviors will inevitably increase. This future may be foreshadowed by recent demands for legislation requiring all women of childbearing age to take vitamins to reduce certain birth defects. This pressure to safeguard the fetus can only further erode the sphere of women's bodily autonomy currently delimited by the thin veneer of privacy rights.

The result is a looming collision in fetal politics, one defined by the contrary moral and legal demands of both wanted and unwanted fetuses. Wanted fetuses impel the development of fetal rights discourse; unwanted fetuses require a woman's right to privacy. The two are incommensurable. Within a legalized political culture, resolution is only possible with further state intrusion. It is a growing conundrum for the country and the courts—one that may define rights theory in the next century. Most importantly, however, it is a crisis for the rights of the women in whom those fetuses will reside.

SEE Ectogenesis; Fetal Abuse; Fetal Protection; Forced Medical Treatment; *International Union, United Auto Workers v. Johnson Controls*; *Planned Parenthood of Southeastern Pennsylvania v. Casey; Roe v. Wade; Secretary of Labor v. American Cyanamid;* Substance Abuse and Pregnancy.

Further References. Robert H. Blank, *Regulating Reproduction* (New York, 1990). Patricia Boling, ed., *Expecting Trouble: Surrogacy, Fetal Abuse and New Reproductive Technologies* (Boulder, Colo., 1995). Joan C. Callahan, ed., *Reproduction, Ethics and the Law* (Bloomington, Ind., 1995). Laura M. Purdy, *Reproducing Persons: Issues in Feminist Bioethics* (Ithaca, N.Y., 1996). Susan Merrill Squier, *Babies in Bottles: Twentieth-Century Visions of Reproductive Technology* (New Brunswick, N.J., 1994). Bonnie Steinbock, *Life before Birth* (New York, 1992).

DEIRDRE CONDIT

FORCED MEDICAL TREATMENT AND PREGNANCY. In the past several decades, numerous issues relating to the concept of "fetal rights" have arisen. These issues extend beyond, but are in part an outgrowth of, the debate over abortion. Extending "personhood" status to the fetus, and granting partial or full citizenship rights to the unborn, has been one attempted strategy of abortion opponents. Advances in medical technology, allowing both early visualization of the fetus (via ultrasound) and medical interventions directly on the fetus, have also contributed to an increasing tendency to view the fetus as a distinct individual endowed with certain rights. Granting legal rights to the fetus would be a significant departure from precedent in Anglo-American law. While this has not occurred in the United States on a broad scale, some state legislatures and courts have begun to grant limited rights to the fetus on an ad hoc basis. These developments raise difficult ethical and legal questions when conflicts arise between the "rights" of the fetus and those of the woman in whose womb the fetus is carried.

One such area of conflict involves forced medical interventions on pregnant women in order to preserve the life or health of the fetus. These interventions include fetal surgery or other therapies during pregnancy, as well as deliveries by cesarean section. Fetal rights advocates and some medical professionals have come to view the fetus as a "second patient" in these situations. In many instances, women are willing to undergo interventions or procedures that they believe will benefit their unborn child. However, some women refuse these interventions for a number of reasons, including fear of surgery or religious objections. Conflict arises in these cases because any procedure performed on a fetus necessarily involves an invasive intervention on the pregnant woman herself. Such an intervention threatens her bodily integrity and autonomy, as well as her liberty and privacy.

U.S. law requires that competent adults consent to medical treatment, indeed to any violation of bodily integrity. But the pregnant woman's bodily integrity has not always prevailed when conflicts have arisen over interventions for fetal health. On several occasions, medical facilities or providers have sought and been granted court orders to perform invasive procedures on pregnant women. The case of Angela Carder in 1987 is perhaps the most notorious instance of forced medical treatment. A long-term cancer survivor, Carder suffered a recurrence in her sixth month of pregnancy. Despite her objection, the hospital petitioned and received a court order to perform a cesarean section against her will. Both she and the premature infant died shortly thereafter. Carder's family sued the hospital. While the U.S. Court of Appeals ruled that the lower court had erred in overruling the pregnant woman's wishes, *in re* A.C. indicated that there might be instances in which a woman's desires must yield to the state's interest in potential life. Indeed, in most states that recognize living wills, a pregnant woman's right to refuse treatment when severely ill is restricted.

Forced medical intervention is not common; there is no evidence that it is becoming more frequent or more popular; and *in re* A.C. remains the most authoritative judicial ruling on the issue. But Angela Carder's fate clearly shows that, however rarely this sort of thing happens, once is too often. Furthermore, it is impossible to determine how many women are persuaded by experts to undergo treatment they do not want.

The possibility of forced medical treatment means that a woman may lose sovereignty over her body by becoming pregnant. Not only does forced intervention abridge a woman's reproductive rights by using her pregnancy as a justification for coercing her, but it also raises issues of class and racial equality. Low-income and minority women are disproportionately the targets of such mandated treatment. If the likelihood of forced medical intervention increases, fear of such treatment may deter women from seeking prenatal care—thereby jeopardizing their health as well as that of their unborn children.

SEE Fetal Abuse; Fetal Rights; Fetal Protection; *In re* (A.C).*;* Lifestyle Restrictions and Pregnancy; Substance Abuse and Pregnancy.

Further References. Cynthia R. Daniels, *At Women's Expense: State Power and the Politics of Fetal Rights* (Cambridge, Mass., 1993). Deborah Mathieu, *Preventing Prenatal Harm: Should the State Intervene?* (Washington, D.C., 1996).

JULIANNA GONEN

G

GAG RULE is a pejorative term used by the opponents of a regulation that forbade any mention of abortion in a federally funded family planning clinic. The gag rule was one of the last in a series of maneuvers by the Reagan administration to weaken the federal family planning program and appeal to anti-abortion, social conservatives. Other policies included the "squeal rule" requiring clinics to notify parents of minors who received birth control (a federal court blocked its enforcement), transferring the Office of Family Planning back to the direct administration of a pro-life political appointee, and disbanding the family planning patient data system. The rule was promulgated in 1988 through family planning regulations issued by the administration in its last year in office. The Department of Health and Human Services (HHS) reinterpreted Title X of the Public Health Service Act of 1970, which provides family funding for low income women and teenagers throughout the United States. Under the new rule, Title X-funded clinic personnel were not allowed to discuss abortion with a pregnant patient; they could inform her only about prenatal care and adoption. This directive was absolute; it applied even if a patient specifically asked for abortion information or if her life were in danger. Although Title X provides only about a fifth of public funds for family planning, the gag rule would have affected the health care of the approximately six million women served by the national family planing program. A clinic that receives *any* Title X funds has to abide by Title X regulations for all of its patients even if the majority of its funds come from other sources.

Proponents of the gag rule claimed that federally funded clinics should not encourage abortion, even if only to mention it as one of a woman's legal options. Opponents of the policy argued that it would discriminate against the indigent women whom Title X serves because they would get less information about their pregnancy options than more affluent women who had access to the private health care delivery system. Because federal courts enjoined enforcement of the gag rule during much of its tenure, its impact is difficult to assess.

After Reagan left office, the Bush administration continued to defend this policy. In May 1991, the Supreme Court issued the 5-4 *Rust v. Sullivan* opinion upholding the federal regulations. Reaction to this decision was vehement and swift. Congress amended Title X to permit abortion counseling. As expected, President Bush vetoed this amendment. An effort to override the veto got the necessary two-thirds majority in the Senate, but fell short in the House. Only days before the 1992 presidential election, the U.S. Court of Appeals for the District of Columbia ruled that the Bush administration had illegally ordered a substantive reinterpretation of the 1988 gag rule banning abortion counseling in federally supported family planning clinics without providing an opportunity for public comment.

Bill Clinton's victory over George Bush in that election sealed the fate of the gag rule—for the time being. On January 22, 1993, President Clinton signed an order initiating the process to repeal the 1988 regulation. However, the Clinton administration never issued new family planning regulations, which would have required a congressional review. Proponents of family planning worry that it would be relatively easy for a future president to reinstate the gag rule in order to placate the anti-abortion lobby.

In the late 1990s, the term "gag rule" was used in a different context: debates over U.S. international family planning assistance. Anti-abortion members of Congress have tried relentlessly to pass a "gag rule" that would prohibit foreign nongovernmental organizations (NGOs) receiving this assistance from using their own funds to provide legal abortions or to engage in a wide range of legal activities, including making public statements about abortion in any context. For several years, Congress has attached riders to United Nations appropriations bills providing that the United States' UN dues cannot be used to fund programs on population control, birth control, or abortion services. President Clinton vetoed these bills. As a result, the U.S. has not paid its UN dues in several years. On his third day in office, president George W. Bush announced that he would block U.S. aid to international family planning organizations which use their own funds for abortions or abortion counseling.

SEE International Law and U.S. Women's Reproductive Rights; *Rust v. Sullivan*

Further References. Deborah R. McFarlane and Kenneth J. Meier, *The Politics of Fertility Control* (New York, 2000). Michele McKeegan, *Abortion Politics: Mutiny in the Ranks of the Right* (New York, 1992).

DEBORAH R. McFARLANE

GEDULDIG v. AIELLO (417 U.S. 484, 1974) is a Supreme Court decision reviewing California's exclusion of pregnancy-related disabilities from its employee sickness and accident benefits plan. Justice Potter Stewart's majority opinion upheld the exclusion under the Equal Protection Clause of the Fourteenth Amendment. Finding no gender discrimination because the classification was not between women and men but between "pregnant women and non-pregnant persons," the Court applied the lowest level of constitutional scrutiny, the "rational basis" test. It concluded that California's legitimate interests in keeping the insurance system solvent and in making benefits adequate for those conditions covered were rationally related to the exclusion of pregnancy-related conditions. Although the Court had used the Due Process Clause to invalidate mandatory maternity leaves in *Cleveland Board of Education v. LaFleur* only a few months earlier, its finding of a rational basis for the policy in *Geduldig* negated the possibility of a ruling against the state on Due Process grounds. Two years after *Geduldig, General Electric v. Gilbert* upheld a similar benefits plan under Title VII of the Civil Rights Act of 1964, which prohibits sex discrimination in employment. *Gilbert* reaffirmed the view that pregnancy-based discrimination is not sex discrimination.

Both *Geduldig* and *Gilbert* were widely criticized for their refusal to characterize pregnancy-based classifications as gender-based. In response to these decisions, Congress passed the Pregnancy Discrimination Act, amending Title VII explicitly to prohibit discrimination on the basis of pregnancy, childbirth, and related medical conditions. By removing some of the economic penalties of motherhood, this legislation greatly enhanced women's reproductive rights.

SEE *Cleveland Board of Education v. LaFleur*; *General Electric Co. v. Gilbert*; Pregnancy Discrimination Act of 1978.

Further References. Lucinda M. Finley, "Transcending Equality Theory: A Way Out of the Maternity and the Workplace Debate," *Columbia Law Review* 86 (1986):1118-1182. Herma Hill Kay, "Equality and Difference: The Case of Pregnancy," *Berkeley Women's Law Journal* 1 (1985):1-38. Wendy W. Williams, "Equality's Riddle: Pregnancy and the Equal Treatment/Special Treatment Debate," *New York University Review of Law and Social Change* 13 (1984/85): 325-380.

CARRIE N. BAKER

GENERAL ELECTRIC CO. v. GILBERT (429 U.S. 125, 1976) involved a class action lawsuit under Title VII brought by employees of General Electric challenging GE's disability plan. Under the plan, GE provided non-occupational sickness and accident benefits to all of its employees but excluded disabilities arising from pregnancy from the plan. The plaintiffs were employees who had been pregnant and had requested disability benefits to cover their absences from work due to pregnancy; GE had denied their claims. The Court's opinion, written by Justice William Rehnquist, relied on *Geduldig v. Aiello* (1974) to hold that GE's plan did not constitute facial discrimination on the basis of sex under Title VII. Although *Geduldig* had been decided on constitutional rather than statutory grounds, Rehnquist approvingly quoted the earlier case on the sex discrimination issue: "There is no risk from which men are protected and women are not." While "pregnancy-related disabilities constitute an additional risk, unique to women," GE's plan provided the same level of benefits to both men and women, and protected both from the same risks. Furthermore, gender-neural grounds existed for differentiating between pregnancy and other conditions; it was often "voluntarily undertaken and desired."

Justice William Brennan dissented, arguing that the exclusion of pregnancy required only women to face the risk of losing their incomes as a result of a temporary medical disability. He also stressed the fact that the plan covered male-only medical procedures, like prostatectomies, and "voluntary" disabilities, like sports injuries. Justice John Paul Stevens also dissented, asserting that "such a rule discriminates on account of sex; for it is the capacity to become pregnant which primarily differentiates the female from the male." The *Gilbert* decision was not popular with the public. Two years later, Congress passed the Pregnancy Discrimination Act, which directly repudiated the Court's holding in *Gilbert*.

SEE *Geduldig v. Aiello*; Pregnancy Discrimination Act of 1978.

JULIE NOVKOV

GRISWOLD v. CONNECTICUT (381 U.S. 479, 1965) was a landmark decision in the development of reproductive rights. In *Poe v. Ullman* (1961) the Court heard a challenge to the 1879 Connecticut law prohibiting the use of contraceptive devices and the giving of medical advice concerning such devices. The majority dismissed the case, holding that it did not present a real controversy because the statute had rarely if ever been enforced. *Griswold v. Connecticut* differed from *Poe v. Ullman* in one crucial respect: the plaintiffs had been charged and convicted of violating the law. Three days after Estelle Griswold, Executive Director of the Planned Parenthood League of Connecticut, and Dr. C. Lee Buxton of Yale University Medical School opened a birth control clinic, they were arrested for dispensing contraceptives to a married couple. They were convicted and fined $100 each.

The Supreme Court, by a vote of seven to two, invalidated the law. Although the justices in the majority all agreed that a constitutional right to privacy protected the right of married couples to use contraceptives, they disagreed on the specific constitutional source of that right. Justice William O. Douglas found the right to privacy in the penumbras "formed by emanations" from the First, Third, Fourth, Fifth, and the Ninth Amendments. Those penumbras, he explained, create zones of privacy, which make the explicit guarantees more secure. Thus, the First Amendment includes the right to association—a right that clearly involves a zone of privacy. Likewise, the Fourth Amendment's prohibition on unreasonable searches and seizures creates a zone of privacy in one's home, one's person, and in one's possessions. The marital relationship, Douglas reasoned, is clearly within the zone of privacy created by those provisions and the law forbidding the use of contraceptives had a "maximum destructive impact" on that relationship.

In order to enforce the law, the police would have to search the marital bedroom for "telltale signs of the use of contraceptives." Obviously, such invasive procedures would be inconsistent with the privacy of marriage. Justice Arthur Goldberg located the right to privacy in the Ninth Amendment's mandate that the enumeration of certain rights in the Constitution must not be interpreted to deny the existence of other rights. Justice John Harlan found the right to privacy in the Due Process Clause of the Fourteenth Amendment.

The actual holding in *Griswold* was quite narrow: it was unconstitutional for states to make the use of contraceptives by married couples a crime. Nevertheless, the justices established that there is a fundamental right to privacy that encompasses decisions about whether to conceive a child. *Griswold* was enormously important in paving the way for the Court's decision in *Roe v. Wade*. Indeed, after *Griswold* only two easy logical steps were required to reach the conclusion that women have a fundamental right to privacy that includes the right to choose to end a pregnancy. First, the Court extended the right to individuals in *Eisenstadt v. Baird* (1972) when it invalidated Massachusetts' law restricting the distribution of contraceptives to married persons. The Court announced that the right to privacy includes the right of the individual to be free of governmental intrusion into decisions concerning whether to have a child. Second, in *Roe v. Wade* it extended the right to privacy to include not only the decision about whether to conceive a child but also the decision about whether to end a pregnancy.

SEE Birth Control Movement; *Eisenstadt v. Baird*; *Poe v. Ullman*; Privacy and Reproductive Rights; *Roe v. Wade*.

Further References. Thomas I. Emerson, "Nine Justices in Search of a Doctrine," *Michigan Law Review,* 64 (December 1965): 219-234. Lee Epstein and Joseph F. Kobylka. *The Supreme Court and Legal Change: Abortion and the Death Penalty* (Chapel Hill, N.C., 1992). Laurence H. Tribe, *Abortion: The Clash of Absolutes* (New York, 1992).

SUE DAVIS

H

_____

H.L. v. MATHESON, (450 U.S. 398, 1981): Soon after *Roe v. Wade*, Utah passed
a statute requiring that the parents of an unmarried minor be notified, "if possible," before an abortion is performed on her. Unlike the laws challenged in
Planned Parenthood v. Danforth and *Bellotti v. Baird*, however, it did not require
parental *consent*. H.L., a pregnant 15-year-old who lived with her parents, alleged
that the law violated her right to privacy and that it was overbroad on its face
because it applied to mature and legally emancipated minors as well as to those
living with and dependent on their parents.

Four justices (one short of a majority) supported the Utah law without qualification. The plurality opinion by Chief Justice Warren Burger found "significant
state interests" in parental involvement in the abortion decision. As applied to this
case, the plurality concluded, the notification requirement was a legitimate exercise of governmental authority. The Court refused to consider the overbreadth
argument. Justices Lewis Powell and Potter Stewart joined in upholding the
statute as applied, but on condition that any pregnant minor must have an opportunity to pursue an alternate course to parental notification via an independent
decision maker. Such a "judicial bypass" would allow a young woman to demonstrate that she was mature enough to make the abortion decision unilaterally or
that notifying her parents was not in her best interests.

Justices Thurgood Marshall, William J. Brennan, Jr., and Harry Blackmun dissented. Marshall's conclusion that the Utah law unconstitutionally deprived minors
of the privacy rights protected by *Roe* was based on the state's failure to demonstrate that its law furthered important state interests. Utah claimed that the law
encouraged minors to seek their parents' counsel during a potentially critical time
in their lives and enabled parents to provide important medical and psychological

information about the minor. But the notification requirement could be met by a perfunctory telephone call minutes before the performing of an abortion.

H.L. v. Matheson was the first in a line of several unsuccessful challenges to statutory restrictions on the reproductive autonomy of minors. This case demonstrates the range of views among the justices on this question, a division has which has continued as the composition of the Court has changed. The splintering of the high Court on the abortion issue in general has been, and remains, equally apparent in the minors' rights cases.

SEE Abortion and Parental Consent and Notification; *Bellotti v. Baird I* and *II*; *City of Akron v. Akron Center for Public Health*; *Hodgson v. Minnesota*; *Ohio v. Akron Center for Reproductive Health; Planned Parenthood of Southeastern Pennsylvania v. Casey*; *Planned Parenthood of Central Missouri v. Danforth*.

Further References. Gayle Binion, "Feminist Theory Confronts U.S. Supreme Court Rhetoric: The Case of Abortion Rights," *International Journal of Law, Policy and the Family*, 11 (April 1997): 63-85. ACLU Foundation, *Parental Notice Laws: Their Catastrophic Impact on Teenagers' Rights to Abortion* (New York, 1986).

GAYLE BINION

HARRIS v. McRAE (448 U.S. 297, 1980) upheld the Hyde Amendment, a federal law originally passed in 1976 which prohibits the use of federal funds to pay for abortions for Medicaid recipients. The law is named after its primary sponsor, Representative Henry Hyde, an Illinois Republican and staunch abortion opponent. The original version of the amendment allowed an exception for abortions that were necessary to save the life of the woman. A later version also permitted exceptions in cases of rape or incest and in situations where carrying the pregnancy to term would result in "severe and long-lasting physical health damage" to the woman. This latter provision for "medically necessary" abortions was subsequently dropped.

A coalition of pregnant Medicaid recipients, abortion providers, and pro-choice groups filed a suit in federal district court challenging the Hyde Amendment on statutory and constitutional grounds. They alleged that: 1) the Medicaid Act required states to pay for abortions not covered by federal funds and 2) the amendment violated several constitutional provisions. The district court rejected the statutory argument but agreed that the amendment was unconstitutional.

By a five to four vote, with Justice Potter Stewart writing for the majority, the Court upheld the amendment. On the statutory claim, Stewart said that the legislative history of the Medicaid Act did not show congressional intent to require states to pay for services for which federal funding was denied. Consequently, states were not required to cover the costs of abortions not covered by the Hyde Amendment. On the critical constitutional issues, Stewart asserted that the Amendment satisfied both the Fifth Amendment due process guarantee and the constitutional right to choose an abortion previously recognized in *Roe v. Wade*. He relied primarily on *Maher v. Roe* (1977) which upheld a state policy limiting the use of Medicaid funds to "medically necessary" abortions. He reaffirmed the holding in *Maher* that the choice to fund childbirth rather than abortion was not arbitrary or irrational, even though it cost more money; therefore, it did not violate due process. On the privacy issue, Stewart wrote, "although government may not place obstacles in the path of a woman's exercise of her freedom of choice, it need not remove those not of its own creation. Indigency falls in the latter category." In short, while women have the constitutional right to have an abortion, the government is not required to provide funds for them to exercise that right.

In dissent, Justice William Brennan declared that the Hyde Amendment clearly discriminated against poor women in the exercise of their constitutional rights. Moreover, Brennan saw the funding restrictions on abortion as having the same effect as "outright denial of [abortion] rights through criminal and regulatory sanctions." Justice Thurgood Marshall's dissent emphasized the fact that a "substantial proportion" of the indigent women burdened by the amendment "are members of minority races," and predicted that upholding the law would "ensure the destruction of both fetal and maternal life." The Court's decisions in *Harris* and related cases have made it difficult for poor women whose health care is provided for by public funding to exercise their constitutional right to obtain abortions.

SEE Abortion and Public Assistance; *Beal v. Doe*; Hyde Amendment; *Webster v. Reproductive Health Services.*

Further References. Barbara Hinkson Craig and David M. O'Brien, *Abortion and American Politics* (Chatham, N.J., 1993). Susan Gluck Mezey, *Women, Public Policy, and the Federal Courts* (New York, 1992).

JOYCE A. BAUGH

HISPANIC/LATINA WOMEN AND REPRODUCTIVE RIGHTS. "Hispanic" and "Latino/a" are umbrella terms used to identify people of diverse racial backgrounds with family origins in Spanish- or Portuguese-speaking cultures of Central and South America and the Caribbean. Hispanics are the fastest-growing segment of the U.S. population, and will soon replace African Americans as the largest minority in the country. Given the numerical strength of U.S. Hispanics, it is surprising that the Centers for Disease Control (CDC) and National Survey of Family Growth did not begin compiling comprehensive data on their reproductive and contraceptive practices until 1988.

Reproductive rights issues and personal choices for Latinas in the U.S. are informed by a complex interaction of cultural and religious values, socioeconomic factors, education level, and degree of acculturation. For example, while reproductive autonomy has been a top priority among non-Hispanic feminists, it has been of secondary importance to Latina feminists. They have concentrated on basic survival issues such as adequate jobs and working conditions, child care, and public safety. Thus, Latinas have often been the subjects, but not the participants, in discussions focusing on reproductive rights. The impact of these factors must therefore be evaluated within the cultural and social context in which Latinas live, and be informed by their past experience with reproductive technologies.

Latinas, even those who are not Roman Catholic, are often constrained by the cultural stereotype of *marianismo*—the "sainted mother." The Virgin Mary is the role model for Latina womanhood as mother, nurturer, one who has endured suffering and is willing to serve. Latinas are expected to emulate these virtues in serving their husbands and children. While these values are a source of subjugation for Latinas, they have also served to comfort and strengthen them in fighting racism and resisting oppression. The devotion that many women have for their families—and the commitment of many men to endure hard work in the agricultural fields, factories, and low-paid, unskilled labor—has made it difficult for Latinas to question traditional values. Nevertheless, while fertility is extremely important to Hispanic identity, the desire to improve the quality of life for their families is also important. It is at this intersection of personal desire and tradition that Latinas make their reproductive choices.

The stereotype that Latinas unilaterally oppose abortion is supported by neither current data nor the historical record. A 1998 CDC study indicates an increase in the abortion rate among Latinas from 9.8 to 16.1 per 1,000 pregnancies during 1990-1996. Although abortions have historically either been self-induced or performed by midwives in Hispanic cultures, more than 5,000 abortions were performed in state-run Puerto Rican hospitals by licensed physicians in 1958. When relations with Cuba deteriorated in the early 1960s, the so-called "Havana weekend" simply became the "San Juan weekend." A 1963 investigation in Puerto Rico revealed that certain hospitals were selling in excess of $1 million of abortion services per year.

Passage of the Hyde Amendment in 1976, which discontinued Medicaid funds for abortion except to save the life of the mother, had its most devastating impact on Latinas. Shortly after its passage, Rosie Jiménez of McAllen, Texas died of a back-alley abortion which she obtained illegally in Mexico. Her death illustrated the consequences of lost abortion rights on poor and minority women. The Supreme Court upheld the Hyde amendment in *Harris v. McRae* (1980), adding that states are not bound under Title XIX of the Social Security Act to fund abortions which are disallowed under the Hyde Amendment. The Hyde Amendment has been modified to include Medicaid funding for abortions in the case of rape or incest.

The Hyde Amendment is far from the only instance of official constraint on the reproductive rights of Latinas. Resisting coercive or imposed fertility choices has long been a major challenge for Latinas in the U.S. For example, the use of Puerto Rico, a colony of the United States, as a place for experimentation and testing of new reproductive technologies is well documented. Oral contraceptives, Emko foam, intrauterine devices, and Depo-Provera were all tested in Puerto Rico before they were distributed on the U.S. mainland. This experimentation extended to the use of sterilization as a method of birth control. While it was not common in the U.S. until the 1960s, "la operación," as it is known colloquially, was introduced and promoted in Puerto Rico in the 1930s in response to what was termed a growing overpopulation problem. By 1982, 39 percemt of all women between the ages of 15 and 45 on the island had been sterilized—not necessarily with their informed consent.

A similar situation existed for Puerto Rican and other Hispanic women on the U.S. mainland. In 1971, the U.S. Department of Health, Education and Welfare (HEW) (now Health and Human Services) included sterilization as part of its health program, with the intent of supporting a variety of family planning services. Soon after, evidence surfaced of attitudes among physicians that endorsed sterilization of poor unwed mothers, the rising incidence of hysterectomies on minority women in teaching hospitals, and the policy in these hospitals that made abortion services conditional on consent to sterilization—known as the "package deal."

The involuntary sterilization of 24 Mexican women at the University of Southern California-Los Angeles County Medical Center between 1971 and 1974 shows the effects of this policy on Latinas. Twelve of these women brought suit in *Madrigal v. Quilligan*, but eventually lost. The judge concluded that the entire matter was the result of a communications breakdown. However, court records reveal that none of the women entered the hospital with an intent to be sterilized; persistent attempts to persuade the women to accept sterilization were made while they were in full labor and/or drugged; consent forms were in English, even though all the women had limited fluency in that language; and the medical staff failed to adequately inform the women of the consequences of the surgery. One of the 12, Guadalupe Acosta, did not learn that she had been sterilized until two months after the surgery, when she returned to the Medical Center to request oral contraceptives. HEW adopted regulations designed to prevent sterilization abuses in 1979. However, a 1995 study correlating elevated hysterectomy rates to areas with high concentrations of Hispanic residents indicates that coerced sterilization may still be a problem.

Today, sterilization is the most common form of contraception among Latinas, particularly Puerto Ricans. In New York City, Latinas have a rate of sterilization seven times greater than that of Euro-American women and almost twice that of non-Hispanic African-American women. The main reason for the popularity of contraceptive sterilization among Latinas appears to be that it is familiar and has a history in Hispanic communities. While the choice of sterilization is voluntary, the history of sterilization abuse among Latinas suggests that the relationship between choice and coercion is complex and problematic.

SEE Birth Control and African-American Women; Federal Sterilization Guidelines (1979); *Harris v. McRae*; Hyde Amendment; Sterilization; Sterilization Abuse.

Further References. Aida Hurtado, "Sitios y Lenguas: Chicanas Theorize Feminisms," *Hypatia*, 13, #2 (1998): 134-161. Ann F. López, "Latinas and Repro

Rights—Silent No More," *Ms.*, 1, #5 (1991): 91. *Madrigal v. Quilligan*, No. 75-2057 (Central District of California, 1975). Rosalind P. Petchesky, *Abortion and Woman's Choice: The State, Sexuality, and Reproductive Freedom*, rev. ed. (Boston, 1990). Annette B. Ramírez de Arellano and Conrad Seipp, *Colonialism, Catholicism, and Contraception: A History of Birth Control in Puerto Rico* (Chapel Hill, N.C., 1983).

ÁNGELA PATTATUCCI-ARAGÓN

HODGSON v. MINNESOTA (497 U.S. 417, 1990) involved a challenge to a Minnesota law requiring that (in the absence of extraordinary circumstances), no abortion be performed on an unemancipated minor until at least 48 hours after written notice had been provided to both her parents if both were living, or to one if the second parent had died or could not be located through reasonably diligent effort. A so-called judicial bypass procedure allowed a minor to petition a court for a determination that she was mature enough to give informed consent or that an abortion without parental notification would be in her best interests. If the court issued the order, the abortion could proceed without notifying either parent. The Supreme Court invalidated the two-parent notification requirement standing alone, but sustained it as combined with the judicial bypass procedure. Justice John Paul Stevens announced the judgment, delivered the majority opinion invalidating the absolute parental notification requirement, and dissented from the ruling on judicial bypass.

Stevens's majority opinion stated that a woman's right to decide whether or not to conceive or bear a child, a right protected by the Due Process clause of the Fourteenth Amendment, is applicable to minors as well as adults. Stevens described the Minnesota statute as the "most intrusive in the nation" in requiring both parents to receive notice without providing for a judicial bypass in all circumstances. To save the statute, Minnesota would have to demonstrate that the obstacles it imposed on women's ability to obtain an abortion were "reasonably related to legitimate, state concerns other than disagreement with the choice the individual has made." The Court found that the state had failed to show that the burdens imposed by the two-parent notification requirement, especially where the parents were divorced or separated, served the claimed interests in protecting pregnant minors or insuring family integrity; indeed, the requirement actually disserved the state interest in the case of dysfunctional families.

Four of the five justices who voted against the absolute notification requirement also found the bypass procedure unconstitutional. Although Stevens had voted to uphold parental consent requirements as early as *Planned Parenthood v. Danforth* (1976), here he dissented. His opinion argued that requiring the bypass procedure to be used when the minor and one parent agree that the other parent should not be notified represents an "unjustified governmental intrusion into the family's decisional process." Justice Thurgood Marshall argued for himself, William Brennan, and Harry Blackmun that the bypass procedure was no less objectionable than the notification requirement alone; it burdened the woman's right to privacy without a compelling state interest for doing so.

Sandra Day O'Connor, who had voted against the notification requirement standing alone, joined William Rehnquist, Byron White, Antonin Scalia, and Anthony Kennedy in sustaining the bypass provision as "a means of tailoring a parental consent provision to avoid unduly binding the minor's limited right to an abortion." O'Connor's switch gave the state's requirement of either two-parent notification or a judicial bypass the majority it needed. As she pointed out, this was not the first decision upholding such a combination. But *Hodgson* was the first, and so far the only, case involving a requirement that *both* parents be notified.

SEE Abortion and Parental Consent and Notification; Abortion and Parental Involvement; *Bellotti v. Baird I* and *II*; *City of Akron v. Akron Center for Public Health*; *H.L. v. Matheson; Ohio v. Akron Center for Reproductive Health*; *Planned Parenthood Association of Kansas City, Missouri v. Ashcroft; Planned Parenthood of Central Missouri v. Danforth;* Youth and Reproductive Rights.

LUCINDA PEACH

HUMAN LIFE BILL/HUMAN LIFE AMENDMENT. Pro-life advocates believe that the U.S. Supreme Court erred in *Roe v. Wade* (1973) by refusing to recognize a right to life from conception. Accordingly, they advocate the passage of a human life bill and/or constitutional amendment in order to circumscribe or overturn the Court's ruling in *Roe* and ultimately to reestablish a constitutional right to life from conception. Human life bills and amendments have been introduced in every session of Congress since 1973. As yet, none has been passed.

The scope of the many human life bills and amendments that have been proposed in Congress varies considerably, relating, in part, to the short and long-term goals of pro-life leaders. Some versions of the human life bill include provisions to establish that human life begins at conception—an issue the Court refused to resolve in *Roe*—and that the rights of all persons from that point forward are protected by the Fourteenth Amendment. Other versions seek to protect a right to life which is deemed superior to all other constitutional rights except the protections afforded to all persons under the Fifth and Fourteenth Amendments. Different congressional proposals have included an outright ban on abortion, an explicit reversal of *Roe*, and a law that would give the states the power to decide whether and when to allow abortion. Despite these variations, each of these alternatives shares a common goal: to circumscribe the constitutional protection of a right to choose protected by *Roe*.

As of 1999, one human life amendment and two bills had been introduced in the 106th Congress. The proposed constitutional amendment would protect the right to life of the unborn at every stage of their biological development, thereby prohibiting abortion, except in cases of rape or incest or where the mother's life is endangered by the pregnancy. The Right to Life Act of 1999 would invoke Congress's enforcement powers under the equal protection clause of the Fourteenth Amendment to protect the right to life of each born and preborn human person from the moment of fertilization. The Unborn Children's Civil Rights Act holds that abortion takes the life of an unborn child, that the right to abortion is not secured by the Constitution, and that the Supreme Court erred in *Roe* by not recognizing the states' compelling interest in protecting the life of each person before birth.

If passed, each of these proposals would drastically abridge women's reproductive freedom. The first two proposals would all but destroy a woman's right to choose to end her pregnancy. The third would permit the states to do so. In addition, legislation which states that life begins at conception would likely jeopardize the availability of various methods of birth control such as oral contraceptives and intra-uterine devices, both of which interfere with the development of a fertilized ovum after conception by inhibiting its implantation in the womb.

Members of Congress have proposed both laws and constitutional amendments because each form of legislation has its advantages and disadvantages. The Supreme Court cannot rule that an amendment is unconstitutional, while it can strike down a federal law. On the other hand, it is far more difficult for a constitutional amendment to be ratified than it is for a bill to be passed. A bill gains approval through the ordinary legislative process, which requires only a simple majority of each house and the president's signature to become law. A constitutional amendment requires a super-majority of both Congress and the states. Proposed amendments which originate in Congress require a two-thirds vote of each house, as well as ratification by three-fourths of the state legislatures. Alternatively, Congress might call a constitutional convention at the request of two-thirds of the states; this convention would have the power to amend any part of the Constitution. Constitutional amendments typically offer a vehicle for more lasting reform than ordinary legislation.

Given the difficulty of attaining the necessary super-majorities, both pro-life and pro-choice supporters recognize that it is unlikely that a human life amendment will be ratified any time in the near future. Therefore, the passage of human life bills is an important short-term goal for the pro-life movement in the United States. John Wilke, the former president of the National Right to Life Committee, has identified the Human Life Amendment as the movement's ultimate goal— but he has also committed his organization to securing passage of a bill that would allow individual states to re-criminalize abortion. It is possible, though unlikely, that the Court will change its mind.

SEE Abortion as a Reproductive Right; Abortion and Political Conflict; *Roe v. Wade.*

Further References. Susan Burgess, *Contest for Constitutional Authority: The Abortion and War Powers Debates* (Lawrence, Kans., 1992). Mark A. Graber, *Rethinking Abortion: Equal Choice, the Constitution, and Reproductive Politics* (Princeton, N.J., 1996). Eileen L. McDonagh, *Breaking the Abortion Deadlock:*

From Choice to Consent (New York, 1996). Up-to-the-moment action on the human life bill and human life amendment proposals in the current session of Congress can be easily tracked through the Library of Congress' World Wide Web site: www.loc.gov. Detailed legislative histories dating from 1973 can be tracked through *Congressional Quarterly Almanac* and *Congressional Quarterly Weekly Reports.*

SUSAN BURGESS

HYDE AMENDMENT. This term refers to provisions in several different federal appropriations bills since 1976 prohibiting the use of federal funds for abortions. These bans affect Medicaid recipients, federal employees, disabled women on Medicare, military personnel, Peace Corps volunteers, Native American women, residents of the District of Columbia, and women in federal prisons. The amendment is named after one of its authors, Representative Henry Hyde (R-Ill.).

In 1974, the first abortion funding ban was introduced in Congress by Representative Angelo Roncallo (R-N.Y.) and Senator Dewey Bartlett (R-Okla.) as an amendment to the 1975 Labor-Health, Education and Welfare (LHEW) appropriations bill. Approximately 33 percent of all abortions were being funded by Medicaid, and members of Congress saw funding bans as a way to reduce the number of abortions without overturning *Roe v. Wade.* Even some supporters of abortion rights concluded that taxpayers who opposed abortion should not be forced to subsidize it.

In 1976, Henry Hyde added the first successful version of a Medicaid funding ban to the 1977 LHEW appropriations bill. Although Silvio Conte (R-Mass.) designed the language signed into law, it was Hyde who became most closely identified with the movement to restrict the use of federal funds for abortion. The regulations have enjoyed considerable bipartisan support. While the most prominent advocates of the bans have been Republicans, the original amendment was passed when Democrats controlled both houses of Congress.

The language adopted in 1976 prohibited the use of Medicaid funds for abortion except when the mother's life was in danger, when two physicians certified that a woman would suffer "severe and long-lasting damage" if she carried to term, and when the pregnancy was the result of rape or incest that was promptly reported to the police. The language adopted between 1981 and 1993 prohibited the use of federal funds except to preserve the woman's life. In 1993, the amendment was expanded to include exceptions for pregnancies that resulted from rape or incest.

Congress extended the abortion funding bans to several other appropriations bills between 1977 and 1998. Groups of women restricted from using federal funds for abortions by these laws include residents of the District of Columbia (1977), military personnel and Peace Corps volunteers since 1979; federal employees (1983), women in federal prisons (1987), Native American women (1988), and disabled women on Medicare (1988).

The Supreme Court has upheld the constitutionality of abortion funding bans in several decisions. The Court issued three rulings sustaining state bans in 1977, while Congress was debating the Hyde Amendment (*Maher v. Roe, Beal v. Doe*, and *Poelker v. Doe*). In 1980, the court upheld the federal amendment in *Harris v. McRae*. The court has also required states to comply with the language used in federal funding bans. Twelve states were ordered to conform to federal law after Congress expanded Medicaid funding to rape and incest victims in 1993. As of 2000, only 19 states funded abortions beyond the restrictions of the Hyde Amendment.

The Hyde Amendment has dominated the political debate about abortion since 1976. Over 75 percent of all reproductive policy legislation in Congress is related to these funding bans. The presidential election campaigns of Jimmy Carter (1976), Ronald Reagan (1980), and Bill Clinton (1992) focused heavily on the public funding debate. The Hyde Amendment has confronted the feminist and pro-choice movements with issues of race and class. While many women who are denied funding manage to obtain safe abortions, the prohibitions have effectively restricted abortion rights to middle-class women—the majority of whom are white.

SEE Abortion and Political Conflict; Abortion and Public Assistance; *Beal v. Doe* et al.; Class and Reproductive Rights; *Harris v. McRae*.

Further References. Patricia Donovan, *The Politics of Blame: Family Planning, Abortion and the Poor* (New York, 1995); National Abortion Rights Action League, *State-by-State Review of Abortion and Reproductive Rights* (Washington, D.C., 1998); Noelle Norton, "Women, It's Not Enough to be Elected: Committee Position Makes a Difference," in Georgia Duerst-Lahti and Rita Mae Kelly, eds., *Gender Power, Leadership and Governance* (Ann Arbor, Mich., 1995): 115-140.

NOELLE H. NORTON

I

_____

IN RE (A.C.) (573 A.2 1235, 1990) overturned, after the fact, a trial court decision that had forced a critically ill woman to undergo a cesarean section. According to George Washington University Hospital, the medical interests of the mother,
Angela Carder (A.C.), and her 26-week-old fetus were in conflict. Carder, a long-
term cancer survivor, had been in remission when she got pregnant, but her cancer recurred. Physicians at the hospital believed her condition was terminal,
although she and her doctor disputed this. The hospital had also determined to its
satisfaction that the fetus was viable and wanted the surgery performed immediately, even though the cesarean was considered likely to hasten the mother's death.

It is not clear whether Carder wanted the surgery or whether she was competent to make the decision. While she had expressed some opposition, she was
sedated and unable to speak because she had a tube in her throat. Her husband,
her parents, and her doctor strongly opposed the surgery. The hospital sought a
court order to permit the procedure and to protect itself from future liability. A
superior court judge quickly issued the order. The U.S. Court of Appeals for the
District of Columbia refused an appeal by Carder's family to stop the medical
procedure. The infant girl died within hours after the surgery; Carder died two
days later.

The family appealed the district court decision to the full appellate court. It
found that "the right of bodily integrity is not extinguished simply because someone is ill, or even at death's door." Therefore, the wishes of the patient should
almost always be binding. When a patient is incompetent to make decisions, the
court must make a "substituted judgment" for the person, choosing what it believes
the individual would if she were competent. This ruling indicated that balancing

the rights of the patient with those of the fetus, as the hospital had urged, is improper. Instead, the right of the woman's bodily integrity must prevail. The court refused to rule out any medical treatment of a pregnant woman against her will, but it did hold that in almost all cases the wishes of the patient will prevail over the interest of the state in protecting the life of the fetus.

SEE Fetal Protection; Fetal Rights; Forced Medical Treatment.

Further References. Ellen Alderman and Caroline Kennedy, *The Right to Privacy* (New York, 1997). Susan Faludi, *Backlash: The Undeclared War Against American Women* (New York, 1991). John F. Tuohey, "Terminal Care and the Pregnant Woman: Ethical Reflections on *in re A.C.*," *Pediatrics*, 6 (December 1991): 1268-1273.

MICHELLE DONALDSON DEARDORFF

INTERNATIONAL LAW AND U.S. WOMEN'S REPRODUCTIVE RIGHTS. Several important international agreements protect the reproductive rights of women and girls worldwide. Many international treaties and declarations prohibit discrimination on the basis of sex. Six of these have particular relevance for the protection of women's reproductive rights. Articles 16 and 25 of the Universal Declaration of Human Rights of 1948 (UDHR), Article 23 of the International Covenant on Civil and Political Rights of 1966 (ICCPR), and Article 12 of the International Covenant on Economic, Social, and Cultural Rights of 1966 (ICESC) implicitly guarantee women's reproductive rights by acknowledging the right to found a family and the right to health. Articles 12 and 16 of the 1979 Convention on the Elimination of Discrimination Against Women (CEDAW), Article 24 of the 1989 Convention on the Rights of the Child (CRC), and Sections C and L of the Beijing Declaration and Platform for Action (1995) explicitly guarantee the right to family planning services and health education. In addition, ICCPR (Article 17) recognizes the right to privacy, and CEDAW (Article 16, Section e) guarantees the right of women to decide on the number and spacing of their children.

A complex and problematic relationship exists between these international laws and the domestic laws that protect the rights of U.S. women. There are two important factors to consider in the analysis of how U.S. reproductive rights laws connect with international legal instruments. First, there is a critical difference between United Nations (UN) Conventions and Declarations. Conventions are considered legally binding as treaties, whereas declarations are not. Declarations do not have the same force as ratified treaties; they require only good faith rather than legal compliance, and are signed by the U.S. Ambassador to the UN with presidential approval. Conventions and covenants, on the other hand, are considered treaties. The U.S. Constitution requires that international treaties be ratified by presidential approval and a two-thirds vote of the Senate before the United States can be officially be party to and legally bound by them.

The second, and related, complicating factor is that, unlike the vast majority of the world's countries, the United States has not ratified several of the important treaties. Although each of the international instruments mentioned above got presidential approval, the Senate did not muster the two-thirds majority votes necessary to ratify the ICESC, CEDAW, or the Convention on the Rights of the Child. The reasons for these rejections have varied with the political climate of the times. ICESC, which came up at the height of the Cold War, aroused suspicions that it granted legitimacy to "communism" by endorsing economic rights over political and civil liberties. Two decades later, CRC ran afoul of conservatives' fears that it would usurp parental rights and permit abortions for minors.

The failure of the United States to ratify these conventions, especially CEDAW, has the effect of denying American women the opportunity for protection under international law. Whereas many women and non-governmental organizations (NGOs) in other countries have used international treaties to pressure their governments to support reproductive rights and freedoms through domestic legislation and/or constitutional amendments, this is feasible only in countries that have ratified the treaties. Non-ratification by the United States consequently de-links U.S. laws that protect women's rights from international laws. This disconnection weakens the already highly contested domestic reproductive rights laws and policies, such as the abortion rights protected in *Roe v. Wade*. The end result is that the federal government essentially becomes the final arbiter in these matters and is not held accountable to any international mechanism such as the United Nations and the International Court of Justice.

For example, CEDAW requires regular reporting on compliance with the treaty and U.S. ratification of CEDAW would subject domestic reproduction rights laws and policies to international scrutiny and accountability. Opponents of ratifying this convention argue that U.S. domestic laws already provide adequate protection of women's reproductive rights and that ratification of the treaties would violate U.S. sovereignty as well as undermine the U.S. legal system. However, these arguments hold little sway since there has been nearly universal ratification of treaties in question. As of February 1, 1998, the United States joins only Afghanistan and Sao Tome and Principe in its refusal to ratify CEDAW and China, Liberia, Sao Tome and Principe, and South Africa in its refusal to ratify the ICESC. The United States is the only country that has yet to ratify the Convention on the Rights of the Child.

We cannot assume that all countries that have ratified these treaties comply fully with them. However, there are 68 countries which, in an effort to comply with international law, have guaranteed the right to equality, the right to health, and/or the right to reproductive decision making in their own constitutions. In the absence of an equal rights amendment to the U.S. Constitution, the failure of the United States to ratify key international treaties that would further legitimize and protect the reproductive rights of women in the United States has two powerful implications for the reproductive rights movement in the United States. First, individual women are limited in their potential course of action since they have no higher law or legal body to appeal to. This is important in light of CEDAW's recent decision to adopt a mechanism by which individuals will now be able report women's rights violations directly to the UN Committee on the Elimination of Discrimination Against Women. Second, U.S.-based women's rights non-governmental organizations do not have the power of issue of compliance with international treaties to pressure the U.S. government into doing more to guarantee reproductive rights of women in the United States.

On January 22, 2001—his third day in office, as well as the anniversary of *Roe v. Wade*—President George W. Bush issued an executive order blocking U.S. financial aid to international family-planning organizations that spend some of their own money to make abortion and abortion counseling available. This decision, which reversed the Clinton Administration's policy, bodes ill for the protection of international reproductive freedom by the United States.

SEE Gag Rule.

Further References. Anne F. Bayefsky, "General Approaches to Domestic Application of Women's International Human Rights Law" in Rebecca J. Cook, ed., *Human Rights of Women: National and International Perspectives* (Philadelphia, 1994):351-374. Center for Reproductive Law and Policy, *Constitutions of the World: Explicit References to Women's Right to Reproductive Freedom* (New York, 1997). United Nations Development Program, *Human Development Report* (New York, 1998).

LAURA PARISI

INTERNATIONAL UNION, UNITED AUTO WORKERS v. JOHNSON CONTROLS (499 U.S. 187, 1991), is the leading Supreme Court case on fetal protection policies in the workplace. Because of concern about birth defects, and the corporate liability for such defects, Johnson Controls, a battery manufacturing facility where lead levels of lead exceeded federal guidelines for exposure for pregnant women, excluded women capable of bearing children from working in the battery plant. Only women who were no longer fertile because they had completed the menopause or undergone surgical sterilization could work in the facility; women using birth control pills, the diaphragm or other forms of reversible birth control were ineligible. The United Auto Workers (UAW) filed suit on behalf of its female members who wished to work in the battery department.

The Supreme Court unanimously decided for the UAW. The opinion for the Court, written by Harry Blackmun and joined by four other justices, rejected Johnson Controls's contention that female sterility was a bona fide occupational qualification (BFOQ). The opinion pointed out that Johnson Controls had failed to show either that lead exposure previous to pregnancy contributed to birth defects or that high lead levels in women previous to pregnancy were more likely to result in birth defects than high lead levels in men who might impregnate their partners. Blackmun had no difficulty finding precedents that had construed the

BFOQ exemption very narrowly. For example, employers could exclude pregnant workers only if pregnancy interfered with the workers' ability to do their jobs safely and efficiently; the same was true for fertility. Tort liability could not establish a BFOQ here because Johnson Controls had not shown that it was vulnerable to heavy damage awards. While "the possibility of injury to future children" was a serious concern, "decisions about the welfare of future children must be left to the parents who conceive, bear, support, and raise them."

In a concurrence, Justice Byron White, joined by William Rehnquist and Justice Anthony Kennedy, wished to allow for future use of a BFOQ defense if companies could show that "exclusion of women from certain jobs was reasonably necessary to avoid substantial tort liability." Such a policy might be necessary because, while employees could waive their own claims against the company, they could not waive their children's rights to sue for any birth defects caused by their parents' employment. Justice Antonin Scalia also concurred, writing an even stronger argument for the UAW's position than Blackmun had. Scalia asserted that it did not matter if there was evidence that male reproductive capacities were also affected by lead or that Johnson Controls had not been able to show a factual basis for excluding women because Congress had unequivocally prohibited "discrimination on the basis of pregnancy" in the Pregnancy Discrimination Act of 1978.

The Court did a masterful job of demolishing Johnson Controls's justifications for its rule. The opinions leave the reader wondering why it took so long to overrule fetal protection policies, and why the case ever had to go as far as the Supreme Court. The prevalence and popularity of fetal protection regulations reveals the vulnerability of women's reproductive rights and the insecurity of their rights to equal employment opportunity. But, as welcome as this ruling was, it represented a hollow victory for women workers. Why, after all, should any worker have to choose between keeping her job and protecting her future children? Sex discrimination law does not address the root problem: the maintenance of an unsafe workplace.

SEE Employment and Reproductive Rights; Fetal Protection; Pregnancy Discrimination Act of 1978; Protective Labor Legislation; Title VII and Reproductive Rights.

DANIEL LESSARD LEVIN

IN VITRO **FERTILIZATION** (IVF) was introduced in the late 1970s, primarily to help women with blocked fallopian tubes conceive. In an IVF cycle, women take fertility drugs to stimulate their ovaries to produce multiple eggs. These eggs are removed and placed in separate glass dishes (whence comes the name of the procedure, from the Latin *in vitro*, in a glass). There, the ova are combined with spermatozoa from the woman's partner or from a sperm donor. If fertilization occurs, the cleaving embryos are transferred to the woman's uterus within 48 to

72 hours. There are now almost 300 clinics in the United States that perform IVF. In one sample year (1995) physicians in the United States initiated 41,000 IVF cycles; fewer than 8,000 deliveries took place. The clinics' birth rate averages 19 to 25 percent, depending on whether the rate is calculated from the start of the IVF cycle (19 percent) or from the time of embryo transfer (25 percent).

The first baby conceived by IVF (sometimes called a "test-tube baby") was born in England in 1978. Since then, IVF has been refined and expanded in numerous ways. First, embryo freezing now allows physicians to store embryos for later transfer to women's uteruses. This technique reduces expenses for patients and avoids the need for repeated hormonal stimulation, which carries risks for the woman. Second, the use of ova donated from younger women has increased the success rates for older women trying to conceive. Third, it is now possible for technicians manually to inject a single spermatozoon into an egg; therefore, IVF can be used by couples for whom the male partner has very few or immature spermatozoa. Fourth, the genetic testing of embryos for couples at risk for passing serious genetic diseases to their children opens IVF to fertile but at risk couples who prefer embryo testing to prenatal testing.

Although IVF has expanded reproductive options for women, issues remain about its safety and practice. One problem is that the risks associated with repeated hormonal stimulation are not fully understood. In addition, reported success rates can obscure the fact that many patients leave IVF clinics without children after only one IVF attempt. Finally, IVF is associated with a growing rate of multiple pregnancies, which occur when more than one embryo is transferred at a time. Multiple pregnancies force women and couples to choose between two difficult options. The decision to try to carry all the fetuses to term poses risks to the health of women, fetuses, and future children. The decision to reduce the number of fetuses through selective abortion of one or more of them is troublesome to many potential parents on moral and religious grounds.

Given the expense of IVF (more than $8,000 per cycle) and the fact that insurance companies generally do not cover the procedure, equitable access to IVF among women of different incomes is an unresolved issue. In addition, because the federal government does not fund embryo research, IVF patients become de facto research subjects in the clinical setting. Debate continues on whether the government should enact consumer protection laws for assisted reproductive technologies; one federal law enacted in 1992 set in motion a system for the systematic record-keeping of IVF success rates. Substantive restrictions on IVF based on such features as marital status and age have been enacted in other countries, but not in the United States.

SEE Artificial Insemination; Ectogenesis; Surrogate Motherhood.

Further References. George J. Annas, "The Shadowlands—Secrets, Lies, and Assisted Reproduction," *New England Journal of Medicine*, 339, #13 (1998): 935-939. "Assisted Reproductive Technologies in the United States and Canada: 1995 Results Generated from the American Society for Reproductive Medicine/Society for Assisted Reproductive Technologies Registry," *Fertility and Sterility*, 69, #3 (1998): 389-398. Laura M. Purdy, "What Can Progress in Reproductive Technology Mean for Women?" *Journal of Medicine and Philosophy*, 21 (October 1996): 499-514. John A. Robertson, *Children of Choice: Freedom and the New Reproductive Technologies* (Princeton, N.J., 1994).

ANDREA L. BONNICKSEN

J

JANE (collective). The unique female capacity for reproduction has always been regulated. Yet everywhere women have attempted, with varying degrees of success, to seize the means of reproduction. Jane, or The Service, furnishes a successful example of women's ability to exercise this control. Between 1969 and 1973, when *Roe v. Wade* legalized abortion, this collective provided 11,000 illegal abortions for women in the Chicago area.

A woman who wanted an abortion could get Jane's phone number from an underground newspaper, the Chicago Women's Liberation Union (to which the collective belonged), from friends and acquaintances, or from surreptitious messages which advised women to "call Jane." A collective member would return the woman's call, take a medical history, and put her in touch with a counselor. The counselor would interview the woman and explain the abortion process. Then the woman was given a time, date and address where she was supposed to go. For security reasons, the woman was taken from that location to a different apartment where the procedure, including a pap smear, was done; she was then returned to the original apartment (termed "the Front"). If the woman did not call during the following week, her counselor would call her, not only to provide support, but also to avoid medical and legal problems. No woman was turned away for lack of funds; Jane maintained a sliding scale of prices. Although the abortions were performed by laywomen, not medical professionals, no woman died because of their care.

When Jane first started, members of the collective negotiated with illegal abortionists. Jane demanded feedback and some free procedures, saving pregnant women from having to negotiate alone in their vulnerable situation. After one abortionist trained a member of Jane, this woman taught the others, and they decided to do the procedures themselves. Although members who did not want to do the dilation and curettage were not forced to perform the procedures, every member was expected to provide individual and/or group counseling for the women who wanted abortions. The primary purpose of the counseling was to demystify the procedure for the clients. This counseling benefitted providers as well as clients; members of Jane did not experience the alienation felt by some other providers of illegal abortion.

Influenced by anarchist philosophy, the collective rejected the rigid, hierarchical division of labor that is common in modern industrialized society. This division is apparent in modern clinics, where physicians perform the abortions, nurses assist the physicians, and the counselors are limited to counseling. By contrast, the Jane women performed as many of the necessary tasks as they could. These workers learned their skills by observation and by performing tasks under the supervision of women with greater skill. Jane had no "patients." According to one member, they were all "partners in the crime of freedom to control our own bodies." The collective felt that the term "patient" implies the subject-object relation that characterizes the medical system and that Jane was trying to change.

The skills, particularly curettage, were not difficult to learn. According to one woman, the curettage was "like making cantaloupe balls—the same motion with the curette." The women also learned the procedures for performing second trimester abortions, inducing labor, and delivering the fetus. At first, Jane started the procedure and told the women to go to a hospital and say they were miscarrying. Eventually, Jane set up an apartment to do the entire second trimester abortions *with* the women. The members of the collective also learned how to deal with doctors, hospitals, police, and medical supply businesses. Learning how to establish and maintain a democratic, efficient and sisterly organization was at least as difficult as acquiring other skills. Although there were some conflicts and schisms, for the most part Jane succeeded here, too.

Jane had relatively little trouble with the law. As far as the police were concerned, Jane provided a useful service for their wives, daughters, and girlfriends (not to mention women officers). Jane did not leave bleeding bodies in motels for police to find, report, and submit paperwork about. On one occasion, however, officers who did not know the situation raided the apartment where the procedures were being performed. Seven women were arrested and jailed overnight, but were never tried.

The women in Jane believed that participating in the collective was the highpoint of their lives. They learned that they could actually solve a problem rather than just talking and demonstrating. By demystifying abortion, they became much more effective consumers of health care. They learned to argue with health workers, including physicians, to get what they needed for themselves and their families. This competence spread to other parts of their lives. They discovered that "if you want to learn how to do something, you can." Medical professionalization was just "a ruse to make you feel powerless in your life." In the case of Jane, sisterhood was indeed powerful. And what is equally important, particularly after the seventies, is that the women "grew" by working with women and helping women, not just by being concerned with being their own best friends or empowering themselves.

SEE Abortion as a Reproductive Right; Abortion Self-Help Movement; Midwifery.

Further References. Pauline B. Bart, "Seizing the Means of Reproduction: An Illegal Feminist Abortion Collective—How and Why it Worked," *Qualitative Sociology* 10, #4, (Winter 1987): 339-357 (also available from the National Women's Health Network, Washington, D.C). Laura Kaplan, *The Story of Jane: The Legendary Feminist Abortion Service* (New York, 1995). Melinda Bart Schlesinger and Pauline B. Bart, "Collective Work and Self-Identity: The Effect of Working in a Feminist Illegal Abortion Collective." In Laurel Richardson and Verta Taylor, eds. *Feminist Frontiers: Rethinking Sex, Gender and Society* (Menlo Park, N.J., 1983): 337-345.

PAULINE B. BART

JOHNSON v. CALVERT (851 P.2d 776, *Calif.* 1993) addressed the legality of a gestational surrogacy contract. Gestational surrogacy involves the implantation of the fertilized ovum of the childless couple into the uterus of the surrogate, who gestates and delivers the child, to whom she is biologically unrelated. Crispina and Mark Calvert entered into a gestational surrogacy agreement with Anna Johnson. Crispina had had a partial hysterectomy, but she still had functioning ovaries. In exchange for $10,000, Anna agreed to relinquish "all maternal rights" after birth and to surrender custody of the newborn infant to the Calverts. Shortly after Anna became pregnant, her relationship with the couple deteriorated. Anna and the Calverts each filed a lawsuit to determine parentage. After the boy was born, the Calverts were awarded temporary custody. Anna was granted visitation rights until a decision regarding parentage was made.

The trial court and the Court of Appeals agreed that Anna's visitation order should be terminated and that the surrogacy contract was legally enforceable. The state Supreme Court upheld this ruling. The justices determined that Crispina Calvert and Anna Johnson had each produced evidence that she was the "natural" mother under California's Uniform Parentage Act. A blood test proved that Crispina was genetically related to the child. However, the fact that Anna gave birth to the child was undisputed. The Court did not directly resolve the question of whether the biological or gestational mother was the "real" mother; nor did it use the traditional "best interests of the child" standard in child custody cases. Instead, the Court used an intent-based analysis. Relying on the intentions of the parties at the time the surrogacy agreement was signed, the majority decided that both parties had to fulfill their part of the bargain. The Calverts got the baby, and Anna Johnson got the money. The Court ruled that Crispina Calvert was the natural mother under California law and awarded full parental rights to her and her husband. Anna lost all visitation rights.

Scholars have disputed the ethical and legal implications of using an intent-based analysis to enforce gestational surrogacy agreements. Some argue that these agreements should be legally enforced, like other contracts—although courts have traditionally been reluctant to enforce specific performance, particularly in "personal service" contracts. Other scholars insist that regardless of the intent of the parties involved in the surrogacy agreement, courts must make decisions based on the child's best interests. Moreover, some critics of surrogacy contracts assert that such agreements exploit poor women and that "selling" babies is unethical. Courts will continue to struggle with these issues as more people rely on gestational surrogacy and other reproductive technologies.

SEE Artificial Insemination; Baby M; *In Vitro* Fertilization; Surrogate Motherhood.

Further References. Janet L Dolgin, *Defining the Family: Law, Technology, and Reproduction in an Uneasy Age* (New York, 1997). Ruth Macklin, *Surrogates and Other Mothers: The Debates over Assisted Reproduction* (Philadelphia, 1994).

LAKESIA D. JOHNSON

JOHNSON CONTROLS. SEE *International Union, United Auto Workers v. Johnson Controls.*

L

LATE TERM ABORTION. SEE Dilation and Extraction (D&X).

LESBIANS AND REPRODUCTIVE RIGHTS. The poet and essayist Adrienne Rich has made a powerful case that heterosexuality has been compulsory for women for most of history. If Rich is correct, reproductive rights for lesbians in the past had mostly to do with establishing the right to refuse heterosexuality and the motherhood that usually went with it. Before the twentieth century, financial need, parental pressure, and social sanctions forced many women, including lesbians, into marriage and motherhood. Early lesbian history also contains the figure of the single woman who plays, or is forced into, the role of surrogate mother to the children of her married siblings (as represented, for example, in Isabel Miller's novel *Patience and Sarah*).

The right *not* to become mothers that American women have won since the 1960s—the ability to control their fertility through birth control, abortion, and voluntary sterilization—are identical for lesbians and heterosexual women. In recent years, an increase in the visibility of gay and lesbian parenting has drawn attention to the rights of homosexuals *to* become, and remain, parents. Controversial issues have included child custody, the termination of the rights of biological fathers (for example, in cases where a lesbian was inseminated by a male friend or sperm donor), the right to adopt children, and the rights of lesbian co-parents after their own relationships end.

Until recently, most lesbian mothers bore their children in the context of heterosexual marriage. Typically, such women discover or assert their lesbianism later, and seek a divorce. The course of their motherhood thereafter depends on many factors: whether or not they are "out," the ages of their children, and the reactions of their children's fathers, other family members, and important third parties like employers. Some lesbians stay in their marriages for fear of losing custody of their children if they "come out."

The legal situation of lesbian mothers is far from uniform. Unlike discrimination based on race or sex, both of which are discouraged by the Constitution and prohibited by several federal statutes, discrimination on the basis of sexual preference is a matter of state law. Therefore, court rulings are highly contextual and local. In every state, courts must decide disputes over custody and/or visitation by determining what arrangement serves "the best interests of the child." Individual states may fall anywhere on a continuum from strongly anti-gay to carefully neutral. Anti-gay states prohibit homosexual custody altogether, while neutral states prevent family courts from considering the sexual preference of parents in determining disputes. In all other states, the homosexuality of a parent is only one of many factors that courts consider in reaching decisions. The local and fact-specific nature of individual custody claims precludes sociological generalizations. The few high-profile cases in this area are of little or no precedential value outside their own states.

In adoptions, the issues are similar to those arising in cases of custody and visitation: "the best interests of the child" standard is the prevailing rule, and the same range of attitudes about homosexuality is evident. Florida and New Hampshire, for example, expressly prohibit adoption or foster-parenting by lesbians and gay men. New York, on the other hand, forbids the rejection of any application for adoption solely on the basis of the applicants' homosexuality. In 1997, New Jersey became the first state to allow adoption by gay couples (and unmarried heterosexual couples) jointly. A court in Washington, D.C. has allowed a gay male couple to adopt a four-year-old girl. Courts in 23 states have approved second-parent adoptions by the same-sex partner of a biological parent. There are reported cases of adoption by lesbian co-mothers, terminating the parental rights of the biological father in favor of the lesbian partner.

What happens to custody and visitation rights when lesbian co-parents end their relationship? As the law stands, biological parents have a presumption of custody against the government, other relatives, stepparents (unless they have adopted the child), and co-parents. Because no state recognizes gay marriage, the rights of the non-biological lesbian parent usually can only be enforced if she has adopted the child or if there is a written contract specifying her rights. Even with such a contract, courts favor biological parents. However, by 2000 a few states had passed laws allowing judges to grant visitation rights to people not biologically related to a child if this was in the child's best interests. A 1995 decision in Wisconsin recognized a category of "functional or psychological parent" and established a test to determine whether former partners of a biological parent had achieved that status. In April 2000, the New Jersey Supreme Court unanimously adopted Wisconsin's test and ruled that a psychological parent has parity with the legal parent.

Recent advances in reproductive technology have introduced new legal and social issues. Access to procedures like physician-supervised artificial insemination and *in vitro* fertilization has not so far been denied to lesbians. In practice, therefore, lesbians who can afford these procedures have "rights" of access to them. Some states have distinguished between medical insemination and impregnation by more informal methods (like having a friend donate sperm), asserting that fathers have no parental rights in the case of medical insemination. Cases are on record, however, in which biological fathers have successfully asserted parental rights after insemination of a lesbian through informal donation of sperm.

At the beginning of the twenty-first century, social and technological practices affecting lesbian reproductive rights are in rapid flux. The legal situation is characterized by diversity among local and state laws and by a continuing focus on the individuality of each parenting situation. In addition, the cultural norms that prevail within individual lesbian communities exert an unpredictable influence.

SEE Adoption; Artificial Insemination; Birth Mothers and Reproductive Rights; Child Custody; *In Vitro* Fertilization.

Further References. Martin Guggenheim, Alexandra Dylan Lowe, and Diane Curtis, *The Rights of Families: The Authoritative ACLU Guide to the Rights of Family Members* (Carbondale, Ill., 1996). Lynn C. Franklin with Elizabeth Ferber, *May the Circle Be Unbroken: An Intimate Journey into the Heart of Adoption* (New York, 1998). Isabel Miller, *Patience and Sarah* (New York, 1969). Adrienne Rich, "Compulsory Heterosexuality and Lesbian Existence," in *Blood, Bread, and Poetry: Selected Prose 1979-1985* (New York, 1986): 23-75. William B. Rubenstein, ed., *Lesbians, Gay Men, and the Law* (New York, 1993).

GEORGE CARR, ESQ. AND GLYNIS CARR

LIFESTYLE RESTRICTIONS AND PREGNANCY. The term "lifestyle restrictions" refers to rules that govern a woman's conduct during pregnancy. In a legal context, the term is usually applied to restrictions on the use of alcohol, tobacco, and illegal drugs, substances known to present risks to the fetus. In the late 1990s, American women who got prenatal care were routinely told to avoid these substances and to seek medical advice even before taking non-prescription drugs. In the twenty-first century, American women who get prenatal care are routinely told to avoid these substances and to seek medical advice even before taking non-prescription drugs. Many pregnant women found that friends, co-workers, acquaintances, and even strangers were eager to remind them of these admonitions.

For "fetal protection" advocates, however, informal sanctions do not go far enough. These activists want to criminalize maternal behaviors like smoking, drinking, and using drugs. In contrast, opponents of these policies contend that criminalization threatens women's rights to privacy and gives the government too much power over individuals. All voices in the fetal rights debate believe that society has a compelling interest in ensuring the health and safety of the next generation. However, they disagree vehemently about the roles of the individual and the state in accomplishing this end.

Supporters of lifestyle restrictions hold that protecting the unborn is a basic obligation of government. They contend that criminalizing such behaviors is the only way to guard against child abuse, and assert that no woman has a legal right to jeopardize the health and safety of her unborn child. While some critics of the fetal protection movement have characterized it as part of an effort by anti-abortion forces to deny reproductive freedom to women, a common defense of these policies grounds them on reproductive freedom: a decision to continue a pregnancy entails a duty of care to the fetus.

Opponents of lifestyle restrictions reject governmental involvement as needlessly intrusive and potentially threatening to individual liberty. They insist that treatment for pregnant addicts (which is rarely available) is a better protection for fetuses than sanctions against pregnant women. Opponents fear that criminalization will discourage these women from seeking prenatal care, resulting in situations potentially more harmful than the drug or alcohol abuse itself. Opponents also emphasize the race and class aspects of fetal protection. Poor women, who often receive Medicaid, are more likely to come in contact with government officials during their pregnancy than women with private doctors and private health insurance, and women of color are disproportionately likely to be poor. Therefore, opponents of fetal protection fear that minority women are more vulnerable to charges of fetal abuse than white, middle class women. The evidence provides considerable support for this contention. According to the American Civil Liberties Union, 70 percent of women charged with crimes against their fetuses are poor and African-American. In general, fetal rights opponents condemn these policies as ill-advised governmental efforts to control women, particularly poor women, and to erode women's hard-won and vulnerable reproductive rights. Fetal rights policies, they suggest, commodify women, making them little more than fetal incubators.

Efforts to criminalize potentially harmful behaviors by pregnant women have been going on for the last two decades of the twentieth century. Currently (2000-01), there is little or no action at the federal level. The U.S. Supreme Court has been silent on fetal rights cases. In contrast, a great deal of activity is occurring at the state level. Legislatures in particular have demonstrated interest in fetal rights policies, although in the past state courts have not been particularly receptive to them. One of the earliest cases occurred in California in 1985. Pamela Rae Stewart was accused but later cleared of contributing to the death of her unborn child by failing to follow medical advice. Since the states child abuse law did not cover unborn children, the prosecutor could not charge Stewart with child abuse. Therefore, charges were brought under a child-support statute. These charges were dismissed as violating due process since the child-support law was not intended to cover this kind of case. Other states have attempted to charge women who used cocaine during pregnancy under statutes meant to cover drug dealers. In 1989, Jennifer Johnson of Florida was the first woman convicted for delivering drugs to her fetus through the umbilical cord, but her conviction was reversed on appeal. The first state supreme court decision upholding a child abuse conviction against a pregnant cocaine user came in 1996, when South Carolina sustained Cornelia Whitner's conviction. In 1999, the Wisconsin Supreme Court deadlocked, three to three, in the case of Deborah Zimmerman. She was charged with first-degree homicide and first-degree reckless injury for attempting to drink herself and her fetus to death.

Cases such as these raise a number of critical legal questions. For example, is a fetus a person? Can it be established in any particular case that drug or alcohol use during pregnancy caused specific harm to the fetus? Should a prosecutor have to prove that a pregnant woman who drank or used drugs intended to harm the fetus? Or could the state charge a woman with some form of reckless endangerment, which does not require the intent to harm usually associated with more serious felonies? Fetal rights policies are a potential slippery slope. For example, if a woman is told by her doctor to exercise during pregnancy and does not do so, could she be charged with endangering her fetus? What other behaviors could be criminalized? Should pregnant women who smoke be charged?

Still more questions arise when we consider how such laws might be enforced. Would every jurisdiction need a special "womb police" to guarantee pregnant women follow a prescribed list of "do's and don'ts?" What if the list itself changes? The routine medical advice pregnant women get today differs dramatically from what their mothers were told. For example, many of the baby boom generation had mothers whose physicians advised them that the occasional cigarette or glass of wine would calm them and prevent premature labor! Opponents of fetal rights policies argue that women need access to all available information concerning the effect of certain behaviors on fetuses, provide appropriate treatment for women who want to change addictive behaviors, and make certain that quality prenatal care is available to all women. Then, they contend, we would have the best possible fetal protection policies.

SEE Fetal Abuse; Fetal Protection; Fetal Rights; Forced Medical Treatment; Substance Abuse and Pregnancy.

Further References. American Civil Liberties Union at http://www.aclu.org. Center for Reproductive Law and Policy at http://www.crlp.org. National Abortion and Reproductive Rights Action League at http://www.naral.org. Bonnie Steinbock, "The Relevance of Illegality: Women's Obligation Toward Their Unborn Children," *The Hastings Center Report*, 22, #1 (1992): 19-23. Ann Pytkowicz Streissguth, *Fetal Alcohol Syndrome: A Guide for Families and Communities* (Baltimore, 1997).

TRUDY STEUERNAGEL

M

MADSEN v. WOMEN'S HEALTH CENTER, INC. (512 U.S. 753, 1994) addresses two crucial constitutional issues: the rights of persons who wish to picket abortion clinics or abortion providers and the practical exercise of the right to an abortion guaranteed by *Roe v. Wade* and subsequent cases. Everyone agrees that persons have as much right to protest the existence of an abortion clinic or per-suade women to carry a pregnancy to term as they do to protest the existence of a factory that makes chemical weapons or to persuade stockholders to change company policy. Still, just as women cannot exercise their right to terminate a pregnancy when they cannot find a person willing to perform an abortion, they cannot exercise their exercise that right when they are physically prevented from entering the appropriate medical facility. *Madsen* and related cases explore the relationship between the exercise of first amendment rights and the rights of per-sons wishing to engage in constitutionally protected behavior.

The specific holdings of *Madsen* are easier to discern than the general principles underlying that decision. *Madsen* arose after a state court determined that an initial injunction against Operation Rescue had not ensured women seek-ing abortions free access to a clinic in Melbourne, Florida. Committed to maintaining both the safety and availability of abortion at that site, the local judge issued a new injunction, establishing a 36-foot buffer zone outside the clinic and a 300-foot zone outside the residences of clinic staff, prohibiting noise and cer-tain pictures at certain hours, and prohibiting certain solicitations unless the women indicated her permission. A divided Supreme Court sustained some fea-tures of this injunction while declaring others unconstitutional. "The buffer zone around the clinic entrances and driveway," Chief Justice William Rehnquist wrote for the majority, "burdens no more speech than is necessary to accomplish the governmental interest at stake." This requirement was generally constitutional, except as it applied to private property owned by third parties. The noise prohibition was sustained, but the prohibition of pictures was struck down because the clinic could shut its windows. The prohibition on solicitation was struck down, as was the ban on all protests within 300 feet of the residence of a member of the clinic staff.

The broader implications of *Madsen* are harder to assess. One difference between the majority opinion and the dissent was over how much deference to give the trial judge. The majority essentially deferred to the lower court's finding of anti-abortion mayhem, but Justice Antonin Scalia claimed that Operation Rescue was conducting a decorous protest that neither threatened violence nor obstructed the clinic entrance. This dispute and the judicial alignment suggest that future cases will be decided on their facts with most justices interpreting the activities of abortion protests through the lens of their opinions on *Roe*.

The general standard of constitutional review that the majority relied on in *Madsen* is not likely to be particularly helpful. Rehnquist set out this standard when he declared that an injunction, which "by its very nature, applies only to a particular group (or individuals)," required "a somewhat more stringent application of general First Amendment principles" than a content-neutral statute directed at all citizens. Thus, the majority held that injunctions would survive constitutional muster only when the court order "burden(s) no more speech than necessary to serve a significant government interest." The differences between this standard and the judicial requirement that legislation imposing time, place, and manner restraints on speech must be "narrowly tailored to serve a significant government interest" is not obvious. The *Madsen* opinion failed to clarify this difference by giving examples of a government restriction that would satisfy one standard but not the other.

The rule that "no more speech should be burdened than necessary" may also have silly applications if taken literally. Courts should not have to determine whether a 35-foot buffer zone will protect the clinic's interest as well as a 36-foot zone, or the precise decibel level at which abortion procedures cannot be performed safely. Rather, free speech concerns should be satisfied whenever the relevant injunction permits speakers to communicate their messages to their intended audiences. Courts should recognize that persons have no constitutional right to speak within a certain distance of an abortion clinic or speak at a certain volume unless some serious concern exists that persons passing by will not see their signs or hear their concerns. If protestors can clearly communicate an anti-abortion message standing 36 feet from a clinic, appellate courts should not tinker with an injunction merely because evidence exists suggesting that abortion rights would not be disturbed if the protestors were allowed to be a foot closer to the clinic.

SEE Operation Rescue; Abortion Providers and Violence.

MARK GRABER

MAHER v. ROE. SEE *Beal v. Doe.*

MARRIAGE AND REPRODUCTIVE RIGHTS. "Reproductive rights," a term in common use only since the 1960s, refers to a range of claims concerning whether, when and how to have children. Cultural attitudes towards marriage, along with the legal regulation of marriage, have affected the way U.S. society has understood reproductive rights. The relationship between marriage and reproductive rights has been and remains complex and dynamic. Race and class have a powerful impact on the exercise of these rights both inside and outside of marriage. And the increasing acceptance of sexual activity outside marriage has led to a gradual extension of reproductive rights to unmarried people.

Marriage has traditionally legitimated sexual activity and reproduction. Both religious and cultural norms have condemned sex outside of marriage, particularly for women. Laws made a distinction between the legal status of children born within a marriage ("legitimate" children) and that of children born outside marriage ("illegitimate" children or bastards). Although state legislatures and courts eliminated many of the legal distinctions between marital and non-marital children by the late 1970s (for example, *Gomez v. Perez*), legitimacy and illegitimacy remained legal categories in most states. The stigma attached to unwed pregnancy and the loss of rights for children born out of wedlock traditionally created strong pressure on women not to engage in sexual activity outside of marriage.

The categories "legitimate" and "illegitimate" were meaningless for the slave population in the United States. Marriage between slaves was not recognized by the law, and slave parents had no legal right to custody of their children (who were always subject to sale). Although the Fourteenth Amendment did not mention "family," those who sponsored and shaped that amendment intended it to protect the family ties of the freed slaves. In the wake of the Civil War, however, many states criminalized marriage between persons of different races. Not until *Loving v. Virginia* (1967) did the Supreme Court finally hold that antimiscegenation laws were unconstitutional.

The idea that only marriage legitimized sexual activity has strongly affected public policy on fertility control. The sale and use of birth control was illegal in many jurisdictions well into the twentieth century. When the Supreme Court finally recognized the right to use birth control, it at first granted this right only to married couples. *Griswold v. Connecticut* (1965) struck down a Connecticut statute prohibiting the prescription, sale and use of contraceptives, on the grounds that the right of married couples to use contraception is protected by a fundamental right to privacy found in the due process clause of the Fourteenth Amendment and the Bill of Rights. In *Eisenstadt v. Baird* (1972) the Court extended this right of privacy to unmarried as well as married persons in their use of contraceptive devices.

Roe v. Wade (1973) did not make a distinction between married and unmarried women when it held that the right to privacy protects a woman's right to have an abortion. Subsequently, the Court held that it was unconstitutional for a state to require a married woman either to obtain her husband's consent (*Planned Parenthood of Central Missouri v. Danforth,* 1976) or to notify her husband (*Planned Parenthood of Southeastern Pennsylvania v. Casey,* 1992) before obtaining an abortion. In *Casey,* the Court upheld a requirement for parental consent for a minor seeking an abortion as long as the law made provision for a judicial bypass of this requirement.

Legal threats to the right to bear and raise children have had a disproportionate impact on unmarried women—particularly poor, unmarried women of color. Women who depend on public assistance for their medical care have been especially vulnerable to forced sterilization and birth control. In the 1970s, women's rights advocates brought to light instances in which poor women were forced to allow themselves or their daughters to be sterilized as a condition of receiving welfare benefits. The welfare system has also impinged on the right to raise children when it prohibited aid to children born while their mothers were on welfare. Since unmarried women are more likely to be poor than married women, these policies have affected them more severely.

The law's tendency to favor the reproductive rights of married over unmarried persons is also evident in the struggles to gain legal recognition of the parental status for lesbian and gay parents. A lesbian who bears a child is regarded as the child's legal parent (although if a heterosexual relative challenges her right to custody, her lesbianism may be taken as evidence that she is an "unfit" mother). Her lesbian partner, however, usually has no legal parental rights, although some states allow her to adopt the child without having the biological mother first relinquish her parental rights. Gay men wishing to become legal parents might seek to have one partner adopt a child born to the other during a prior heterosexual marriage, or utilize contract pregnancy (surrogate motherhood), or seek to adopt a child biologically unrelated to either partner. The lack of legal recognition for same-sex marriages has profoundly affected the establishment of parent-child relationships in many lesbian and gay households.

Legal recognition of a man's parental rights has been affected by whether or not he was married to the child's mother. Traditionally, many state statutes did not allow unwed fathers to be heard concerning custody, and many states precluded nonmarital children from inheriting from their fathers if their fathers died intestate (without having drawn up a will). The courts sometimes cut unwed fathers off from their children simply because the parents were not married, but in other cases they have given considerable weight to the genetic tie, regardless of whether the man had any relationship with or had taken responsibility for his offspring. In the widely publicized "Baby Jessica" and "Baby Richard" cases of the 1990s, state courts invalidated adoptions to which the mothers had consented without the fathers' knowledge. In each case, after the men learned of the adoption and sued for paternity, the court took the child from the adoptive home and gave custody to the biological parents. Feminists are divided over these issues. Some feminists assert that recent efforts to increase recognition of legal paternity give unmarried fathers unwarranted power over women and their children, while others argue that such efforts increase men's assumption of responsibility for their offspring in beneficial ways.

New reproductive technologies have raised new questions concerning marriage and reproductive rights. Should use of procedures like in vitro fertilization and gamete donation be restricted to married couples? If married persons divorce after having conceived children using a third party's egg or sperm, should the parent with a genetic relationship to the child have a stronger claim to custody? Who should have the authority to decide on the disposition of frozen embryos when the couple for which they were created disagree on what should be done?

Meaningful freedom to have and raise children depends on more than the absence of prohibitions and restrictions. It also requires those social supports and services (like housing and health care) that enable adults to meet children's needs. Those concerned with procuring reproductive freedom for women (and men) must consider not only laws governing personal liberty, privacy and marriage, but also the social context in which children are raised to adulthood.

SEE Class and Reproductive Rights; Federal Sterilization Guidelines; *Eisenstadt v. Baird*; *Griswold v. Connecticut*; *Planned Parenthood of Central Missouri v. Danforth*; *Planned Parenthood of Southeastern Pennsylvania v. Casey*; *Roe v. Wade*; Sterilization Abuse.

Further References. Peggy Cooper Davis, *Neglected Stories: The Constitution and Family Values* (New York, 1997). Janet Dolgin, *Defining the Family: Law Technology and Reproduction in an Uneasy Age* (New York, 1997). *Gomez v. Perez*, 409 U.S. 535 (1973). *Loving v. Virginia*, 388 U.S. 1 (1967). Dorothy Roberts, "The Genetic Tie," *University of Chicago Law Review* 62 (Winter 1995): 209-273. Mary Lyndon Shanley, "Fathers' Rights, Mothers' Wrongs: Reflections on Unwed Fathers' Rights, Patriarchy, and Sex Equality," in Joan Callahan, ed., *Reproduction, Ethics, and the Law* (Bloomington, Ind., 1995): 219-248.

MARY LYNDON SHANLEY

MATHESON. SEE *H.L. v. Matheson.*

McCORVEY, NORMA. The "Jane Roe" of *Roe v. Wade*. In March, 1970, 21-year-old Norma McCorvey became the lead plaintiff in the lawsuit filed to challenge the strict anti-abortion laws in Texas. McCorvey never got the abortion she sought. She gave birth to a girl whom she gave up for adoption. On January 22, 1973, three years after the lawsuit was filed, the U.S. Supreme Court vindicated McCorvey's claim.

While *Roe v. Wade* was not about a single individual, one individual was needed to bring the case to court. In order to test the constitutionality of state laws, lawyers had to have a woman who was pregnant, wanted an abortion, but was prevented by state law from obtaining a safe and legal abortion. Norma McCorvey became that person. In her autobiography, she described herself as a 9th-grade dropout who had suffered physical and emotional abuse as a child, spent some time in reform school, and was raped as a teenager. She wrote that she was married at 16 and beaten by her husband. She also wrote of her experiences with lovers of both sexes and with alcohol and drug abuse. She drifted through a series of dead-end jobs, including work as a bartender and a carnival barker. In 1970, McCorvey became pregnant for the third time. Her first child was raised by her mother and her second by the child's father.

McCorvey's accounts of the circumstances surrounding her third pregnancy and her feelings about the case have varied. She told her lawyers, Sarah Weddington and Linda Coffee, that the pregnancy had resulted from a rape, but later denied this. Her autobiography recounts the anger she felt when she read Weddington's book about the case and learned that the lawyer herself had obtained an illegal abortion in Texas. McCorvey wondered why Weddington did not help her to do the same. She came to believe that Weddington had used her, sacrificing her interests for a legal principle.

Several years after the *Roe* decision, Norma McCorvey identified herself as Jane Roe in her first book, *I Am Roe.* After she went public, she worked in several clinics where abortions were performed and did some public speaking in favor of reproductive choice. However, in 1995, while working at a women's clinic, she became friendly with members of the anti-abortion group, Operation Rescue. She was baptized into the Protestant faith on August 8. With her conversion, she reversed her position on abortion. She became anti-abortion, starting a ministry called "Roe No More" to fight against abortion rights with the aim of creating a mobile counseling center for pregnant women in Dallas. During this time she wrote *Won by Love.* In 1998, she converted to Roman Catholicism.

SEE Abortion as a Reproductive Right; Operation Rescue; *Roe v. Wade.*

Further References. Norma McCorvey, *I Am Roe: My Life, Roe vs. Wade, and Freedom of Choice* (New York, 1994). Norma McCorvey and Gary Thomas, *Won by Love: Norma McCorvey, Jane Roe of Roe v. Wade, Speaks Out for the Unborn* (Nashville, Tenn., 1999). Sarah Weddington, *A Question of Choice* (New York, 1992).

MARY LOU KENDRIGAN

MIDWIFERY AS A REPRODUCTIVE RIGHT. "Midwife," Middle English for "with woman," aptly describes women's traditional role as birth attendants. Throughout history and across cultures, women have provided and continue to provide direct assistance and support during childbirth. Professional midwives attend the majority of normal births in developed countries today. But in the United States, physicians wrested control over birthing from midwives in the early twentieth century. The proportion of midwife-attended births decreased from approximately half in 1900 to one-eighth in 1935. Obstetricians remain the dominant providers of birthing care, attending 93 per cent of American births in 1997.

The obstetrics profession achieved dominance over birthing not by demonstrating scientific superiority or better clinical outcomes relative to midwives but by political action. Early professionalization, the political power of the American Medical Association, and heavy lobbying at state and federal levels secured to obstetricians the legally based right not only to define the scope of their own practice but to limit that of others. Obstetricians marketed birth technology like forceps and anesthesia to middle- and upper-class women and stigmatized midwifery as substandard care for the poor. The obstetrics lobby frustrated midwives' efforts to practice safely by opposing licensing for midwives and by refusing to collaborate with them.

Obstetrics and midwifery represent fundamentally opposing philosophical approaches to birthing care. The medical model views birth as an inherently risky process with a high potential for pathology, thereby requiring routine technological monitoring and intervention. The midwifery model, in contrast, regards birth as an inherently normal process with only a small potential for pathology. Thus, the midwifery model combines trust in the normal process with vigilance for complications that might require medical intervention. This model assumes a holistic approach that seeks to empower women and facilitate their ability to give birth. These two models depict the dominant philosophies of their respective fields; individual obstetricians and midwives may merge aspects of the two or adopt the opposite model in their own practices.

The safety and efficacy of midwifery care has been well documented. Studies have consistently shown that midwifery care results in lower infant mortality rates, less intervention in birth, better physiological and psychological outcomes, and lower costs than obstetrical care. The perinatal mortality rates achieved by midwives are the same as those achieved by physicians attending low-risk hospital births. In normal, low-risk pregnancies and births, midwifery care has significant advantages over obstetrical care and poses no greater risk.

Since the 1970s, the feminist and childbirth reform movements have stimulated new interest in midwifery care that persists to the present day. Two main categories of midwives now practice in the United States. Certified nurse-midwives (CNMs) have completed educational programs in both nursing and midwifery. Direct-entry midwives (DEMs) have completed midwifery training only, through formal education and/or apprenticeship. Both groups embrace the midwifery model of care, but they represent two historically divergent paths to practice and to effecting change in birth care.

CNMs, who work primarily in hospitals where the vast majority of American women give birth, have attempted to effect change from within, working to humanize hospital birth practices and make them more woman-centered. To gain integration into the system, they have had to make many compromises, including adapting to the technological interventions in birth that are standard in most hospitals, and accepting physician supervision. CNMs are licensed or regulated in all 50 states and the District of Columbia; they attend 6 percent of American births. DEMs have adopted the strategy of working outside the system to effect change; they attend births primarily at home. Their outsider status has enabled them to maintain the midwifery model in a more unadulterated form and to hold open the home birth option for American women. But they are licensed or regulated in only 14 states, often face legal repercussions for their independent practice, and attend only 1 percent of American births. Both groups are professionally organized, CNMs through the American College of Nurse-Midwives and DEMs through the Midwives' Alliance of North America.

Access to midwifery care is a basic reproductive right that women in the United States have long been denied. As the century ends, American midwives are gaining in numbers and political strength. Their excellent outcomes and women's satisfaction with their care are placing increasing pressure on the health care system to further incorporate them, but the battle to make midwifery care available to all women is not yet won. CNMs too often find themselves pushed out of practice by physicians seeking to eliminate the competition, while DEMs are still fighting in many states for the right to practice legally. Midwives continue to struggle to make their profession the primary provider of birthing care and to enable all women to reclaim this basic reproductive right.

SEE Abortion Self-Help Movement; Breast-Feeding and the Law; Jane (collective).

Further References. Judith Pence Rooks, *Midwifery and Childbirth in America* (Philadelphia, 1997). Jan Tritten and Joel Southern, eds., *Getting an Education: Paths to Becoming a Midwife*, 4th ed. (Eugene, Ore., 1998).

DEBORAH CORDERO FIEDLER AND ROBBIE DAVIS-FLOYD

MIFEPRISTONE. SEE RU-486.

MULLER v. OREGON (208 U.S. 412, 1908) was the first Supreme Court decision on protective labor legislation for women. When Louis Brandeis agreed to defend Oregon's law establishing a maximum 10-hour day for women laundry workers before the Court, he knew it had struck down similar laws for men (*Lochner v. New York*, 1905). Since the Court was unlikely to reverse such a recent decision, Brandeis decided to emphasize sex differences in his argument. He submitted an innovative brief claiming that such a law was necessary to protect women's reproductive capacities and their ability to take care of their families. It asserted that the "dangers of long hours for women" resulted from "their special physical organization" and that "the evil effect of overwork before as well as after marriage upon childbirth is marked and disastrous." "When the health of women has been injured by long hours," the brief continued, "the deterioration is handed down to succeeding generations" and harm is done to "the welfare of the nation." The brief cited similar statements by physicians and commissions from around the country, Great Britain, France and Germany.

Anxious to have the Court validate a maximum hours statute, Brandeis deliberately held back data showing that a worker's being adversely affected by excessive hours of labor had nothing to do with the worker's sex. The tactic worked. The Court, impressed by the "family values" argument, unanimously upheld the law. Justice David Brewer stressed "woman's physical structure and the performance of maternal functions" in his conclusion that "legislation designed for her protection may be sustained, even when like legislation is not necessary for men, and could not be sustained."

This ruling encouraged Brandeis and his researchers to prepare a gender-neutral defense of maximum hours laws, which was used successfully in *Bunting v. Oregon* in 1917. However, courts continued to rely on *Muller* to sustain special laws for women until Title VII of the Civil Rights Act of 1964 prohibited sex discrimination in employment. The *Muller* approach has been criticized for contributing to the societal and legal view of women as needing "protective legislation" and denying them equal opportunity because of their reproductive role.

SEE Employment and Reproductive Rights; Protective Labor Legislation; Title VII and Reproductive Rights.

Further References. Louis B. Brandeis and Josephine Goldmark, *Women in Industry* New York, n.d). *Bunting v. Oregon*, 243 U.S. 426 (1917). Josephine Goldmark, *Fatigue and Efficiency* (New York, 1912). *Lochner v. New York*, 198 U.S. 45 (1905). Philippa Strum, *Louis D. Brandeis: Justice for the People* (Cambridge, Mass., 1984).

PHILIPPA STRUM

MUÑOZ v. HARO (572834 San Diego Superior Court, 1986) involved a surrogacy contract between three Mexican citizens residing in the United States. Nineteen-year-old Alejandra Muñoz was the second cousin of Nattie Haro, who lived in San Diego, California, with her husband, Mario. The Haros were both in the United States legally. After unsuccessful attempts at *in vitro* fertilization, Nattie and Mario arranged for Alejandra and her daughter to cross the Mexican border illegally. Alejandra signed a hand-written contract that she later claimed she could not read. This contract stipulated that she would be inseminated with Mario's sperm. If she became pregnant, she would carry the baby for the full pregnancy and relinquish him or her to the Haros after birth for $1,500. Alejandra later claimed that she agreed only to be inseminated and to carry the embryo for two to three weeks, until it could be transferred to Nattie.

When Alejandra realized that she was expected to carry the baby for the full pregnancy, she decided she wanted to keep the baby. She remained with the Haros because she felt she could not afford to continue the pregnancy on her own. Alejandra and the Haros carried out a nine-month deception. Alejandra rarely left the house during this time, while Nattie stuffed her clothes with pillows to appear pregnant. Alejandra used Nattie's name when she attended Lamaze classes and visited her doctor. After the delivery, Nattie signed her own name on the birth certificate which Alejandra could not read, thwarting Alejandra's intention to keep her baby.

Alejandra went to a lawyer, who arranged a temporary visa and instigated a lawsuit. At trial, the judge ruled that the contract was not enforceable. Before he ruled on custody, the parties reached an agreement that gave the Haros primary custody and Alejandra visitation rights on a graduating scale. The arrangement broke down due to a complete lack of communication between the parties that resulted in such incidents as different doctors prescribing different medications for the child. At a second hearing, both sides moved for primary custody with limited visitation rights for the other party. The judge ruled for shared custody. The resulting arrangement is similar to the first agreement. The Haros retain primary custody, while Alejandra has gradually increasing visitation rights. Although custody is shared, tensions between the two parties remain unresolved.

While this case received less media attention than the Baby M case a year later, it presents a more dramatic contrast between the parties. In some ways Alejandra Muñoz was more of a victim than Mary Beth Whitehead Gould was. Alejandra was not only poorer and less educated than the Haros; she was also an illegal alien, illiterate in English, with a small child. The amount of money Alejandra was promised by the Haros—$1,500—was considerably less than the rate for surrogacy at that time, which was about $10,000. This case raises grave questions about the exploitation of poor and immigrant women for surrogate motherhood.

SEE Artificial Insemination; Baby M; *In Vitro* Fertilization; Surrogate Motherhood.

Further References. Lori Andrews, *Between Strangers: Surrogate Mothers, Expectant Fathers, & Brave New Babies* (New York, 1989). Patricia Boling, ed., *Expecting Trouble: Surrogacy, Fetal Abuse, & New Reproductive Technologies* (Boulder, Colo., 1995). Phyllis Chesler, *Sacred Bond* (New York, 1988). Janice Raymond, "Reproductive Gifts and Gift Giving: The Altruistic Woman," *Hastings Center Report,* 20 (November-December 1990): 7-11.

NIKKI GRAVES

N

NATIONAL ABORTION AND REPRODUCTIVE RIGHTS ACTION LEAGUE (NARAL) is the largest national political pro-choice organization in the United States. Its mission is to develop and sustain a constituency that uses the political process to guarantee every woman the right to make personal decisions regarding the full range of reproductive choices, including preventing unintended pregnancy, bearing healthy children, and choosing legal abortion.

Before *Roe v. Wade*, women facing unwanted pregnancy also faced punitive restrictions to legal abortions, risk of sterilization or death from underworld abortions, prohibitive costs, and ostracism. Advocates for non-discriminatory legal abortion, seeing the need for a unified pro-choice movement, held the First National Conference on Abortion Laws in February 1969. At that time, they founded the National Association for the Repeal of Abortion Laws. NARAL activists wanted to end women's deaths from unsafe, illegal abortions and to achieve legal autonomy for women for personal reproduction decisions. They supported grassroots efforts to repeal state abortion bans and lobbied Congress for legislation to legalize abortion. After abortion was legalized in 1973, the coalition's name and focus changed. The National Abortion Rights Action League protected legal access to safe abortion and women's reproductive rights from erosion by opponents. In 1993, the organization became the National Abortion and Reproductive Rights Action League, reflecting its comprehensive approach to reproductive health policy. Kate Michelman has been president of NARAL since 1985.

NARAL, Inc., a non-profit organization, conducts grassroots organizing and lobbying efforts to secure reproductive choice for all Americans. NARAL-PAC, a political action committee, campaigns for pro-choice candidates and against anti-choice candidates. It supports legislation to hold anti-choice terrorists financially liable for acts of violence against abortion clinics, women seeking abortions, and doctors who provide abortions. The NARAL Foundation, a charitable organization founded in 1977, conducts research, legal work, leadership training for grassroots activists, and publishes policy reports to protect women's autonomy and dignity. It advocates the creation of comprehensive sexuality education programs and funding for contraceptive research and education, family planning services, and maternal and child health services.

SEE Abortion as a Reproductive Right; Abortion and Political Conflict; Common Ground; National Right to Life Committee; Operation Rescue; *Roe v. Wade.*

Further References. http://www.naral.org. Flora Davis, *Moving the Mountain: The Women's Movement in America Since 1960* (New York, 1991). Lawrence Lader, *Abortion II: Making the Revolution* (Boston, Mass., 1973). Karen Schneider, ed., *Choices: Women Speak Out About Abortion* (Washington, D.C., 1997).

BETTY J. GLASS

NATIONAL RIGHT TO LIFE COMMITTEE (NRLC) is the largest and most influential anti-abortion organization in the United States. It began as a small group with a limited constituency. Founded by Monsignor James McHugh shortly after the 1973 *Roe v. Wade* decision, NRLC was first housed in the offices of the National Council of Catholic Bishops. But the new group soon moved away from its roots, both physically and symbolically. As a new organization striving for legitimacy in the anti-abortion movement, NRLC tried early in its existence to distance itself from the Roman Catholic Church and broaden its appeal. These efforts have continued throughout the group's history and persist to the present. However, NRLC numbers many Catholics among its active supporters. Today, NRLC is a non-profit, grass roots organization. The group claims affiliates in all 50 states, with approximately 3,000 local chapters. The size and influence of local NRLC affiliates varies widely. Total national membership has been reported as high as 12 million (although Judie Brown, former NRLC Public Relations Director and current President of the ultra-conservative American Life League, has admitted to inflating membership figures).

NRLC was established to work for the re-enactment of restrictive anti-abortion laws. It has long supported a federal constitutional amendment to outlaw abortion. The group first achieved national recognition for its role in the passage of the first Hyde Amendment in 1976. This provision forbade the use of Medicaid funds for low-income women seeking abortions. NRLC continues to focus on abortion funding restrictions, as well as parental notification statutes for minors seeking abortions, restrictions on late-term abortion procedures, and opposition to clinical research with fetal tissue or human embryos. The primary strategies of NRLC now emphasize public education and political action.

The main ideological focus of NRLC is to uphold the sanctity of human life. In recent years, the group has expanded its focus beyond abortion to oppose euthanasia and physician-assisted suicide. For example, it was heavily involved in the challenge to Oregon's assisted suicide law. Despite its dedication to the preservation of human life, NRLC does not hold a position on capital punishment or contraception. It does, however, distinguish between contraceptive methods that prevent fertilization (i.e., barrier methods) versus those that do not (i.e., mifepristone, also known as RU-486). In particular, the organization has actively blocked the development and introduction of mifepristone in the United States, but has been silent on the availability of emergency contraception (the "morning-after" pill). Because opposing all methods of birth control would run grossly counter to American public opinion, NRLC has been cautious in its position on birth control. Nevertheless, the Planned Parenthood Federation of America, the nation's most recognizable provider of contraception and abortion, is a frequent target of NRLC.

The leadership of NRLC has consisted of mostly white professionals (physicians, attorneys, academics, etc). These leaders have often publicly asserted their independence from the Roman Catholic Church. In 1978, for example, Dr. Carolyn Gerster, the incoming president, began her first press conference by saying, "I would like to note that I am a Protestant." Gerster's successor, John C. Willke, may have been NRLC's most prominent leader. Also a physician, Willke served as NRLC President throughout the tumultuous 1980s, a time of massive clinic protests, high-profile court decisions, and escalating rhetoric. During Willke's tenure, anti-abortion rhetoric became increasingly visceral, emphasizing the omnipresent use of fetal imagery and the words "kill" and "unborn baby."

The NRLC officially condemns violence (though they did endorse direct action tactics like clinic sit-ins and picketing at their 1978 annual convention) and disassociates itself from the radical, often-violent wing of the anti-abortion movement. Even during the era of clinic blockades and mass arrests, NRLC publications (such as the *National Right to Life News*) omitted references to militant groups like Operation Rescue. When John Willke was president, he defended such omissions on the grounds that the organization might face lawsuits if it were perceived as supporting illegal tactics. NRLC issues press releases condemning violence after high-profile shootings and clinic bombings. However, pro-choice leaders have held NRLC and other anti-abortion groups accountable because of their inflammatory rhetoric.

Evidence does exist of links between NRLC and more militant groups. It is worth noting that two prominent radical anti-abortion activists have employed NRLC venues in their rise to prominence. During the 1983 NRLC annual convention in Orlando, Florida, Joseph Scheidler, a former head of the Illinois NRLC affiliate and then a rising militant anti-abortion leader, held a meeting with sympathizers. Disillusioned with NRLC's "marginal [legislative] victories," Scheidler went on to form the Pro-Life Action Network, a group not bound by NRLC's limits on "aggressive action." In 1998, a federal jury found Scheidler and his associates' national campaign of intimidation and harassment at abortion clinics to be in violation of federal racketeering laws (*NOW, et al. v. Scheidler et al*). In the same year, John Kavanagh O'Keefe, similarly disillusioned with mainstream anti-abortion ideology, began spreading ideas about civil disobedience at abortion clinics. O'Keefe's audiences, like Scheidler's, included NRLC conventioneers. O'Keefe would go on to be known as the "father of the [clinic] rescue movement."

Although the NRLC describes itself as non-partisan, it has become prominently identified with conservative special-interest politics and the right wing of the Republican Party. The organization has been aggressive in supporting presidential and congressional candidates who hold anti-abortion beliefs. During the 1998 elections, the NRL-PAC was active in 106 House and Senate races. For the 2000 presidential election, the NRLC endorsed Republican nominee George W. Bush. NRL-PAC spent $340,000 in nine states alone prior to the March 2000 "Super Tuesday" primaries. (Suggesting the political power of the national office, a South Carolina affiliate board member resigned due to what he called "coercion" from the NRLC to endorse Bush).

The political relationship between conservative Republicans and the NRLC is increasingly close and strong. In a controversial move in late 1999, the National Republican Congressional Committee gave the NRLC $250,000 as a bequest to its "general pro-life activities." Critics view this donation as an ethically questionable strategy for Republicans to commandeer the NRLC's influence in energizing that party's conservative base. The lobbying efforts of the NRLC are far-reaching; *Fortune* magazine has ranked the NRLC in the top 10 of its 1997, 1998 and 1999 "Power 25" Washington lobbying groups. With its political clout firmly established, the NRLC has ardently opposed campaign finance reform in recent years—including restrictions on political action committee spending and activities.

The likelihood of achieving the NRLC's highest goal—a constitutional "Human Life Amendment"—seems remote at best. But the vast sociopolitical influence of the NRLC has allowed abortion to become a deciding factor, if not an overt litmus test, in elections at the congressional, gubernatorial, and presidential levels. And while other factions of the anti-abortion movement jockey for influence and survival, the NRLC continually emerges as the immutable center of the American anti-abortion landscape.

SEE Abortion and Parental Consent and Notification; Abortion and Political Conflict; Abortion and Political Rhetoric; Abortion and Public Opinion; Dilation and Extraction; Human Life Bill/Amendment; Hyde Amendment; National Abortion Rights Action League; Operation Rescue; Planned Parenthood; Religion and Reproductive Rights.

Further References. Frederick S. Jaffe, Barbara L. Lindheim, and Philip R. Lee, *Abortion Politics: Private Morality and Public Policy* (New York, 1981). James R. Kelly, "Toward Complexity: the Right-to-Life Movement," in Monty L. Lynn and David O. Moberg, et al., eds., *Research in the Social Scientific Study of Religion*, vol. 1 (Greenwich, Conn., 1989): 83-107. James Risen and Judy L. Thomas, *Wrath of Angels: The American Abortion War* (New York, 1998).

TRACY SEFL

NATIVE AMERICAN WOMEN AND REPRODUCTIVE RIGHTS. Approximately 1.6 million Native Americans (or American Indians) live in the United States. They represent a small percentage of the 42 million people, belonging to 480 distinct ethnic groups, who make up America's indigenous population. The reproductive health of these indigenous populations is affected by the lack of clean water, sanitation, health services, housing, and food. For these peoples, land is central to culture and reproductive survival. The severing of the interdependent relationship between indigenous peoples and the land has given rise to a host of problems that endanger the reproductive health of Native Americans. Indigenous women must survive living conditions that weaken immune systems, early pregnancies, complications of pregnancy and delivery, and iron deficiency anemia. In industrial areas, these problems are accompanied by alcoholism (and consequently by fetal alcohol syndrome), hazardous mining, waste, polluted agricultural environments, AIDS, diabetes, and malnutrition. Other factors which endanger the reproductive health of American Indians include interpersonal violence; alcohol and drug abuse; sexually transmitted diseases and other infectious diseases; the contamination of living habitats and work environments; and malnutrition and micro-nutrient deficiencies. These condition lead to a high incidence of birthing complications, short life expectancies, and high mortality rates among people of fertile age.

Historically, the over-exploitation of natural resources, the lack of health care, and high mortality and morbidity rates are all associated with an imposed colonial cultural cycle of health—disease—death. In this historical process, local health wisdom, access to land, and the resources necessary for a sustainable culture have been systematically removed by Western European theft of the land base for the purpose of creating colonies on it. These colonies have lacked any recognition of the value of mutual cultural respect, reciprocity, or interdependence. The personal and technological violence perpetrated upon displaced indigenous groups has created a diaspora. The separation of indigenous peoples from our traditional lands has endangered our cultures, our sense of home and of belonging interdependently with our land base, and our very survival.

Throughout the Native American diasporas from our homelands, a consistent and ongoing reproductive genocide of Indians has been carried out by the U.S. government. Methods of genocide during U.S. wars against Indians included not only using the known technologically advanced warfare techniques against our warriors, but also the systematic murder of women (reproducers), children (the next generation), and elders (the keepers and conveyors of tribal survival wisdom). The U.S. government hoped to exterminate Indians completely, thereby eliminating the genetic pool. As conventional warfare became less frequent, biological warfare (for example, providing smallpox-infested blankets and handkerchiefs) replaced other methods of extermination.

In the twentieth century, the health policies of the U.S. government, influenced by the historical and contemporary eugenics movement, inflicted modern methods of reproductive sterilization on Indians. President Theodore Roosevelt's call to prevent a race suicide among whites was a political boost for the racist lynch mobs and rioters, providing tacit government acceptance of population control against people of color. Race suicide for whites was to be prevented by birth control among women of color. By 1932, 26 states had compulsory sterilization laws for "undesirables," morons, mental defectives, epileptics, illiterates, paupers, unemployables, criminals, prostitutes, and dope fiends; they were all to be sterilized or segregated into labor camps. Nothing less than the complete extermination of Blacks and Indians was acceptable. In 1972, the Department of Health, Education and Welfare (HEW) supported between 100,000 and 200,000 sterilizations, as compared to the 250,000 sterilizations during the Third Reich under the Nazi Hereditary Health Laws. From 1970 to 1977, HEW funded between 192,000 and 540,000 sterilizations each year.

Reproductive technologies have played a central role in contemporary genocide practices. By the mid 1970s, some 25,000 Indian women of childbearing ages were permanently sterilized; by the mid 1980s 42 percent of Indian women in the U.S. had been sterilized. Most of these operations were performed in federally funded programs, often by medically questionable surgery techniques, such as hysterectomy, and often without full, informed consent. Techniques of harassment and coercion included failing to provide foreign language consent forms, misinforming women about their ability to have children after the operations, secretly performing tubal ligations or even hysterectomies during abortion procedures, especially on women who were labeled "uncooperative" or "alcoholic," and threatening to remove federal benefits for refusing the procedures. These were only some of the techniques used by government health care providers to insure that Indian reproduction would come to a halt.

Depo-Provera (10 months' injectable contraceptive) and Norplant (five years' implant under the skin) have been supplied to Indian women since 1986 with little or no informed consent about the high contraindications (diabetes, obesity, and smoking) for their use in Indian communities. Long-term serious health side effects, ineffectiveness in obese women, and non-prevention of sexually transmitted diseases, which affect fertility, are only a few of the undesirable elements of these drugs for Indian women. By the mid-1980s, the eugenic policy of exterminating "undesirables" according to a white racist criterion was well on its way to success in destroying Indian nations and Indian peoples. As the twentieth century ended, "white" women were using the media to fight for the right not to have to bear children, while Indian women were quietly engaged in struggles to have the right to bear children.

The effects of diaspora and genocide on Native Americans have been devastating and profound. The early, pre-industrial methods of genocide created a response of grief and loss for Indians. This era was followed by a sense of helplessness and hopelessness in the struggle against ongoing battles of colonization. Various leaders, such as Tecumseh, Osceola, and Geronimo, began to notice patterns of intergenerational warfare in reaction to broken promises, U.S. policies which permitted genocidal practices, and the confinement to barren and empty reservations when acculturation methods were too successful, or not successful at all. The response to these situations was anger at oneself, at one's clan, tribe, and Indianness, and then, finally, at the government itself.

More recent historical conditions of poverty as a result of broken treaty promises have severely damaged the physical, mental, and reproductive health of Native Americans. Suicide rates are high. The current primary causes of death among Indians are accidents, alcohol and drug use, stress-related heart disease, malnutrition, and, most recently, breast cancer. These health problems have their roots in behavioral diseases, and might be drastically reduced, if not prevented within a few generations by means of Indian-centered psychological intervention. Eliminating these behavioral diseases would lead to healthier communities, and hence to higher reproductive rates.

A vicious cycle of poverty reproducing poverty has been fostered by the United States, creating dependent care systems for Indians. One-half of Native American children under age six now live in poverty. Factors contributing to Natives' poverty include the shift from kinship clan family systems to a capitalist nuclear family system; the erosion of self-esteem, due to the outlawing of cultural survival practices such as the use of language and spiritual activities; biological warfare causing the death of elderly Indians, and loss of land.

For indigenous people, the land is fundamental to maintaining the interdependent, sustainable lifestyles of living conditions and respect for the relationship among the environment, the clan, and the self (the "we" relationship). But economic necessity has forced more than 50 percent of American Indians to live in urban areas. In these areas, mental health problems, obesity from improper diet resulting in diabetes, and kidney failure, breast cancer, AIDS risk, and poverty conditions all contribute to the inability of Native women to reproduce in a supportive environment.

Native Americans living in urban areas are isolated from family members, traditional tribal religious and medical support systems. These strong traditional social structures might lessen the high rates of hypertension and suicide and generally improve people's health. As the few tribes that have been able to regain economic sufficiency for their members have proven successful, many urban Indians are trying to return and reintegrate into the tribal culture. This process has resulted in increased efforts to heal the open wounds from city dwelling while continuing the healing of reservation Indians.

Revived and reinvigorated tribal cultures may go a long way toward creating a supportive environment in which women can reproduce in health and safety. These changes might lead to the availability of good quality health care in Native American communities, which may be a precondition for safe and effective birth control. In the near future, Native Americans will be faced with important and difficult reproductive choices. New innovations in reproductive technologies, such as artificial insemination, egg transference, surrogacy, and genetic manipulation, may engender exploitative repercussions among least advantaged social groups. These groups tend not to be in positions of decision-making power, nor to have access to accurate information about these innovations. These problems are intensified by the social context in which reproductive innovation is occurring. Pre-existing racial, class, and sexual biases and prejudices, and overt as well as covert individual and group racism, classism, and sexism, and genetic engineering carried on by groups funded with the same monies that funded the earlier eugenics movement, will all affect the uses to which new technology is put.

There is still a dominant mentality in the Americas that Indians belong naturally at the bottom of the race/social/class scale, and that natural selection justifies any means of keeping them there. (The flaw in this reasoning often goes unnoticed: if nature puts a group at the bottom, what need is there for force?) Embracing reproductive technologies which may do no more than pander to the newly created desires for novelty and experimentation among those who are the most advantaged would, therefore, be self-defeating in the Indian community, where "race suicide" has a long history. The familiar argument that reproductive technologies are not harmful so long as the most advantaged members of the society do not impose genocidal reproductive measures on the least advantaged does not fully apply to Native Americans. Even where economic improvement has occurred, policy can shift dramatically in very short time. Indians are not yet out from under the historical racism and sexism of genocide.

American Indians have much to lose and little to gain by participating in the technological advances of the new reproductive engineering. Genetic engineering has not yet been tested enough for any population with a history of genocide to use. It would be unfortunate for Indians to experiment with this technology when the mechanisms of control and means of production are not within our means. Capitalist benefit is invested in extensive testing and research on our targeted groups.

Despite centuries of boastful claims of equality made by Americans of Western European descent, Americans remain unsocialized to diverse cultures. They continue to support forms of genocidal practices on peoples of color, both within and without the Americas. This information is a warning to all nations, and especially our red nations, that the use of technology will be most effective when our own communities control the means of its production and use. In this context it may be wise to accelerate the reclaiming and maintaining of traditional reproductive sources of control, while at the same time learning about the fruits of Western science that have historically led to a 50 percent sterilization of Native American women. Caution ought to be our guide.

SEE African-American Women and Reproductive Rights; Class and Reproductive Rights; Eugenics; Federal Sterilization Guidelines (1979); Sterilization Abuse.

Further References. Ward Churchill, *A Little Matter of Genocide: Holocaust and Denial in the Americas, 1492 to the Present* (San Francisco, 1997). Brint Dillingham, "Indian Women and HIS Sterilization Practices, *American Indian Journal*, 3 (January 1977): 27-28. M. Annette Jaimes with Theresa Halsey, "American Indian Women: At the Center of Indigenous Resistance in Contemporary North

America," in *The State of Native America: Genocide, Colonization, and Resistance,* ed., M. Annette Jaimes (Boston, 1992): 311-344. Robin H. Jarrell, "Native American Women and Forced Sterilization, 1973-1978," *Caduceus,* 8 (Winter 1992): 45-48. Native American Women's Health Education Resource Center (nativewoman@igc.apc.org). Rosalind P. Petchesky, "Reproduction, Ethics, and Public Policy: The Federal Sterilization Regulations," *Hastings Center Report,* 9 (October, 1979): 29-41. H. Temkin-Greener et al., "Surgical Fertility Regulation among Women on the Navajo Indian Reservation, 1972-1978," *American Journal of Public Health*, 71 (April 1981): 403-407. Russell Thornton, *American Indian Holocaust and Survival: A Populations History since 1492* (Norman, Okla., 1987). Anne Waters, *Morality, Law, and Politics: Reproduction and Surrogacy* (unpublished Ph.D. dissertation, Purdue University, 1992).

ANNE WATERS

NEWPORT NEWS SHIPBUILDING & DRY DOCK CO. v. EQUAL EMPLOYMENT OPPORTUNITY COMMISSION (462 U.S. 669, 1983) was a Supreme Court decision interpreting the Pregnancy Discrimination Act (PDA) of 1978. A male employee of Newport News Shipbuilding charged that the company's employee benefits plan discriminated on the basis of sex in violation of Title VII of the Civil Rights Act of 1964 as amended by the PDA. This policy limited insurance coverage for the pregnancies of the spouses of male workers (denying coverage for pregnancy-related hospitalization), but put no limitation on the benefits afforded the spouses of female workers. Since the PDA refers specifically only to the treatment of pregnant employees, it is not clear from the language of the statute whether it applies to employees' spouses. The Court heard *Newport News* to determine the scope of the PDA, and to resolve conflicts among the lower federal appellate courts, which had spilt on this question.

The Court ruled, seven to two, in favor of the employee. Justice John Paul Stevens's majority opinion construed the PDA as a statement that discrimination based on a woman's pregnancy is sex discrimination on its face. "Since the sex of the spouse is always the opposite of the sex of the employee," Stevens continued, "it follows inexorably that discrimination against female spouses in the provision of fringe benefits is also discrimination against male employees." Because "petitioner's plan unlawfully gives married male employees a benefit package for their dependents that is less inclusive than the dependency coverage provided to married female employees," that limitation discriminates against male employees and thus violates Title VII. *Newport News* extended the reach of the PDA, thereby affording a higher level of protection to a class of women in terms of pregnancy-related health benefits. Therefore, even though the immediate plaintiff was male, the ruling was a victory for both reproductive freedom and gender equality.

SEE Pregnancy Discrimination Act of 1978; Title VII and Reproductive Rights.

Further References. Stephen Tarnoff, "Court Decisions or Benefits Increase Employers' Costs," *Business Insurance* 21 (November 2, 1987): 93-95. "The Supreme Court, 1982 Term: Sex Discrimination in Employment Benefits," *Harvard Law Review* 97 (November 1983): 252-261.

SARA C. BENESH

NEW YORK v. SCHWEIKER (557 Fed. Supp. 354 S. D. N.Y. 1983): In this ruling, District Judge Henry Werker issued an injunction against the "squeal rule." This was a regulation proposed by the Department of Health and Human Services (HHS). In keeping with the social conservatism and "family values" emphasis of the Reagan administration, the rule required all family planning clinics receiving federal funds under Title X of the Public Health Service Act to notify the parent or guardian of any minor to whom they provided contraceptive drugs or devices. A second regulation would have forbidden Title IX grantees to disregard family income when setting fees for unemancipated minors. The New York State Department of Health and several clinics and doctors asked the Court for a preliminary injunction against enforcement of both regulations.

The decision was based not on constitutional interpretation but on statutory construction. Judge Werker, a Nixon appointee, rejected HHS's argument that the regulations were compatible with Congress's intentions in enacting Title X. The department relied on a 1981 amendment providing that grantees "will encourage family participation." The judge's language was vigorous and unequivocal. In refusing HHS's request to dismiss the case for lack of standing, he characterized the agency's argument as "fatuous." He described HHS's argument on the merits as "an exercise in mere sophistry." For Werker, the legislative history of the disputed amendment clearly indicated that "parental or family participation is not mandated; rather, what is required is that Title X grantees *encourage their clients* to include their families" (emphasis original). The judge also accepted the plaintiffs' argument that the fee-setting regulation "is another form of a parental notice requirement."

A preliminary injunction prevents enforcement of a law only while litigation is pending. If a higher court had reversed Judge Werker, the regulation would have gone into effect. However, the government dropped the case. The squeal rule was dead.

SEE *Carey v. Population Services International*; Youth and Reproductive Rights.

JUDITH A. BAER

NORPLANT, which arrived on the U.S. market in November 1991, is one of the newest methods of birth control to become available in recent years. Different from all other contraceptives, Norplant consists of six matchstick-size capsules that are inserted into a woman's upper arm by a health care provider. The synthetic hormone progestin levonorgestrel, the same hormone used in some types of birth control pills, is slowly and steadily released into a woman's body and prevents conception in part by inhibiting ovulation. The capsules remain implanted for up to five years; they can be removed at any time during that period. Removal, like insertion, requires a trained provider.

Women's rights supporters, who have long argued that access to contraceptives is a crucial prerequisite to women's independence and self-sufficiency, have generally been enthusiastic about Norplant. It is reliable, safe, convenient, and easily reversible if a woman wants to get pregnant. With a failure rate of less than one percent, Norplant is second only to tubal ligation as an effective method of preventing conception. But its usefulness is limited, not only because it requires advance planning and professional intervention but because not all women can afford it. Implantation costs approximately $600, and removal approximately $200. Averaged over Norplant's five-year life, this amount is approximately equal to the cost of oral contraceptives—but it must be paid in lump sums. While many women have access to Norplant through Medicaid and private insurance, the cost can be prohibitive to uninsured women who are not eligible to receive Medicaid.

The potential for mandatory or coercive use of Norplant is a serious concern to feminists and reproductive rights advocates. From the time Norplant received FDA approval in December 1990, it has been hailed by some public health and criminal justice professionals as ideally suited for use by low income women because of its long-term but reversible contraceptive effect. Several states, including Louisiana, Texas, and South Carolina, have considered laws that would provide incentives to welfare recipients who choose the device. Elsewhere, some judges have mandated Norplant use as a condition of probation for women convicted on substance abuse or child abuse charges. Such policies, women's rights supporters insist, have a negative and disproportionate impact on poor women and women of color and, in effect, limit their reproductive choice. Given the lack of consensus over the status of women's reproductive freedom with respect to abortion, sterilization, and other forms of contraception, questions over the ethics of state intervention in Norplant use are not likely to be resolved soon.

SEE Birth Control Movement; Oral Contraceptives.

Further References. Boston Women's Health Book Collective, *The New Our Bodies, Ourselves: A Book by and for Women* (New York, 1992). Sarah Gehlert and Sarah Lickey, "Social and Health Policy Concerns Raised by the Introduction of the Contraceptive Norplant." *Social Service Review* 69 (June 1995): 323-337. Lenore Kuo, "Secondary Discrimination as a Standard for Feminist Social Policy: Norplant and Probation, a Case Study." *Signs: Journal of Women in Culture and Society,* 23 (Summer 1998): 907-944.

MARIA BEVACQUA

O

OHIO v. AKRON CENTER FOR REPRODUCTIVE HEALTH (497 U.S. 502,
1990) upheld a parental notification/ judicial bypass requirement. House Bill 319
required doctors to notify the parent or guardian of any unmarried, unemancipated minor seeking an abortion, unless she acquired court permission to bypass
notification. This permission could be granted on the basis of her maturity to make
the decision or her ability to convince the court that parental notification was not
in her best interest. A doctor could perform an abortion without parental notification if efforts to reach a parent or guardian failed or if the court procedures
were not completed in a timely manner.

When a young woman, the Akron Center for Reproductive Health, and one of
its doctors questioned the constitutionality of sections of HB 319, a federal district court issued an injunction preventing the bill from being enforced. The
Supreme Court ruled that the bill was not unconstitutional and upheld its enforcement. On the same day it decided *Hodgson v. Minnesota*, the justices argued that
HB 319 was in agreement with legal precedents like *Planned Parenthood v.
Ashcroft* regarding parental notification bypass procedures, confidentiality, and
expedited court proceedings. The dissenting justices argued that the bill was a thinly
veiled parental consent law, intended to prevent young women who seek abortion
from obtaining it by placing a series of complicated legal procedures in their way.

SEE Abortion and Parental Consent and Notification; Abortion and Parental
Involvement; *H.L. v. Matheson; Hodgson v. Minnesota; New York v. Schweiker,
Planned Parenthood of Kansas City v. Ashcroft; Planned Parenthood of South-
eastern Pennsylvania v. Casey*; Youth and Reproductive Rights.

MOLLY DRAGIEWICZ

OPERATION RESCUE is an anti-abortion group that specializes in confrontational tactics, especially in the blockading of abortion clinics and the harassment of doctors and patients. Randall Terry, a lay minister, who had long been involved in picketing abortion providers, founded the organization in 1988. Over the next two years, Operation Rescue became highly visible, staging blockades at a number of sites across the country. Operation Rescue leaders faced heavy fines—usually paid by benefactors—and spent time in jail.

Operation Rescue's rhetoric is more explicitly fundamentalist and inflammatory than that of most other anti-abortion groups. For example, the organization's Web page compares abortion providers to child molesters and Nazis, and the clinics to Nazi death camps. Yet the organization attracts a mix of activists from a variety of religious traditions, including some who are generally liberal on other issues, who identify themselves as feminists, and/or who have had personal experiences of abortion. The group is much more confrontational than most other anti-abortion organizations. Operation Rescue's blockades seek not only to express the pro-life point of view but also to prevent women from entering clinics to receive abortions. In addition to silent protests, placards and signs, members may bring graphic props, engage in hostile verbal exchanges with clinic staff and patients, and resort to physical jostling and contact.

However, Operation Rescue explicitly rejects violence against clinics, doctors and patients; group members who participate in clinic protests must sign a pledge of non-violence. This policy has caused internal disputes, resulting in the formation of several splinter organizations which advocate the use of deadly force and which publish lists of abortion providers as targets. Operation Rescue has also faced heavy fines and civil damages. Now headed by Flip Benham, the organization has splintered and been driven partly underground. Terry has filed for bankruptcy.

SEE Abortion and Political Rhetoric; Abortion Providers and Violence; Common Ground; National Abortion Reproductive Rights Action League; National Right to Life Committee; Pro-Life Feminism.

Further References. Carol J.C. Maxwell, *Moral Mosaic: Meaning and Motivation in American Pro-life Direct Action* (New York, 2000). Karen O'Connor, *No Neutral Ground? Abortion Politics in an Age of Absolutes* (Boulder, Colo., 1996).
CLYDE WILCOX AND RACHEL E. GOLDBERG

ORAL CONTRACEPTIVES. No method of birth control has received more attention than oral contraceptives (OCs) or "The Pill." Oral contraceptives prevent pregnancy by suppressing ovulation through the combined actions of the hormones estrogen and progestin. These hormones, which also occur naturally in women's bodies, act upon many different organ systems and produce a broad range of effects, including the suppression of ovulation and the thickening of cervical mucus, which makes it more difficult for sperm to enter the uterus. Millions of women have benefitted from the Pill's effectiveness in preventing pregnancy, its facilitation of spontaneous sexual activity by separating contraception from intercourse, and some health benefits unrelated to birth control.

By improving women's access to reasonably safe and effective fertility management, oral contraceptives represent a major victory for reproductive rights. However, the history of oral contraceptives has also been marked by widespread criticism. The origins of hormone-based contraception have been linked to eugenicist and racist motives. Feminists have condemned the medical establishment for inadequate testing of the Pill and under-emphasis of its negative health effects. Some feminists also fear that oral contraceptives may reduce rather than increase women's sexual autonomy. Forty years after it became available in the United States, the Pill remains a controversial subject.

The development of oral contraceptives was made possible by changes in social attitudes after World War II. Both public opinion and public policy displayed a new openness toward family planning. Even the medical profession was rethinking its traditional conservatism about birth control. Concern for reproductive autonomy was not the only reason for this change. Many doctors and public officials interpreted current fertility trends as a "threat" to the social order. Fertility rates were shrinking among upper-middle class whites, while the fertility rates of minorities and the poor remained high.

Many scholars have argued that eugenicist and racist attitudes increased federal willingness to become involved in family planning services, both domestically and abroad. These experts cite the disproportionate number of family planning clinics and services placed in poor and minority communities with high fertility rates, the increasing number of states that tried to make birth control a condition of receiving welfare benefits, and the ongoing scandals surrounding sterilization abuse in medical facilities serving poor and minority clienteles. Concerns over the "overpopulation" of certain social groups helped stimulate federal, medical, and pharmaceutical interest in the development of contraception that was both more effective and more "scientific" than the condoms, jellies, and diaphragms available at the time.

The medical, pharmaceutical, and population control communities greeted the Pill with great fanfare when it appeared in the late 1950s. While this invention is credited primarily to physician-researchers Gregory Pincus, John Rock, and Min-Cheuh Chan, the Pill was also born from significant recent developments in biology, chemistry, and the burgeoning field of endocrinology. The U.S. Food and Drug Administration (FDA) approved the oral contraceptive pill in May of 1960. Two years later, 1.2 million American women used it. By 1973, the number had risen to an estimated 10 million (the annual number of OC users today).

In 1964, the American Medical Association recognized birth control as a "major responsibility" of the medical profession. This policy was not without benefit for doctors. The Pill was, and remains, available only by medical prescription. As medical historian James Reed has argued, "suddenly physicians had a much sought-after service that commanded good fees, lent the prestige of science to the general practitioner, and involved none of the awkwardness of diaphragm fitting."

Some feminists have argued that the medical profession's endorsement of oral contraceptives had as much to do with their mode of distribution as with their effectiveness and medical respectability. The medical profession's control over access to the Pill became more conspicuous when physicians had to confront concerns about the safety of high-dose estrogen OCs. Although medical literature confirmed dangers of the Pill as early as 1962, very few professionals cautioned against using it too widely or too quickly. The authors of *Our Bodies, Ourselves* have suggested that to do so meant fighting against the prevailing ideology, which supported medical progress and accepted the associated risks. Supporters of the Pill countered attacks by citing the millions of women who had found the Pill to be an excellent alternative to the methods then available.

Barbara Seaman's book, *The Doctors' Case Against the Pill* (1969), was one of the first mass-market publications to inform women of the medical dangers of the Pill. Many stopped taking it and found alternative methods. Others joined consumer activists in the public hearings conducted by Senator Gaylord Nelson in 1970. Testimony from numerous physicians, scientific researchers, and professionals from the pharmaceutical industries dominated the early phases of the Nelson hearings. Later, dissatisfied with the conduct of the subcommittee, several feminist and consumer activist organizations became involved as well. These well-publicized hearings led to modifications of the Pill as well as special patient package inserts. Since 1978, the FDA has required physicians and pharmacists to hand out comprehensive information sheets on its possible negative effects and complications.

Today's oral contraceptive pills have much lower estrogen levels than earlier versions. These lower doses have diminished many of their negative health effects. Nonetheless, a number of physiological disadvantages remain associated with the Pill. These effects included menstrual cycle changes, nausea or vomiting during the first several cycles, headaches, aggravation of depression, and alleged increased risk of cervical ectopy, chlamydia, and cardiovascular disease. The Pill has also been shown to alter the nutritional requirements of those who take it, increasing some women's requirements for vitamins C, B_2 (riboflavin), B_{12} and especially B_6 and folic acid. Adolescents and poor women are at greatest risk for this nutrition depletion due to their propensity toward poorer nutritional health.

At the same time, a number of physiological advantages are associated with taking OCs. These include: reduced menstrual flow (and therefore less anemia); decreased menstrual cramps and pain; decreased premenstrual tension, decreased risk of endometrial cancer, ovarian cancer, ovarian cysts, and pelvic inflammatory disease; management of pain associated with endometriosis; and acne improvement. Another benefit of OCs is that they can be used as an emergency contraceptive regimen just after intercourse.

Some reported effects may be considered either beneficial or disadvantageous to women, depending on one's perspective or on the individual user. For example, in terms of sexual enjoyment, some OC users have reported increased vaginal dryness and decreased sexual desire and pleasure. Other users have found that diminished fear of pregnancy is conducive to enhanced sexual enjoyment. Oral contraceptives also allow for more spontaneous sexual activity, since users do not have to insert or apply a barrier method at the time of sexual intercourse. The Pill's cost is another potential benefit or drawback of the method, depending on a number of factors. Oral contraceptives cost between $100 and $300 per year, depending whether they are generic or brand name and the type of insurance/payer system. Public clinics and college health services usually have reduced prices.

The Pill is frequently praised for its effectiveness. However, efficacy is highly dependent on the individual user and how challenging she finds taking the Pill every single day. Inconsistent or incorrect use significantly raises the risk of pregnancy. Among *perfect* users (those who miss no Pills and follow instructions perfectly), only about 1 in 1,000 women (0.1 percent) will become pregnant in the first year. However, among *typical* users, about 1 in 20 women (5 percent) will become pregnant in the first year. The women who are the least likely to receive adequate counseling on proper Pill taking are women with sub-par health care—often poor women, African-American and Hispanic women, and adolescents.

Oral contraceptives have been viewed as both an improvement and hindrance to women's reproductive autonomy. Millions have praised the Pill for allowing women more control in managing their fertility. Unlike condoms, vasectomy, or withdrawal, the Pill does not necessitate participation from male partners. A woman can take it without her partner even knowing. This independence from men has been an enormous gain for women's reproductive freedom. But other commentators have criticized oral contraceptives for the very same reason: they allow men to evade responsibility in the prevention of pregnancy. Ideally, feminists argue, this is a task for which both partners should be accountable. A related problem is that OCs provide no known protection against sexually transmitted diseases. Many users have found it difficult to persuade their partners use condoms if the man knows that the woman is already protected from pregnancy via the Pill. Some feminists fear that a man's knowledge that his partner is on the Pill—or his expectation that she should be—may make it harder for a woman to refuse sex.

Research on oral contraceptives remains a high priority of the pharmaceutical, medical, and scientific communities. Scientists seek to minimize the remaining negative effects of OCs while increasing their health benefits. Progress has also been made on the development of a male contraceptive pill, although researchers warn that they are a long way from a finished product. We eagerly await further improvements and developments. In the meantime, today's oral contraceptives remain an extremely important reproductive option for millions of women and their partners.

SEE Birth Control and African-American Women; Birth Control Movement; Class and Reproductive Rights; Eugenics; Hispanic/Latina Women and Reproductive Rights; Norplant; Sterilization Abuse; Youth and Reproductive Rights.

Further References. Boston Women's Health Collective. *The New Our Bodies, Ourselves.* (New York, 1992). Robert A. Hatcher, ed., *Contraceptive Technology.* 17th edition. (New York, 1998). Constance A. Nathanson, *Dangerous Passage: The Social Control of Sexuality in Women's Adolescence.* (Philadelphia, 1991). James Reed, *From Private Vice to Public Virtue: The Birth Control Movement and American Society Since 1830.* (New York, 1978). Barbara Seaman, *The Doctors' Case Against the Pill.* (New York, 1969, updated, 1979, 1995). Senate Subcommittee on the Monopoly of the Select Committee on Small Business, *Competitive Problems in the Drug Industry: Present Status of Competition in the Pharmaceutical Industry; Oral Contraceptives,* 91st Cong., 2d session (Washington, D.C.,1970).

JENNY HIGGINS

P

PARTIAL BIRTH ABORTION. SEE Dilation and Extraction (D&X).

PILL. SEE Oral Contraceptives.

PLANNED PARENTHOOD is an affiliation of reproductive health organizations. These organizations have two primary functions: as health service providers and as political interest groups. Planned Parenthood grew out of the birth control movement of the early twentieth century. The most prominent of the activists and reformers associated with this movement was the activist and reformer, Margaret Sanger. She had worked as a nurse in England, where she saw the positive effect birth control had on the lives of women and their families. Upon returning to the United States, she began a lifelong struggle to make birth control available to American women.

In 1921, Sanger helped found Planned Parenthood's predecessor, the American Birth Control League. The League merged with the Birth Control Clinical Research Bureau in 1939, adopting the name Birth Control Federation of America. The organization's current name, the Planned Parenthood Federation of America (PPFA), was adopted in 1942. Ten years later, the PPFA helped establish the International Planned Parenthood Federation to advocate family planning worldwide. Both organizations are structured as a federation of autonomous family planning affiliates. Membership in the international federation links state and local affiliates of PPFA to other national federations such as Planned Parenthood of Canada.

Planned Parenthood affiliates are the descendants of Margaret Sanger's birth control clinic and her fight to bring safe, legal birth control and reproductive services to all women. They provide low-cost health care, HIV testing, counseling, contraception, and, in some cases, abortion services. But this is not all Planned Parenthood does. Throughout its history, the organization has been forced to becoming politically active, lobbying legislators and bringing lawsuits in order to fulfill its mission.

The Birth Control League was founded partly in response to legal threats. In 1916, Sanger, Ethel Byrne, and Fania Mindell opened a birth control clinic in Brooklyn, New York—and ran afoul of the law. All three women were arrested that year and convicted of violating state and federal statutes known as "Comstock laws." (During the late 1860s and 1870s, Anthony Comstock, backed by the Young Men's Christian Association, led a moral crusade to outlaw birth control by including it under anti-obscenity statutes, thereby prohibiting the advertisement, sale or dissemination of birth control information or devices). Sanger's first brush with the law was far from her last. In 1921, she was again arrested, along with Mary Winsor, when they attempted to speak publically about birth control at the first American Birth Control Conference. The protests and appeals instigated by these early arrests and police raids on Sanger's clinic led to the founding of a powerful voluntary organization and eventually to a legal redefinition of birth control.

An important victory came in 1936, when Judge Augustus Hand of the Second Circuit Court of Appeals ruled that the Tariff Act of 1930, which forbade the importing of contraceptives, would never have been enacted if Congress had been aware of the medical necessity of contraception. Hand's decision meant that birth control was no longer defined as obscenity and was therefore not criminalized by obscenity statutes. *Griswold v. Connecticut* (1965) overturned the last vestiges of the Comstock laws. The Supreme Court overturned an 1879 state law prohibiting the use of birth control even by married couples, on the grounds that it violated the constitutional right of marital privacy. At 86, Margaret Sanger had lived to see the last legal obstacle to birth control fall.

This victory won, Planned Parenthood turned its political focus to the liberalization of abortion laws. *Roe v. Wade* (1973) represented the group's second landmark victory in court. Since then, PPFA and its affiliates have opposed spousal and parental consent/notification policies, prohibitions and restrictions on abortion procedures, and laws like mandatory waiting periods which are designed to discourage abortions. Sometimes Planned Parenthood wins and sometimes it loses, but it continues its political activity with the same energy and commitment that Sanger and her successors evinced.

Throughout its existence, Planned Parenthood has consistently been ahead of the American mainstream in support of reproductive freedom. The organization supported birth control long before public consensus existed in support of this right. As the twenty-first century began, Planned Parenthood's support of unlimited access to abortion was similarly ahead of the opinion curve. Because of the organization's controversial reputation, the United Way has never included it among the beneficiaries of its annual fund drive.

One of Planned Parenthood's goals is to influence public opinion with respect to abortion as it did with respect to birth control. But Planned Parenthood has changed, too, in response to popular influence. The change in terminology from *birth control* to *planned parenthood* implied that the organization's purpose was to help people limit the size of their families, not to avoid having them. And Planned Parenthood long ago disassociated itself from the "eugenics" philosophy favored by Sanger, with its elitist and racist overtones. Faye Wattleton, one of PPFA's most prominent recent presidents, is an African-American woman. Today, the Planned Parenthood Federation of America has more than 50 affiliates in the United States. The International Planned Parenthood Federation includes more the 180 family planning associations in more than 150 countries. Together these affiliates form the largest, non-governmental health organization in the world. Their goal is to promote and provide sexual and reproductive health for all people in every part of the world.

SEE Abortion and Public Opinion; Birth Control Movement; Eugenics; *Griswold v. Connecticut*; Sanger, Margaret.

Further References. Margaret Sanger, *Margaret Sanger: An Autobiography* (New York, 1938). Margaret Sanger, *The Woman Rebel* (New York, 1976). Faye Wattleton, *Life on the Line* (New York, 1996).

VON BAKANIC

PLANNED PARENTHOOD OF CENTRAL MISSOURI v. DANFORTH (428 U.S. 52, 1976) is the first Supreme Court ruling on one of the many state laws seeking to discourage and restrict abortion which were passed after *Roe v. Wade*. This law, from Missouri, imposed several restrictions on both abortion providers and women seeking abortions. It required doctors to preserve the life and health of the fetus throughout pregnancy, defined viability as occurring "when the life of the unborn child may be continued indefinitely outside the womb by natural or artificial life-support systems" and required providers to keep records for public health officials of the number and type of abortions performed, The law also prohibited the use of saline amniocentesis, the standard method for abortions after the first trimester, and imposed several consent requirements. All women seeking abortions must consent in writing; married women needed their husbands' consent; and unmarried minors needed the consent of one parent.

The Court did not take this opportunity to retreat from the position it had taken three years earlier. *Danforth* upheld only the viability, women's consent, and record-keeping provisions. A majority of six, speaking through Justice Harry Blackmun, found the fetal care and saline amniocentesis regulations "inconsistent with the standards enumerated in *Roe v. Wade*." The same justices refused to allow the state "to give the spouse unilaterally the ability to prohibit the wife from terminating her pregnancy, when the state itself lacks that right." Five justices invalidated the parental consent requirement because it did not provide an alternative such as a judicial waiver. Later statutes took the hint, and the Court has relaxed the standard of review on state regulation. But *Danforth*'s ruling on spousal consent still stands.

SEE Abortion as a Reproductive Right; Abortion and Parental Consent and Notification; Abortion and Parental Involvement; Abortion and Spousal Consent; *Bellotti v. Baird*; *City of Akron v. Akron Center for Reproductive Health*; *H.L. v. Matheson*; *Planned Parenthood of Southeastern Pennsylvania v. Casey*; *Roe v. Wade*; *Thornburgh v. American College of Obstetrics and Gynecologists*; *Webster v. Reproductive Health Services*; Youth and Reproductive Rights

MELISSA MOORE

PLANNED PARENTHOOD OF KANSAS CITY v. ASHCROFT (462 U.S. 476, 1983) is one of a trio of cases that reaffirmed the fundamental right for a woman to obtain an abortion but also delineated the boundaries of that right. Along with *City of Akron v. Akron Center for Reproductive Health, Inc.* and *Simopoulos v. Virginia*, *Ashcroft* dealt with several state and local restrictions on abortion procedures. Specifically, Missouri's statute required that all second-trimester abortions be performed in a hospital; that a pathology report be completed after every abortion; that two physicians be present during every abortion procedure where the fetus is viable; and that parental or judicial consent be given before a minor could obtain an abortion. In an opinion authored by Justice Lewis Powell, the Supreme Court ruled six to three that the requirement that a second-trimester abortion be performed in a hospital was unconstitutional, reiterating its holding in *City of Akron*. However, the Court upheld the other three provisions of the Missouri law by a vote of five to four.

The Court ruled that the pathology report requirement was valid because it comported with generally accepted medical standards and furthered the state's health objectives. Therefore, this regulation did not place a significant burden upon the right to an abortion, despite the added cost to the patient. In upholding the rule requiring a second physician at the abortion of a viable fetus, the Court held that Missouri could legitimately protect the life of a fetus who survived the abortion procedure, even though instances of this are quite rare. It was reasonable, Powell wrote, for the state to assume that the first physician would concentrate on the mother and, therefore, to require the presence of a second physician who could focus on the child.

The Court's reasoning in this section of the opinion is neither convincing nor logically consistent. The Court relied upon accepted medical practices to justify its ruling on post-abortion pathology analysis, but ignored the fact that Missouri did not require two physicians to attend any other medical procedure, including childbirth. The Court's selective reliance upon generally accepted medical procedures disregarded the fact that the two-physician requirement is unnecessary, burdensome, and constitutionally overbroad.

Finally, the Court upheld the Missouri parental consent statute because it contained a judicial bypass procedure which allowed the minor child to demonstrate her maturity to consent to an abortion procedure to a judge without notifying her parents. Therefore, the law did not establish an absolute parental veto on a minor's decision. The Court had struck down parental consent statutes in other states because they did not include the judicial consent alternative. This provision was the first parental consent law that the Court sustained.

Ashcroft represents mixed results for both proponents and opponents of abortion rights. There is no question that the abortion cases of 1983 reaffirmed the constitutional validity of *Roe v. Wade*. However, *Ashcroft* also granted significant latitude to states wishing to impose medical and procedural restrictions upon the abortion process. The parental consent ruling, in particular, was a major setback for abortion rights supporters (not to mention children's rights advocates). Viewed in retrospect, *Ashcroft* foreshadows the scope and direction of future legal battles over reproductive choice.

The respondent in the case was John Ashcroft, then attorney general of Missouri. On February 1, 2001, Ashcroft became attorney general of the United States.

SEE Abortion and Parental Consent and Notification; Abortion and Parental Involvement; *City of Akron v. Akron Center for Reproductive Health*; *H.L. v. Matheson*; *Planned Parenthood of Southeastern Pennsylvania v. Casey; Roe v. Wade*; *Simopoulos v. Virginia; Thornburgh v. American College of Obstetricians and Gynecologists*; *Webster v. Reproductive Health Services*; Youth and Reproductive Rights.

Further References. David J. Garrow, *Liberty and Sexuality: The Right to Privacy and the Making of Roe v. Wade* (New York, 1994).

DAVID L. WEIDEN

PLANNED PARENTHOOD OF SOUTHEASTERN PENNSYLVANIA v. CASEY 505 U.S. 833, 1992) was the case that confounded prognosticators by *not* overturning *Roe v. Wade*. When the U.S. Supreme Court agreed to hear *Casey*, it was widely anticipated that this would be the occasion for reversing *Roe* and annulling the right to abortion. During the 1980s, abortion rights advocates viewed with increasing apprehension the shifting composition of the Court as conservative Justices replaced liberal members. By the time *Webster v. Reproductive Health Services* was heard in 1989, the abortion right appeared to have the support of only four Justices. However, the right survived in *Webster* because Justice Sandra Day O'Connor refused to join Chief Justice William Rehnquist and Justices Byron White, Antonin Scalia, and Anthony Kennedy in reexamining *Roe*. But three years later, after Justices William Brennan and Thurgood Marshall had retired and President George Bush had replaced them with David Souter and Clarence Thomas, it seemed inevitable that the seven to two margin that created

Roe would become a seven to two vote to overturn it. Instead, the Court stunned the public by reaffirming, though in weakened form, the abortion right recognized in *Roe*.

What brought the Court to this moment was a Pennsylvania statute that imposed several restrictions on the abortion right. It required that a woman seeking an abortion wait 24 hours after a state mandated counseling session to give her informed consent; that a married woman notify her husband before procuring an abortion; that a minor obtain the informed consent of one parent or the permission of a judge; and that facilities follow certain reporting requirements. Five abortion clinics and a physician challenged the statute as a deprivation of liberty under the Due Process Clause of the Fourteenth Amendment. But the Pennsylvania law was clearly not the only item the Court would review. Since the holding in *Roe* was implicated throughout this case, *Casey* invited the Court to reexamine and reevaluate this precedent as well.

In addressing both the validity of *Roe* and the constitutionality of the Pennsylvania statute, the Court fractured into three coalitions, each too small to form a clear majority. Therefore, it was a plurality of three, Justices O'Connor, Kennedy, and Souter, who spoke for the Court. Justices Harry Blackmun and John Paul Stevens joined them in sustaining *Roe*'s central holding that a woman has a right to abort a nonviable fetus. This majority of five unequivocally stated that both the liberty clause of the Fourteenth Amendment and the rule of *stare decisis* (adherence to precedent) compelled the recognition of an abortion right. Whatever reservations the justices had about *Roe*, O'Connor wrote, "the destiny of the woman must be shaped to a large extent on her own conception of her spiritual imperatives and her place in society."

However, these five justices departed significantly from *Roe* by accepting "the principle that the state has legitimate interests from the outset of the pregnancy in protecting the health of the woman and the life of the fetus that may become a child." This implicit rejection of *Roe*'s trimester scheme was made explicit by the plurality of three. They replaced it with the concept of a two-part pregnancy divided at the point of viability. The women's abortion right extended only to this point. The plurality opinion also effectively demoted abortion from its status as a constitutional right, replacing *Roe*'s strict scrutiny with an "undue burden" test. This approach invalidated only those laws that had the "purpose or effect of placing substantial obstacles in the path of a woman seeking an abortion of a nonviable fetus." Other less burdensome but still restrictive measures would be upheld. And, for the first time, discouraging abortion was recognized as a legitimate state purpose.

Applying these principles to the Pennsylvania statute, the plurality voted to uphold the waiting period, the informed consent provision, the parental consent rule, and the reporting requirements. Rehnquist, White, Scalia, and Thomas, all of whom wanted to reverse *Roe* outright, joined these portions of the opinion. But Stevens and Blackmun joined the plurality in creating a majority which voided as unduly burdensome the spousal notification provision.

Reactions to the decision were swift as both sides claimed defeat. "*Roe* is dead," lamented Patricia Ireland, president of the National Organization for Women. "Three Reagan-Bush appointees stabbed the pro-life movement in the back," declared Operation Rescue leader Randall Terry. But in truth, the decision was a compromise that recognized the abortion right even while it invited state legislatures to be creative in restricting it. Under that standard, the bans imposed by Louisiana, Utah, and Guam would be invalidated, but the many state laws that left poor women, rural women, and minors without access to abortions would be sustained under the tolerant undue burden test. Within hours of the decision, Democrats in Congress were promising to push passage of the Freedom of Choice Act, but it was clear that the real forums for the continuation of this battle would be the states. While promising years of future litigation, *Casey* seemed to signal that this would be the Court's final word on the constitutionality of the abortion right—at least for the foreseeable future.

SEE Abortion as a Reproductive Right; *City of Akron v. Akron Center for Reproductive Health; Roe v. Wade*; Undue Burden; *Wester v. Reproductive Health Services*; Youth and Reproductive Rights.

Further References. Barbara Hinkson Craig and David M. O'Brien, *Abortion and American Politics* (Chatham, N.J., 1993). Roy M. Mersky, ed., *A Documentary History of the Legal Aspects of Abortion in the United States: Planned Parenthood of Southeastern Pennsylvania v. Casey*, Vol. I-VI (Littleton, Colo., 1996).

SUSAN M. BEHUNIAK

POE v. ULLMAN (367 U.S. 397, 1961), narrowly upheld Connecticut's 1879 statute criminalizing the use of contraceptives. This controversial law, a relic of the "Comstock era" of anti-obscenity legislation, was rarely if ever enforced. Nevertheless, it had been the target of birth control activists and Yale University professionals for years. During the 1950s, law school professor Fowler V. Harper and Dr. C. Lee Buxton, the chair of the medical school's department of obstetrics and gynecology, joined the Planned Parenthood League of Connecticut (PPLC) in challenging the statute on both legislative and judicial fronts. Buxton convinced "Paul and Pauline Poe," (court-approved pseudonyms), who had lost three infants in three years from congenital defects, to join him in a test case to get the law declared unconstitutional. Dr. Buxton, the Poes, and three other couples filed cases in the state court. When Connecticut's supreme court upheld the law, the plaintiffs filed in federal court.

Only the Poes' and Dr. Buxton's case reached the U.S. Supreme Court. The Poes asserted their "constitutional right to marital intercourse in the privacy of their homes" and alleged that the statute unduly restricted their liberty and jeopardized their lives and health. The Court, however, disappointed the plaintiffs. The justices declined to reach the constitutional merits of the case. They dismissed the appeal on the grounds that the case did not present a justiciable question.

Justice Felix Frankfurter's opinion for the Court emphasized Connecticut's "undeviating policy of nullification" of the law. The resulting "lack of immediacy of the threat" of prosecution under the statute meant that the plaintiffs faced no real threat of injury if they violated the law.

Justices John Marshall Harlan II and William O. Douglas issued powerful dissents arguing that marital privacy was inherent in the "liberty" guaranteed by the Due Process Clause of the Fourteenth Amendment. These dissents, combined with the majority's observation's about the history of non-enforcement, paved the way for the case that would successfully challenge the statute four years later. The PPLC opened a highly publicized clinic in New Haven shortly after the Court's decision. The arrest of Dr. Buxton and Estelle Griswold, the clinic's director, initiated the case of *Griswold v. Connecticut.*

SEE *Griswold v. Connecticut; Eisenstadt v. Baird;* Privacy and Reproductive Rights.

Further References. David J. Garrow, *Liberty and Sexuality: The Right to Privacy and the Making of* Roe v. Wade (New York, 1994). Amy Kesselman, "Women versus Connecticut," in Rickie Solinger, ed., *Abortion Wars: A Half Century if Struggle, 1950- 2000* (Berkeley, 1998), 42-67.

KIRSTEN RAMBO

POELKER v. DOE. SEE *Beal v. Doe.*

POPULATION POLICY AND REPRODUCTIVE RIGHTS. In general, a "population policy" is an explicit attempt by a government to affect demographic trends. The usual ways in which governments do this are through immigration law and/or regulations designed to influence reproductive decision-making. The latter, typically referred to as "fertility policy," usually brings to mind efforts in poorer nations to combat rapid population growth by lowering birth rates. Some nations, however, attempt to raise fertility, whether in the entire population or only in some segments of the population.

Explicit fertility policies can involve an array of "carrots and sticks." Governments may offer tax breaks, family benefits, subsidized housing, low-cost child care and/or any number of other incentives to encourage people to have fewer or more children. On the other hand, leaders may impose more repressive measures, such as banning abortion or forcing women to have abortions, in order to achieve demographic goals. Currently, approximately 43 percent of the world's nations have explicit anti-natalist policies, designed to lower birthrates, and about 25 percent have pronatalist policies, explicitly intended to maintain or raise birthrates.

The United States has never adopted an explicit fertility policy. From a feminist perspective, that should be a good thing—because when the state becomes involved in trying to raise or lower fertility rates, women's ability to control their reproduction can be compromised. But though the United States has no explicit policy, it has enacted laws and regulations that could be interpreted to constitute an implicit policy. An implicit population policy exists when social policies, even though they may have no explicit demographic goals, have the potential to influence population trends. During the nineteenth century, for example, the U.S. government and many states instituted restrictions on contraceptives and abortion, thus implicitly encouraging people to have children. These restrictions, of course, continued well into the twentieth century.

In the absence of an explicit population policy, various interest groups have attempted to convince lawmakers to institute programs to influence fertility. Two of the most noteworthy include the eugenics movement of the late nineteenth and early twentieth centuries and the population control movement of the 1960s and 1970s. While these groups failed to attain the explicit policies they would have liked, they were successful in swaying public opinion and gaining the support of many lawmakers. Their efforts can be linked to implicit policies.

Eugenics claimed to promote a scientific agenda designed to "improve the human race;" but the "improvement" eugenicists sought was, in fact, highly correlated with race, ethnicity, and class. Early eugenicists promoted fertility control among poor immigrant women while accusing native-born, white women of "race suicide." By 1931, in response to the eugenics movement, 30 states had instituted laws calling for the sterilization of "socially inadequate" persons. By 1935, about 20,000 sterilizations had been performed. Contraceptives, though still subject to numerous restrictions, became more easily available during this same time period in part due to support by eugenicists, who hoped to discourage the poor and "less fit" from having children by helping them gain access to birth control. Somewhat ironically, Margaret Sanger was able to get support for her Planned Parenthood clinics by aligning herself with the eugenics movement.

After World War II, the eugenics movement was discredited by its association with Nazi atrocities, like the sterilization and even murder of "unfit" persons, and ceased to be a viable movement. However, vestiges of eugenics ideology have remained embedded in policy and medical practice over the past several decades. Some critics accused the population control movement of the 1960s and 1970s of being more concerned with controlling the fertility of "minority" groups and the working class than with controlling the fertility of the population as a whole. Women of color and poor women were often pressured by health care providers to be sterilized; sometimes, the procedure was performed without their knowledge or consent. Sterilization abuse continued at least until 1979, when the Department of Health, Education and Welfare (now Health and Human Services) issued regulations prohibiting sterilization without informed consent. During those same decades, white, middle-class women often complained of lack of access to sterilization. The women's health movement of the 1970s helped curb sterilization abuses and helped ensure access for those actively seeking the procedure.

One result of the population control lobby's efforts during the 1960s and 1970s was federal funding for contraceptives for the poor. Since the late 1960s, Medicaid has covered the entire cost of all contraceptives for Medicaid clients.

In addition, the United States provides funding, through Title X, for birth control clinics to distribute free or low-cost contraceptives to low-income clients. Meanwhile, middle-class women must often pay the cost of contraceptives out-of-pocket. Some have argued that federal policy on contraceptives is classist or racist—that the goal of the program is to reduce the numbers of poor and "minority" citizens. However, some conservatives would argue that providing welfare benefits to poor mothers encourages them to have more children—thus, they would say, the United States has an implicit pronatalist policy for its poorer citizens. Some activists, researchers, and politicians would like to see the United States adopt a fertility policy explicitly discouraging births to poor welfare mothers.

The history of population policy reminds us that while many view the decision to have children as a private matter, reproductive decision-making is, in fact, political. The demographic trends of today influence the population composition of tomorrow and are therefore important to political leaders and many activists. This connection is less obvious in the United States than it is in countries with explicit fertility policies. France, for example, has a pronatalist fertility policy; national leaders openly discuss tax laws, family leave policy, housing regulations and other government programs in terms of their potential affect on birth rates. In the United States, leaders are less likely openly to address the possible demographic implications of government programs. Nonetheless, the programs may have demographic consequences—whether intended or not—and thus deserve to be considered in any discussion of population policy.

SEE African-American Women and Reproductive Rights; Birth Control and African-American Women; Birth Control Movement; Eugenics; Federal Sterilization Guidelines; Sanger, Margaret; Sterilization Abuse.

Further References. Angela Y. Davis, *Women, Race, and Class* (New York, 1981). Linda Gordon, *Woman's Body, Woman's Right* (New York, rev. ed., 1990). Andrea Tone, ed., *Controlling Reproduction* (Wilmington, Del., 1997).

LESLIE KING

PREGNANCY DISCRIMINATION ACT OF 1978 (PDA). The passage of the Pregnancy Discrimination Act of 1978 (PDA) was prompted by the Supreme Court's decision in *General Electric v. Gilbert* (1976). In this case, the Court held that General Electric's disability insurance policy did not violate Title VII of the 1964 Civil Rights Act; denying disability benefits to pregnant women did not constitute sex-based discrimination. The Court rejected the Equal Employment Opportunity Commission's guidelines, issued in 1972, which characterized pregnancy as a disability and stated that denying pregnancy disability benefits violated Title VII. In refusing to equate pregnancy with other temporary disabilities, the Court ignored the financial burden of pregnancy on women workers and allowed employers to penalize them for having children. Within days after *Gilbert,* more than 300 groups formed a coalition to lobby Congress to reverse the Court's decision.

Composed mostly of union groups, the Campaign to End Discrimination Against Pregnant Workers also included members of the National Organization for Women, the National Women's Political Caucus, and the Women's Equity Action Alliance.

On October 31, 1978, Congress enacted the PDA. It declared that discrimination on the basis of pregnancy constituted illegal sex discrimination under Title VII. The heart of the PDA, § 701(k), provided; "women affected by pregnancy . . . shall be treated the same for all employment-related purposes . . . as other persons not so affected but similar in their ability or inability to work . . . " Thus, in enacting the PDA, Congress reversed *Gilbert* and placed pregnancy on a par with other disabilities. However, the law only required employers to cover pregnancy-related disabilities if they offered disability benefits to all workers.

Although the PDA stressed gender neutrality and nondiscrimination, Congress was also concerned about specifically promoting equal opportunity for women in the workplace. It intended the PDA, in the words of one senator, "to assure equality of employment opportunity and to eliminate those discriminatory practices which pose barriers to working women in their struggle to secure equality in the workplace." Passage of the PDA led to public debate about whether pregnant women workers could be afforded special benefits not given to men or non-pregnant women. In the 1970s, some states enacted laws granting pregnant workers reasonable periods of leave time, reinstatement, and protection of fringe benefits. Shortly before the PDA was passed, California enacted legislation guaranteeing female employees covered by Title VII up to four months of unpaid pregnancy disability leave and reinstatement. In *California Federal Savings and Loan Association v. Guerra* (1987), the Court held that California's law was consistent with the PDA's principle of nondiscrimination because while the PDA did not "require" preferential treatment, neither did it "prohibit" it.

An extension of the PDA, the Family and Medical Leave Act (FMLA), was enacted on February 5, 1993. In signing the bill, President Bill Clinton said: "now millions of our people will no longer have to choose between their jobs and their families." The FMLA provided that workers in companies with 50 or more employees were entitled to take up to 12 weeks of unpaid leave for their serious illness, or for the birth or adoption of a child, or to care for a sick family member. Although it furthers the nondiscrimination principle of the PDA, because it only provides for unpaid leaves of absence, the FMLA does not ease the financial burden of pregnancy on working women and falls short of achieving Title VII's goal of equal opportunity for women in the workplace.

SEE *California Federal Savings and Loan Association v. Guerra*; Family and Medical Leave Act of 1993; *General Electric v. Gilbert.*

Further References. Susan Gluck Mezey, *In Pursuit of Equality: Women, Public Policy, and the Federal Courts* (New York, 1993). Christine Neylon O'Brien and Gerald A. Madek, "Pregnancy Discrimination and Maternity Leave Laws," *Dickinson Law Review* 93 (Winter 1989): 311-337. Wendy W. Williams, "Equality's Riddle: Pregnancy and the Equal Treatment/Special

Treatment Debate," *New York University Review of Law and Social Change*, 13 (1984-85):325-380.

SUSAN GLUCK MEZEY

PRISONERS AND REPRODUCTIVE RIGHTS. The reproductive rights of women prisoners are limited in a variety of ways relative to the female population at large. These limitations operate along four main dimensions: (1) a male-dominated justice and prison system; (2) the limited services available to pregnant inmates; (3) the separation of incarcerated mothers from their children, sometimes including eventual termination of parenting rights, and (4) constraints on prisoners' access to birth control, abortion and sterilization that differ from those imposed on non-incarcerated women. All of these factors, singly and in combination, have a powerful impact on incarcerated women.

First, in a nation where judges, wardens and guards are still predominantly male, female offenders are especially vulnerable, from sentencing through incarceration. In addition to instances of sterilization imposed as part of sentencing, female prisoners are often exposed to sexual abuse and exploitation. Litigation and media reports—reflecting cultural bias of the public in the use of the headline *Sex Scandal* instead of *Human Rights Violation*—have revealed a systematic pattern of sexual exploitation and abuse in several state prison systems. This behavior ranges from the eliciting of sexual favors from inmates in return for contraband to outright rape, resulting in a number of unintended pregnancies. Inmates' concerns for their personal safety are particularly acute in maximum security units. Indeed, studies report that, while mothers incarcerated in the general-population prison system are mainly concerned with separation from their children, those confined to maximum security units are concerned with personal safety and even survival.

Second, health care for pregnant inmates is jeopardized by the reduced availability of specialty medical services compared with the general population. While court cases over health care disputes are helpful in drawing public attention to prisoners' problems, women prisoners rarely win them. For example, a Louisiana court ruled in *Williams v. Delcambre* (1982) that prison personnel did not violate a female inmate's constitutional rights by failing to provide her with medical care, and further that this failure did not cause the spontaneous abortion of the inmate's child. Another factor affecting female inmates' health is the high incidence of HIV and its effect on the fetus in case of pregnancy. The combination of these two health factors with the increased risk of unwanted pregnancy in the prison system reduces inmates' reproductive freedom relative to that of the general population.

Third, increasing numbers of prisoners become permanently separated from their children. While parental rights are terminated for some, incarceration in itself is insufficient cause for termination. The inability to arrange for relatives or friends to serve as caretakers may lead to the loss of parental rights for women prisoners. Many incarcerated mothers maintain a strong bond with their children with the help of family members. Others, despite generous prison visitation policies and the involvement of family members, become disconnected from their children—one third in a 1997 study of the Minnesota correctional system. Risk factors include chemical dependency, recidivism, and lack of consistency in intimate relationships. In states where correctional facilities provide less generous visitation, or where inmates are relocated to facilities distant from their loved ones, parent-child relations are even more difficult to maintain.

Fourth, prisoners' sexuality is regulated in a variety of ways by a combination of birth control, abortion and sterilization. Where such means are made available on a voluntary basis, one might draw the uneasy conclusion that female inmates have more reproductive freedom than women in the general population. However, the use of these techniques is not always voluntary in prison. Reproductive choice means that a woman can have a child when and where she wants. Coercive contraception takes away this choice. While Norplant—surgically implanted silicone capsules that release progestin over time—was hailed as a method of enhancing reproductive freedom, it has negatively affected the reproductive freedom of women convicted of child abuse or drug use during pregnancy since its approval by the Food and Drug Administration in 1991. Although judges claim to offer Norplant as a choice to avoid incarceration or to receive welfare benefits, the choice involved is a coercively structured one. Some women in prison may be there partly because they chose to refuse Norplant. The fact that male batterers are not punished for fetal abuse by forced contraception or sterilization indicates a persistent cultural bias against women.

Abortion is another contested issue for women prisoners. They are vulnerable both to coerced abortion and to denial of access to abortion. In 1998, an Ohio judge sentenced a pregnant woman to an unusually long prison sentence of six months to prevent her (successfully) from getting an abortion. Furthermore, prisoners are often the targets of the efforts of anti-choice legislators to deny access to abortion to marginalized subgroups of women. A recent rider to a congressional spending bill prohibited abortion for female federal inmates, except in cases of rape or threats to life. It is clear that the reproductive choices of female prisoners are reduced relative to those of the general population. Of course, this is true of prisoners' freedom in general; restrictions are part of the very purpose of punishment. But people do not lose all their rights when they are incarcerated, and there is no justification for women prisoners' losing the right to abortion or being forcibly sterilized. In fact, the status of prisoner entails the rudiments of certain benefits like access to food, clothing, shelter and health care. Overall, preservation of the reproductive rights of female inmates calls for a combination of efforts by policy makers in several areas, including safety, access to health care in general, specialized services to deal with the needs of pregnant prisoners, and sensitivity to the need for visitation and geographic proximity between mothers and their children. The enhanced attention given to these matters in the literature will help orient policy priorities accordingly.

SEE Breast-feeding and the Law; Class and Reproductive Rights; Fetal Abuse; Norplant; Sterilization Abuse.

Further References. Agnes L. Baro, "Spheres of Consent: An Analysis of the Sexual Abuse and Sexual Exploitation of Women Incarcerated in the State of Hawaii." *Women & Criminal Justice,* 8, #3 (1997): 61-84. Barbara J. Bowman, "The Impact of Mandatory Relocation on Female Maximum Security Inmates," *International Journal of Offender Therapy and Comparative Criminology,* 41, #4 (1997): 375-377. Mary Martin, "Connected Mothers: A Follow-Up Study of Incarcerated Women and Their Children," *Women & Criminal Justice* 8, #4 (1997): 1-23. Michael Welch, "Regulating the Reproduction and Morality of Women: The Social Control of Body and Soul," *Women & Criminal Justice* 9, #1 (1997): 17-38. *Williams v. Delcambre,* 413 So. 2nd 324 (La. App., 1982).

BRIGITTE H. BECHTOLD

PRIVACY AND REPRODUCTIVE RIGHTS. The word "privacy" appears nowhere in the U.S. Constitution or in any of the constitutions of the original states. However, English common law formed the basis for a right of privacy in the United States through its protections against eavesdropping, trespassing, and other violations of property rights. America's colonial experience prompted the adoption of the Fourth Amendment, with its guarantee against unreasonable searches and seizures and its requirement of probable cause for specific search warrants. The Fifth Amendment's protection against self-incrimination likewise incorporates a sense of personal autonomy and integrity. Expanding on this implied notion of privacy, lawyer (later Supreme Court justice) Louis Brandeis co-authored an 1890 *Harvard Law Review* article which argued that judges would eventually recognize "man's spiritual nature" and his "right to be let alone."

Griswold v. Connecticut (1965) marked the first U.S. Supreme Court case in which privacy and reproductive rights were at issue. The case challenged Connecticut's criminal law prohibiting the use of birth control devices or the dissemination of information about them. The Court held that the law violated a constitutional right of privacy. Seven justices found this right in the Constitution, but they did not all find it in the same place. Justice William O. Douglas's opinion for the Court discovered this right in the "penumbras and emanations" of the First, Third, Fourth, Fifth, and Ninth Amendments. These provisions created "zones of privacy" that protected "the sacred precincts of marital bedrooms" and encompassed "the notions of privacy surrounding the marriage relationship." Arthur Goldberg's concurring opinion emphasized the Ninth Amendment, which he read as a statement that the framers of the Constitution recognized additional fundamental rights that existed alongside those guarantees specifically mentioned in the Bill of Rights. Another concurring opinion, written by John Marshall Harlan II, invoked the controversial notion of "substantive due process." Harlan maintained that the right of privacy was implicit in the Fourteenth Amendment's

Due Process Clause; it was part of the "liberty" of which no state could deprive any person consistently with due process of law.

The dissenting opinions of Hugo Black and Potter Stewart represented the opposite side in the debate over the right of privacy. The dissenters came down firmly on the side of popular sovereignty over judicial activism. Black labeled the Connecticut law "offensive," and declared that he valued his own privacy. Nevertheless, he argued, the government had the power to restrict it in the absence of any "specific constitutional provision" protecting privacy. Black recommended passage of a constitutional amendment as a way out of this impasse. Likewise, Justice Stewart conceded that Connecticut's statute was "uncommonly silly." But it was up to the voters of the state "to persuade their elected representatives to repeal it."

Since *Griswold,* judicial activism and substantive due process have prevailed in a considerable number of decisions. Reproductive privacy, however, has experienced triumphs and losses. *Roe v. Wade* (1973) exemplifies a victory. Justice Harry Blackmun, writing for another seven-person majority which included Justice Stewart, based a woman's right to abortion on the guarantee of privacy implicit in the liberty component of the Fourteenth Amendment's Due Process Clause. But this right was not absolute; like First Amendment freedoms, it could be abridged when a "compelling state interest" existed. *Roe* created a trimester test by which to make this determination. In the first three months of pregnancy, the woman's right to privacy and autonomy over her own body meant that the decision to obtain an abortion was solely between her and her physician. In the second trimester, the state's interest in maternal health could legitimate regulations "reasonably" related to preserving the health of pregnant women. By the last trimester, the state's interest in protecting the life of a viable fetus justified the proscription of abortion, except "to preserve the life or health of the mother."

The Court's refusal to allow legislatures to resolve "the difficult question of when life begins" by basing their laws on the premise that life begins at conception angered opponents of abortion and disturbed numerous students of the democratic process. The pro-life movement hoped, and pro-choice groups feared, that the Court (with six members appointed by the conservative Reagan/Bush administrations) would overturn *Roe* in 1992's *Planned Parenthood of Southeastern Pennsylvania v. Casey.* At issue were regulations that applied even in the first trimester, including a 24-hour waiting period for, and informed consent of, women seeking abortions. Married women had to notify their spouses that they intended to abort their pregnancy, and minors had to obtain the informed consent of one parent.

In ruling on the Pennsylvania statute, the Court fractured into three distinct camps. A bloc of four dissenters, led by Chief Justice William Rehnquist, voted to uphold all of the abortion strictures and strike down the *Roe* precedent. Two justices, led by *Roe*'s author Justice Blackmun, would have upheld *Roe* in its entirety and used it to invalidate the Pennsylvania law. In a highly unusual step, Justices Sandra Day O'Connor, David Souter, and Anthony Kennedy drafted, and then read from the bench, their controlling opinion. It upheld all of the Pennsylvania restrictions (except spousal notification), but asserted that the central holding of *Roe* must remain intact in order to follow the Court's tradition of confirming its own precedents as a way of protecting its legitimacy. Moreover, the trio's opinion noted that society had come to rely on the right to abortion established in *Roe*. Yet the plurality opinion did not leave *Roe* intact. It jettisoned Blackmun's trimester framework and replaced it with the "undue burden" test. Henceforth, the Court would evaluate state abortion restrictions by whether they had "the purpose or effect of placing a substantial obstacle in the path of a woman seeking an abortion of a nonviable fetus." This ruling had the effect of demoting abortion from the status of a constitutional right, abridgeable only for compelling reasons, to something ranking somewhere between fundamental rights and ordinary interests that the state can override whenever it has a legitimate reason. The text of *Casey* reaffirmed judicial activism and the privacy doctrine. The subtext, however, showed the indirect but powerful influence of the democratic process on the judiciary.

SEE Abortion as a Reproductive Right; Abortion and Public Opinion; *Eisenstadt v. Baird*; *Griswold v. Connecticut*; Human Life Bill (Amendment); McCorvey, Norma; *Planned Parenthood of Southeastern Pennsylvania v. Casey*; Undue Burden.

Further References. Louis Brandeis and Charles Warren. "The Right to Privacy," *Harvard Law Review*, 4 (1890-91): 193-220. John Hart Ely, *On Constitutional Ground* (Princeton, N.J., 1997). David M. O' Brien and Barbara Hinkson Craig, *Abortion and American Politics* (Chatham, N.J., 1993).

BARBARA A. PERRY

PRO-LIFE FEMINISM could be described as the belief that abortion is injustice against fetuses caused by injustice against women. Although it has become a minority, and often invisible, stance, pro-life feminism was actually the majority opinion in the American women's movement for most of its history. Susan B. Anthony, Elizabeth Cady Stanton, Dr. Elizabeth Blackwell, Victoria Woodhull, Matilda Joslyn Gage and other early feminists were practically unanimous in opposing what they termed "child-murder" and "infanticide." They strongly believed, as Woodhull stated, that "the rights of children as individuals begin while yet they remain the fetus."

Early feminists' anti-abortion stance was of a piece with their opposition to war, the death penalty, slavery, and cruelty to animals. Most of all, their concern for fetal life was interwoven with a deep concern for female life. Blackwell spoke of abortion as "a gross perversion and destruction of motherhood" which violated the pregnant woman as much as the fetus. While supporting legal restrictions upon abortion, early feminists focused more upon alleviating its root causes. Often risking prosecution under the "anti-obscenity" Comstock Act, they promoted "voluntary motherhood": the right of women to choose whether and when to risk conception. Early feminists provided education about prenatal development, family planning, and other aspects of sexual and reproductive physiology. They promoted a view of pregnancy as a normal, healthy condition rather than a disease state which necessarily excluded women from the public sphere. They championed women's right to earn decent wages and develop their whole range of talents while raising families. They challenged society's tolerance of men's parental irresponsibility and sexual coercion of women while women and children involved in crisis pregnancies, especially nonmarital ones, were ostracized and deprived of the most basic material needs.

It was not until the current wave of the women's rights movement that the majority of feminists considered a moral and legal right to abortion an essential part of voluntary motherhood. The complex reasons for this change of opinion await thorough exploration by historians. Anxieties about overpopulation played some role, although some feminists, especially women of color, have criticized population control as a racist, classist threat to reproductive freedom. Perhaps more importantly, illegal abortion was a pivotal life experience for many 1960's and 1970's era feminists, one which awakened them to the severe hardships women faced before, during and after pregnancy.

Support for abortion rights has never been unanimous among feminists, however. From the start of the current feminist movement, a significant minority of feminists has argued that abortion is an act of life taking with negative physical and emotional repercussions for woman as individuals and as a gender. This steadily growing feminist minority has described abortion not as a choice, but as a product and perpetrator of the reproductive hardships it is meant to resolve. The National Organization for Women (NOW) did not adopt an abortion-rights platform until a year after its 1966 founding, and then only after heated debate. One of NOW's founding members, the Chicana activist Graciela Olivarez, objected that legalized abortion would sabotage "an equal sharing of responsibilities by and as men and women." She added: "To talk about the 'wanted' and the 'unwanted' child smacks too much of bigotry and prejudice. Many of us have experienced the sting of being 'unwanted.' . . . The poor cry out for justice, and we respond with legalized abortion." Feminist leaders who expressed similar views in the 1970's included Fannie Lou Townsend Hamer, the African-American civil rights leader and co-founder of the National Women's Political Caucus; Constance Redbird Uri, a Cherokee-Choctaw physician who exposed the federal government's sterilization abuse of Native Americans; and Alice Paul, author of the original 1923 Equal Rights Amendment.

In 1972, Pat Holtz, an Ohio woman who had been expelled from her local NOW chapter for her anti-abortion views, joined with linguist Catherine Callahan to found a national organization for feminists with similar views. Feminists for Life (FFL) is today the oldest, largest and most visible pro-life feminist organization. Others include the Feminism and Nonviolence Studies Association and the Pro-life Alliance of Gays and Lesbians. All of these organizations are affiliated with the Seamless Garment Network, a loose coalition of groups and individuals whose "consistent life ethic" opposes abortion, militarism, the death penalty, poverty, racism, and euthanasia and strives to create nonviolent alternatives to these practices.

Contemporary pro-life feminists have adopted a range of positions on the legal status of abortion, from a ban on almost all abortions to a policy of "permit-but-discourage." However, these feminists share a general dissatisfaction with *Roe v. Wade* (1973). They criticize the decision not only for its failure to give due recognition to an interest in protecting fetal life, but also for casting abortion as an issue of privacy. This approach, they argue, absolves the community of responsibility to provide women with better alternatives, ones that do not occasion the grief and trauma so often involved in abortion.

Whatever their views of abortion legislation, pro-life feminists give the highest priority to alleviating the demand for abortion by transforming the social context in which women conceive, bear and raise children. FFL, for example, has campaigned for child support enforcement, parental leave, and anti-domestic violence initiatives. Its College Outreach Program mobilizes parenting and adoption resources for students who wish to continue their unplanned pregnancies without interrupting their education. FFL has also joined with the American Civil Liberties Union to support single pregnant teens barred from the National Honor Society on charges of "immorality."

The intense polarization of the abortion debate has often led both pro-choice feminists and anti-abortion activists to dismiss pro-life feminists as walking oxymorons. However, pro-life feminists have successfully promoted dialogue between the anti-abortion and women's rights movements, allowing the discovery of common ground. Through dialogue, pro-choice feminists have developed more respectful attitudes toward pro-life feminists. For example, abortion rights activists assert, not that all true feminists must support legalized abortion, but that asking women to refrain from abortion in the present imposes too many hardships on them, or that the goal of eventually eliminating abortion altogether is too idealistic. Pro-life feminists have responded: "There is no way to peace; peace is the way." Like the history of the American women's movement, this contemporary dialogue confirms that disagreement between pro-choice feminists and those who identify themselves as pro-life feminists is an integral part of the women's movement. The two groups differ, not over voluntary motherhood, but over the validity of abortion as a means to that shared end.

SEE Abortion as a Reproductive Right; Abortion and Public Opinion; Class and Reproductive Rights; *Roe v. Wade;* Sterilization Abuse.

Further References. Feminists for Life of America, http:/www.feministsforlife.org. Angela Kennedy, ed., *Against the Tide: Feminist Dissent on the Issue of Abortion* (Dublin, 1997). Rachel MacNair, Mary Krane Derr, and Linda Naranjo-Huebl, eds., *Prolife Feminism Yesterday and Today* (New York, 1995).

MARY KRANE DERR

PROTECTIVE LABOR LEGISLATION. During the nineteenth century, social reformers pushed for legislation to protect American workers laboring long hours under sweatshop conditions for low wages. Protective legislation took many forms in various states, including maximum hours and minimum wages, time off for breaks and meals, and weight-lifting limits. Although some laws applied to all workers, many applied only to women. Organized labor supported protective legislation for all workers, but it also endorsed protective legislation applicable only to women when it gave male workers competitive advantages over female workers.

Protective legislation applicable only to women was often easier to enact than general legislation. Employers were less vehement in their opposition, partly because women-only legislation was consistent with cultural attitudes toward the "weaker sex." For a time, such legislation also more likely to survive constitutional challenge. In 1905, the Supreme Court struck down state maximum hours legislation applicable to all workers in certain jobs, but three years later it sustained a similar statute applicable only to women because "healthy mothers are essential to vigorous offspring, the physical well-being of woman becomes an object of public interest and care in order to preserve the strength and vigor of the race" (*Muller v. Oregon*, 1908). This opinion clarifies the classic relationship between protective legislation and women's reproductive rights; women's work responsibilities were limited so that they might be healthier and better mothers.

Many of the progressive reformers who fought for protective legislation, like Jane Addams, Lillian Wald, and Florence Kelley, were women who provided direct services to poor and immigrant communities. These activists were particularly concerned about the labor conditions of women who worked a "second shift" at home. Often, women's labor was beneficial to women. If employers continued to employ women for jobs despite requirements of special treatment—such as breaks every four hours or only ten hours of work a day—such legislation was probably good for most women. But if employers found the limits onerous enough to switch to male workers (which would usually require paying higher wages), women were hurt by being denied employment. Laws banning women from certain occupations, such as night work in factories, hurt women by closing doors to relatively well-paying jobs. There is no way to assess whether such legislation was, overall, good or bad for women.

Protective legislation became a source of frustration among women activists in the decades after suffrage was achieved in 1919. The National Women's Party, organized by Alice Paul during the final drive for suffrage, proposed an Equal Rights Amendment (ERA) to the U.S. Constitution during the early 1920s. Supports and opponents of the ERA agreed that it would invalidate protective legislation applicable only to women workers. Supporters believed, with some justification, that protective legislation hurt women workers, closing jobs to them and giving men an edge in employment. These activists tended to be elite women who had little if any contact with the working-class women covered by the legislation. ERA supporters included many Republicans opposed in general to government regulation of business.

Opponents of the ERA included progressives, women who had worked in settlement houses providing direct services workers and their families, organized labor, Democrats with close links to both the reform movement and labor, and social conservatives opposed to changes in women's status. Progressive women feared that ERA would eliminate protections needed by women workers as well as sex-specific legislation beneficial to women in other areas, such as the obligation of a husband to support his wife and children. More fundamentally, the individualistic approach of the ERA was inconsistent with progressives' basic frames of reference and their analysis of social causes for class problems. The vast majority of the members of the suffrage coalition and of politically active women opposed ERA for these reasons during the 1920s.

From the 1920s through the early 1960s, women activists remained divided on the ERA. By the early sixties, both sides were anxious to move forward. The Presidential Commission on the Status of Women, appointed by President Kennedy, adopted a compromise proposed by Pauli Murray, a black lawyer and longtime activist in the civil rights movement. Murray suggested that rather than seeking an ERA *now*, women could use the existing Equal Protection Clause of the Fourteenth Amendment to argue that laws discriminating against women were unconstitutional. This approach was seen as giving the Supreme Court the leeway to strike the bad and uphold the good so that both sides could climb on the same bandwagon. By 1969, courts were beginning to strike sex-specific protective legislation as inconsistent with Title VII of the Civil Rights Act of 1964, which banned discrimination on the basis of sex in employment. By 1973, such cases had made the decades-old battle moot.

Ironically, because of Title VII's ban on sex discrimination in employment, new protective policies applicable only to women emerged as the old disappeared. The new polices were adopted by employers as women moved into previously male jobs in unionized industries dealing with hazardous chemicals and as pregnant women gained the right to work under a 1978 amendment to Title VII, which redefined sex discrimination to include discrimination on the basis of pregnancy. These policies took one of two forms. If the workforce was traditionally male, some employers excluded all fertile women from jobs seen as hazardous. If the workforce was traditionally female (for example, nurses giving X-rays), some employers fired pregnant workers. Employers "protected" fetal health when women were marginal workers (because vying for traditionally male jobs or because pregnant). In adopting fetal vulnerability policies, employers ignored women's economic responsibilities to their living children, the actual needs and alternatives facing women denied employment, the (comparable) hazards in low-paying women's jobs, and the risks associated with paternal employment. The lower federal courts held that reasonable policies to protect fetal health were legal. But in *International Union, UAW v. Johnson Controls, Inc.*, (1991), the Supreme Court held that such policies discriminate on the basis of sex in violation of Title VII.

Title VII replaced the old *Muller* doctrine with a rule of strict formal equality for men and women workers. Whereas law once treated women as a special class of workers because of their reproductive role, law now treats women as if they had no reproductive role. As a result, reproductive hazards in the workplace continue to be a problem for women. Even when pregnant, women have only the right *to* jobs. Women working in hazardous jobs have no right to transfer to an equivalent less-hazardous position during pregnancy. There is no duty to accommodate the needs of pregnant workers under Title VII, though in other contexts, discrimination law does sometimes impose such a duty. Until there is such a duty, an important aspect of reproductive freedom—the ability to safely bear a child—will continue to elude women workers.

SEE American Cyanamid; Employment and Reproductive Rights; *International Union, UAW v. Johnson Controls, Inc., Muller v. Oregon*; Title VII and Reproductive Rights.

Further References. Mary Becker, "From *Muller v. Oregon* to Fetal Vulnerability Policies," *University of Chicago Law Review*, 53 (1986): 1219-1273. Mary Becker, "Reproductive Hazards After *Johnson Controls*," *Houston Law Review* 31 (1994): 43- 97. Mary Becker, "The Sixties Shift to Formal Equality and the Courts: An Argument for Pragmatism and Politics," *William and Mary Law Review*, 40 (October 1998): 209- 277. Eleanor Flexner, *Century of Struggle: The Woman's Rights Movement in the United States* (Cambridge, Mass., rev. ed. 1975).

MARY BECKER

R

RELIGION AND REPRODUCTIVE RIGHTS have proved a controversial mix in American politics and culture. The nature and extent of reproductive control raises questions about personhood itself. Questions like these are fundamentally important to religious traditions of all kinds. The issue of birth control is illustrative. Contraception has been discouraged, if not rejected outright, throughout most of the history of the Jewish and Christian faiths. Both traditions have interpreted scriptural mandates—for example, God's command to "be fruitful and multiply" in Genesis 1:28—as precluding the use of artificial barriers to conception. Indeed, many early church fathers and rabbinical scholars insisted that it was immoral to engage in sexual intercourse without the intent to conceive.

The Roman Catholic Church officially reaffirmed many of these historical teachings as recently as 1968, when Pope Paul VI issued the controversial encyclical, *Humanae Vitae*. The Church today forbids the use of artificial birth control, but does make provision for "natural family planning" (monitoring changes in a woman's temperature or cervical mucus to determine the time of ovulation). Despite its official position, however, public opinion surveys indicate that most self-identified American Catholics disagree with the Church hierarchy on the issue. Their support (and use) of artificial birth control is on a par with that of the majority of their contemporary Protestant and Jewish counterparts. Most of these religionists do not view sexual intercourse as linked necessarily to procreation. Hence, at least within the marital relationship, the use of birth control is generally considered acceptable and legal restrictions have met with relatively little support.

Abortion, of course, is another matter. The Catholic Church, an early leader in the abortion debate, began to develop its political opposition to abortion rights in the 1960s, many years before the landmark *Roe v. Wade* decision in 1973. The Second Vatican Council, Pope John XXIII's church reform campaign in the early 1960s, declared abortion an "unspeakable crime." The U.S. bishops responded with a series of statements against abortion rights beginning in the late 1960s. Many in the Catholic laity (including such notables as Eunice Shriver, sister of John F. Kennedy) heeded the message and pushed for closer attention to the issue.

Religious opposition to abortion rights became increasingly organized in the early 1970s. Plans for a "Human Life Amendment" to the U.S. Constitution surfaced even before *Roe* was decided. In 1973, the bishops helped create the National Right to Life Committee (NRLC), which served as an umbrella organization for myriad groups formed at the state level to oppose repeal of abortion laws. Today the NRLC is a lay organization that claims members from a wide variety of faiths, but the bishops' leadership remains decisive. Soon after the *Roe* decisions, other organizations connected to religious traditions—the American Life League, Catholics United for Life, the Christian Action Council, the Moral Majority, and Concerned Women for America, among many others—joined the NRLC in active opposition to abortion rights. While strongly committed Catholics and evangelical Protestants continue to be the most prominent religious voices against abortion, some Muslim and Orthodox Jewish groups have also expressed their opposition. (It should be noted, however, that the low numbers, scarce resources, and particular interests of many minority religions prevent a highly visible presence on the issue of abortion).

Religious groups in favor of abortion rights include such organizations as Catholics for a Free Choice and most mainline Protestant and liberal Jewish groups. In 1973, these groups formed a broad-based alliance, the Religious Coalition for Reproductive Choice (RCRC), to counter pro-life politics. There is increasing political sophistication among religious proponents of abortion rights, but members of the RCRC have only a fraction of their opponents' resources.

Tactically, the NRLC and similar organizations focus on legislative lobbying, electioneering, public education, and litigation at both national and state levels. Unlike the NRLC, some groups are more inclined to unconventional tactics, and this has caused considerable tension among opponents of abortion rights. Religious leaders have regularly denounced civil disobedience—blocking access to or occupying abortion clinics, among other things—for its apparent ineffectiveness and its propensity to violence. Nevertheless, civil disobedience became an increasingly attractive approach throughout the past two decades, reaching a high water mark with the "Summer of Mercy" in 1993, an effort by Operation Rescue and its leader, fundamentalist Randall Terry, to shut down abortion clinics.

The theological foundations for opposition to abortion are quite complex. Most traditions argue that the fetus is an individual human life from the moment of conception and therefore deserving of legal protection. Yet, even though a religious tradition may oppose abortion in principle, it may discourage its followers from expressing that opposition in the political arena. This partially explains why many fundamentalist and evangelical Protestants were absent from the abortion debate in the years immediately following *Roe*. They were activated only after religious leaders, including the Rev. Jerry Falwell of the Moral Majority, exhorted them to greater political awareness and direct involvement. In contrast, the Catholic Church had a stronger tradition of translating theological tenets into policy agendas.

It is also important to recognize that the rhetoric of the abortion debate, especially its highly charged "rights talk," can mask the underlying religious values of participants. The language of "pro-choice," for example, does not always convey the expressed religious beliefs of abortion rights advocates. Some religious groups argue in favor of abortion rights by invoking respect for "individual conscience," a phrase which has traditionally referred to actions taken out of a sense of religious obligation, not choice.

Similarly, declaring a "right to life" is a political and legal expedient, but it does not fully capture the notion of the "sanctity" or "sacredness" of human life embodied in most religious traditions. Some activists have sought to deepen the "pro-life" stance by showing that it does not imply a single-issue politics. The "seamless garment," for example, was an idea championed by the late Cardinal Joseph Bernardin, archbishop of Chicago, as a consistent life ethic that coupled opposition to abortion, the death penalty, weapons of mass destruction, and euthanasia with support for the welfare of the poor. Pope John Paul II has also articulated a position on the dignity of human persons that has implications not only for abortion but also for a host of other issues (see, for example, his encyclical, *Evangelium Vitae*, or "The Gospel of Life," published in 1995). These uniquely religious understandings have implications for various new reproductive technologies as well. There is a direct connection between the values underlying the contraception and abortion debates and religious views of such issues as *in vitro* fertilization, artificial insemination, and surrogacy. In *Donum Vitae* (1987), for example, the Catholic Church urged its members to reject *in vitro* fertilization and artificial insemination as alternatives to conception through marital intercourse. Both alternatives would separate the "unitive" meaning of sex—a sacred bond between a man and woman—from its "procreative" implications. (Surrogacy is rejected by the Catholic Church and many Protestants and Muslims for similar reasons).

Moreover, embryos are often discarded in the *in vitro* process, raising the specter of abortion for some religious groups. To solve this problem, some groups have encouraged the legal adoption of frozen embryos. Other groups, including the Christian Medical and Dental Association, find artificial insemination and *in vitro* fertilization permissible as long as it is done between married partners and the couple intends to attempt implantation of all frozen embryos. Still others, especially those religious groups in favor of abortion rights, embrace new reproductive technologies as opening the door to a greater range of choices for women.

SEE Abortion as a Reproductive Right; Abortion and Political Conflict; Abortion and Public Opinion; Abortion and Political Rhetoric; Birth Control Movement;

Ectogenesis; Human Life Bill/Amendment; National Right to Life Committee; Surrogate Motherhood.

Further References. Timothy Byrnes and Mary Segers, *The Catholic Church and the Politics of Abortion: A View from the States* (Boulder, Colo.,1992). John Noonan, Jr., ed., *The Morality of Abortion: Legal and Historical Perspectives* (Cambridge, Mass., 1970).; James Risen and Judy L. Thomas, *Wrath of Angels: The American Abortion War* (New York, 1998). Kathy Rudy, *Beyond Pro-Life and Pro-Choice: Moral Diversity in the Abortion Debate* (Boston, 1996).

KEVIN R. DEN DULK

RESTELL, MADAME. "Madame Restell" was the name by which "New York's notorious abortionist" was known. She was born Anna Trow in 1812 in Painswick, England into a farm family. Anna married her first husband, Henry Sommers, before she was 20. The couple left England for the United States and arrived in New York City in 1831. Sommers died two years later. Anna seems then to have taken up midwifery in order to support herself, and may have begun her practice of assisting women with birth control and abortion during this period. She continued her work after she remarried, to Charles Lohman, a printer. Anna advertised in the New York papers in the early 1830s, under the name "Madame Restell." The origin of the name is a mystery, but Allan Keller, one of her biographers, speculates that it may have sounded more exotic than her legal name, or that she may have wanted to use an alias in order to safeguard her privacy.

Madame Restell offered the very services in demand among many American women of the period: abortion, birth control, and the placement of illegitimate children. The first two of these were illegal at the time; the third was illegal in the way that Restell was accused of practicing it. Early in Restell's career, Mary Applegate, an unhappy young mother, accused Restell of having given her infant to unknown persons without her consent. Restell was charged with numerous offenses, but eventually the charges were all mysteriously dropped. During her lifetime, several other women charged her with the same offense; in each case the charges were either dropped or not filed. In 1847, Restell was charged with aborting the child of Maria Bodine. Amid a media circus, Restell's attorney attacked Bodine's credibility and reputation, obtaining his client's conviction on a misdemeanor instead of the felony with which she was originally charged. Restell spent 12 months in prison, while her activities remained front page news. She continued to be the object of public derision for the rest of her life.

Anthony Comstock, the well-known crusader against "obscenity," brought Restell's career to an end in 1878 by representing himself as an impoverished man whose wife needed assistance with an abortion. When she agreed to help, he had her arrested and charged with the illegal possession of certain medical instruments. On April 1, 1878 she committed suicide, apparently unwilling or unable to face the prospect of yet another trial.

Restell was a pioneer in the struggle for women's reproductive freedom. She and individuals like her represented a source of assistance for both rich and poor women who found themselves faced with unwanted children at a time when neither public nor private services were available to address the problem. She risked her life and liberty by providing desperately needed but illegal services. Her motivations seem not to have been solely the desire for money, since she seems always to have assisted those who could not pay her. She is certainly among the victims of Comstock's exaggerated sense of morality which dominated the United States during the last quarter of the nineteenth century.

SEE Abortion as a Reproductive Right; Abortion Self-Help Movement; Birth Control Movement; Jane (collective); Sanger, Margaret.

Further References. Frederic Dan Huntington, *Restel's* [sic] *Secret Life: A True History of Her from Birth to Her Awful Death by Her Own Wicked Hands* (Philadelphia, 1897). Allan Keller, *Scandalous Lady: The Life and Times of Madame Restell, New York's Most Notorious Abortionist* (New York: 1981). Marvin Olasky, "Advertising Abortion during the 1830s and 1840s: Madame Restell Builds a Business," *Journalism History* 13 (Summer 1986): 49-55. Madame Restell, defendant, *The Wonderful Trial of Caroline* [sic] *Lohman, alias Restell*, (reported in full for the National Police Gazette) (New York, 1847).

CHRISTINE A. CORCOS

ROE v. WADE (410 U.S. 113, 1973): On January 22, 1973, the U.S. Supreme Court handed down a landmark decision declaring virtually all restrictive abortion laws unconstitutional. *Roe v. Wade* brought to a close a series of debates, initiated in the mid-sixties and conducted, for the most part, among reformers and an elite of concerned professionals, most of whom considered this a question of public health and safety. *Roe* also followed a nationwide trend toward liberalized abortion and, in this respect, merely accelerated what might otherwise have been a slow, uneven process of state-by-state reform. With public opinion polls favoring liberalization and with opposition to abortion seeming both small and sectarian, there was every indication that the Court's action in *Roe* would simply resolve the issue. And, in one sense, it did: the Supreme Court narrowly defined abortion as a medical issue and, drawing on what it took to be the medical and legal history of the practice, organized or dismissed the many competing interests at stake in the case accordingly. Almost immediately, however, this somewhat abridged definition and the priorities it established were widely criticized; within a decade, both would be forcefully challenged in the context of a sometimes violent, nationally divisive struggle over the rights of prenatal life.

Speaking for the majority in *Roe v. Wade*, Justice Harry Blackmun declared that the right of privacy recognized in *Griswold v. Connecticut* eight years previously "is broad enough to encompass a woman's decision whether or not to terminate her pregnancy." Blackmun noted that stringent laws proscribing abortion were of relatively recent vintage and had their origins not in ancient or even common law, but "in statutory changes effected for the most part in the latter part of the nineteenth century." Throughout the major portion of that century, as at the time of the adoption of the constitution, "women enjoyed a substantially broader right to terminate their pregnancies than in most states in [1973]." What minimal legal regulation existed followed the English common law doctrine of "quickening" and proscribed the undertaking only of late abortions—those performed after the fetus had manifested some semblance of existence through movement, usually sometime during the fourth and sixth months of gestation. Aside from this rarely enforced and virtually unenforceable standard, abortion was treated both popularly and legally with a certain degree of indifference.

Why, then, was it criminalized? As Blackmun read the medical and legal history, the original impetus for state curtailment of abortion in the nineteenth century had to do with public safety: the high mortality of women who were undergoing the procedure in the absence of widely accepted antiseptic techniques. In Blackmun's words, "a state's real concern in enacting a criminal abortion law was to protect the pregnant woman . . . to restrain her from submitting herself to a procedure that placed her life in jeopardy." This concern, he maintained, had largely disappeared in the wake of modern medical techniques, "even while other important state interests in the area of health and medical standards remained."

Arguing that abortion was "in all its aspects . . . inherently and primarily a medical decision," a decision in which the dual questions of public health and medical safety were paramount, the Court formulated a fairly straightforward scheme of pregnancy that divided the management and regulation of the procedure by trimester. In the first trimester of pregnancy, a woman's right to determine whether or not to terminate a pregnancy, *in consultation with her physician*, was established over any possible state interest in regulating abortion. In the second trimester, the Court reasoned that the dangers of abortion were relatively greater to maternal health than during the first. For this reason, the state could legitimately impose certain regulations on abortion, but only those "reasonably related" to the preservation and protection of a woman's health. In the third stage of pregnancy, following viability or that point at which the fetus is "potentially able to live outside the womb, albeit with artificial aid" the state's interest in protecting potential life prevailed. The undertaking of any abortion during the final 12 weeks of pregnancy might, therefore, be prohibited, except when necessary to preserve the life or health of the woman.

Roe v. Wade did not grant women an unlimited right to control their bodies. In fact, it was to medical professionals rather than to women that the Court acceded control of pregnancy ("the abortion decision and its effectuation must be left to the medical judgment of the pregnant's woman's attending physician"). Nevertheless, the radical potential of the ruling was unmistakable. *Roe* provided many women with an expanded sense of freedom, power, and control over their lives. *Roe* appeared to challenge, if only symbolically, traditional assumptions regarding the organization of gender and sexuality. Although legalized abortion did not and can not in itself guarantee reproductive freedom for women, the acrimonious debates of the last two decades over the personhood status of pre-natal life nevertheless demonstrate the degree to which it is, unquestionably, an essential constituent of that freedom.

Finally, any rendering of *Roe v. Wade* would not be complete without men-tioning the issue of fetal personhood. Although this issue has transformed the meaning of abortion and now dominates contemporary debate, it was dismissed by the Court in *Roe* as legally irrelevant. The Court determined that within the language and meaning of the Fourteenth Amendment, the word "person" did not include the unborn and, further, that the "unborn [had] never been recognized in law as persons in the whole sense." As Blackmun put the matter: "We need not resolve the difficult question of when human life begins. When those trained in the respective disciplines of medicine, philosophy, and theology are unable to arrive at any consensus, the judiciary, at this point in man's knowledge, is not in a position to speculate as to the answer." Many assume that it is only a matter of time before this question is definitively settled by advances in science and med-icine. It seems more likely that even with such advances, conclusive answers to the many issues that together comprise what we call "the issue of abortion" will remain beyond our reach.

SEE Abortion as a Reproductive Right; Abortion and Political Rhetoric; Abortion and Public Opinion; *Griswold v. Connecticut*; *Planned Parenthood of Southeast-ern Pennsylvania v. Casey*; Privacy and Reproductive Rights; *Webster v. Reproductive Health Services*.

Further References. Jay L. Garfield and Patricia Hennessey, *Abortion: Moral and Legal Perspectives* (Amherst, Mass., 1984). David J. Garrow, *Liberty and Sex-uality: The Right to Privacy and the Making of* Roe v. Wade (New York, 1994). Kristin Luker, *Abortion and the Politics of Motherhood* (Berkeley, Calif., 1984). James C. Mohr, *Abortion in America: The Origins and Evolution of National Pol-icy* (New York, 1978).

VALERIE HARTOUNI

RU-486 (mifepristone or mifegyne) is a progesterone receptor blocker used to induce abortion. It is a synthetic hormone, given in pill form, that causes the resorption or shedding of uterine lining, thus inducing menstruation, or, if the sub-ject is pregnant, abortion. Named for Roussel-Uclaf, the French company that developed the pill, it was approved for use in France and other European coun-tries beginning in 1988. Although the U.S. Food and Drug Administration (FDA) finally approved the drug in 1997, it was not available for use in the United States until November 1999. Since late 1999, it is becoming widely used as a non-surgical form of abortion at clinics and hospitals across the United States.

RU-486 is used in conjunction with a low-dose prostaglandin, such as Miso-pristol, administered 48 hours after RU-486. Misopristol expels the conceptus without increasing the side effects. A World Health Organization study looking at the use of the RU-486-prostaglandin regimen since 1982, concluded that when this combination is given within seven to eight weeks from the first day of the last menstrual period, a complete abortion occurs in 64 to 85 percent of women. A smaller study conducted in the United States included 2,121 women requesting termination of a pregnancy of less than 64 days duration. This study yielded a success rate of 92 percent for women less than 50 days pregnant, 83 percent for women between 50 and 56 days, and 77 percent in the for women more than 56 days pregnant. Side effects of this drug include bleeding, cramping, nausea, vomiting, short-term fatigue or weakness, and occasional diarrhea. In about 2 percent of cases, the drug does not work, and a conventional abortion procedure is necessary. But, despite these problems, RU-486 has an enormous advantage over a conventional abortion from the pregnant woman's perspective. As one journalist wrote, the drug eliminates the "trek to a clinic, where anyone watching her enter and leave could make a reasonable surmise about her business there."

In 1996, the Population Council, a New York-based research organization and holder of the United States patent rights to RU-486, submitted an application for approval of RU-486 to the FDA. Eleanor Smeal, President of the Feminist Majority Foundation, announced: "Submission of an FDA application is a long-awaited milestone in our eight-year campaign to license Mifepristone in the United States. The day is finally approaching when the women of this nation will join the women of France, Great Britain, Sweden and China in having access to this medical breakthrough." Smeal's optimism has been vindicated, but only after considerable frustration and delay. The efforts of President Bill Clinton, women's groups, and the Population Council to bring the drug to this country have been met by consistent, vigorous opposition from religious organizations and right-to-life groups. Their objections focus upon the possibility that RU-486 might become a routine method of "morning after" birth control and thus blur the distinction between contraception and abortion. Such opponents have labeled the drug a "human pesticide." Impressions of use of RU-486 and similar drugs as a "morning after" pill are highly anecdotal and are not supported by medical practice either in Europe or the United States.

When the FDA finally gave the drug conditional approval in 1996, pro-life organizations organized boycotts of Hoechst and other companies that manufactured it and were successful in delaying its availability in the United States for three years. However, a similar drug, Methotrexate, has been available in the U.S. for some time. Commonly used in the treatment of cancer and certain chronic diseases such as endometriosis, Methotrexate stops the rapid growth of embryonic and placental cells in early pregnancy. Methotrexate has been used on a limited basis to treat ectopic pregnancies and in clinical trials in early normal pregnancies. These procedures have shown that this drug is an effective and safe abortifacient in pregnancies of less than seven weeks. The FDA gave RU-486 final marketing approval in September 2000. Future medical breakthroughs may well make non-surgical abortion safer, more effective, and more widely available.

SEE Abortion as a Reproductive Right; Abortion Self-Help Movement.

Further References. A chronological history of the Feminist Majority's eight-year struggle to legalize the use of RU-486 in the United States may be found at http://www.feminist.org/ru_486. The site includes many links to medical studies as well as to the ongoing political struggles over the drug. See also, Margaret Talbot, "The Little White Bombshell," *The New York Times Magazine* (July 11, 1999): 38-43, 48 and 61-63.

VIKI SOADY

RUST v. SULLIVAN (500 U.S. 173, 1991) allowed the executive branch to deny federal funds to family planning clinics that provided information about abortion to their patients. The "gag rule," as critics of the policy called it, was part of the Reagan administration's strategy to narrow the scope, and eventually negate the effect, of *Roe v. Wade*. At issue was a new interpretation of the provision of Title X of the Public Health Service Act of 1970 (PHSA) that no federal funds "shall be used in programs where abortion is a method of family planning." Until 1988, the Department of Health and Human Services (HHS) and its predecessor, the Department of Health, Education, and Welfare, interpreted this language to deny government aid only to those clinics that provided abortions for their patients. But in 1988, the administration decided to exploit the linguistic ambiguity of the term "method of family planning" to include not only the provision of abortion, but also counseling about this procedure. Title X grantees who were thus denied federal funding brought suit against HHS. By the time the case reached the Supreme Court, George Bush was president and Louis Sullivan was HHS secretary.

The Court upheld the rule by a five to four vote. The majority opinion, authored by Chief Justice William Rehnquist, rejected the three primary challenges to the regulations. Rehnquist first held that the Public Health Service Act's failure to precisely specify what it meant by a "method of family planning" introduced an element of ambiguity that Secretary Sullivan was legitimately exploiting in the instant case. The fact that the government had interpreted it differently between 1970 and 1988 did not negate the current administration's reading of the law. Second, the Court held that the First Amendment free speech rights of clinic personnel were not violated by the Secretary's understanding of Title X. So long as the government does not actively suppress the speech of clinic workers, the First Amendment is not implicated. "The government may choose not to subsidize speech" with which it disagrees. Finally, the regulations did not violate a woman's due process rights to abortion. "The government has no constitutional duty to subsidize activity merely because the activity is constitutionally protected."

Justice Harry Blackmun wrote a passionate dissent that was joined, entirely or in part, by three other justices. He insisted that, absent clear congressional intent to deny federal monies to clinics that merely provide information about abortion, Secretary Sullivan lacked the power to do so himself. Blackmun further argued that these regulations embodied "viewpoint-based suppression of speech," thereby violating the First Amendment rights of clinic personnel. Blackmun's most serious objection to HHS's creative interpretation of the PHSA was the burden that it would impose on a woman's right to seek an abortion if she so chooses. He argued that the Court does not leave "intact a woman's ability to decide without coercion whether she will continue her pregnancy to term." He lamented the Court's determination to negate *Roe v. Wade* by rendering a woman's right to abortion "nugatory" and "unenforceable."

Congress responded to the Court's decision with an amendment to the PHSA that would again allow federal funding of family planning clinics that provided information about abortion. The Congress was unable, however, to override President Bush's prompt veto. In his first week in office in January 1993, President Bill Clinton reversed Sullivan's reading of the PHSA, thereby restoring federal funding to these clinics.

SEE Abortion and Political Conflict; Gag Rule.

Further References. Neal E. Devins, *Shaping Constitutional Values: Elected Government, the Supreme Court, and the Abortion Debate* (Baltimore, 1996). Ted G. Jelen, ed., *Perspectives on the Politics of Abortion* (Westport, Conn., 1995).

FRANCIS CARLETON

S

SANGER, MARGARET (1879–1966). Margaret Higgins Sanger is the most famous, and perhaps the most effective, birth control activist in U.S. history. She emerged on the American scene in those halcyon days before World War I, when it was fashionable to believe in the inevitability of human progress. She first became politically active in the radical labor movement, and was called to her life's mission by the tragedies of unwanted pregnancy and illegal abortion that she witnessed while working as a nurse and midwife among the immigrant poor in New York.

In 1917, Sanger went to jail for distributing an early version of the diaphragm from a makeshift clinic in a tenement storefront in Brooklyn. She was convicted under obscenity statutes dating from the nineteenth century. On appeal, she won an interpretation of New York law that allowed doctors—though not nurses, as she intended—to prescribe contraception for medical purposes. Under those constraints, she built the modern family planning movement.

With the victory for women's suffrage finally achieved in 1920, Sanger found new supporters among its adherents, many of them women from the middle and upper classes. Birth control, she argued would liberate women in the bedroom, the home, and the larger community. It was essential to women's freedom but also to social reconstruction, since birth control, in Sanger's vision, would alter the balance of supply and demand for labor and help eradicate poverty.

Through the 1920s and 1930s, Sanger built the thriving organization that later became the Planned Parenthood Federation of America. She named it the American Birth Control League when she founded it in 1921. Six years later, she sponsored the first world population conference in Geneva, which gave rise to the International Union for the Scientific Study of Population, the world's first formal association of demographers. Meanwhile, Sanger's clinic in New York provided contraception and preventive gynecology, along with pioneering services in sex education, marriage counseling, and infertility counseling. The clinic even made quiet referrals for safe, illegal abortions. It was, in many ways, a model for the comprehensive and integrated approach to service delivery that remains an ideal of women's health reformers today.

However, the birth control movement stalled during the long years of the Great Depression and World War II, and in the pro-natalist environment that followed. The movement was stymied by the cost and complexity of trying to reach the women most in need, engulfed by internal dissension, and overwhelmed by a barrage of opposition. The always-fragile alliance Sanger tried to forge with America's social, professional, and business establishments became a distinct liability. She formally resigned from the Birth Control League in 1928 because of the eugenicist leanings of some of its leaders. Although Sanger had been favorably disposed toward the eugenics movement and welcomed its support of birth control, she balked at its bold advocacy of contraception as a means of slowing birthrates among the poor. Nor did she find an ally in her close friend, President Franklin Roosevelt, for her more democratic family planning message. Roosevelt yielded to pressure from the northern urban Catholics and southern rural populists who formed the base of his New Deal coalition.

Embittered by birth control's failure to secure a place in America's social welfare and public health systems, Sanger turned much of her attention abroad after World War II. She founded the International Planned Parenthood Federation in London in 1948. Until her death at the age of 87 in 1966, she struggled valiantly to build family planning associations in the developing world. She helped develop the oral anovulent birth control pill. She lived to see the first public funding of family planning programs and the historic Supreme Court ruling in *Griswold v. Connecticut* (1965). This ruling gave constitutional protection to the use of contraception by married couples. Margaret Sanger never wavered from her commitment to advancing the status of women.

SEE Birth Control Movement; Eugenics; *Griswold v. Connecticut*; Planned Parenthood.

Further References. Ellen Chesler, *Woman of Valor: Margaret Sanger and the Birth Control Movement in America* (New York, 1992, 1993). Linda Gordon, *Woman's Body, Woman's Right: A Social History of Birth Control in America* (New York, 1976, 1990). James Reed, *From Private Vice to Public Virtue: The Birth Control Movement and American Society Since 1830* (New York, 1978; Princeton, 1984).

ELLEN CHESLER

SECRETARY OF LABOR v. AMERICAN CYANAMID, OSHRC Docket No. 79-5762 (1979), 886 F. 2d 871 (7th Circ. 1989): This widely publicized case involved an employer's efforts to establish a "fetal protection" policy in the workplace. These regulations, which limited the freedoms and opportunities of women workers, were contemporaneous with two parallel developments of the 1960s and 1970s: advances in medical knowledge about the harmful effects of lead, benzene, radiation, and other toxic substances on fetuses, and the increased availability of traditionally male jobs to women after the passage of Title VII of the Civil Rights Act of 1964. Supporters of fetal protection policies praised them as conscientious efforts to prevent birth defects, but opponents regarded them as attempts to keep women out of good jobs. The *American Cyanamid* case lends credence to the opponents' interpretation.

The American Cyanamid company manufactures chemical lights, engineering materials, industrial chemicals, plastics and pharmaceuticals. Prior to the federal government's investigation in 1973, the company employed women only in low-paying clerical or kitchen worker jobs. As a result of this investigation, management at the Willow Island plant in Pleasant County, West Virginia, was put on notice to hire women for their production lines. The women who went to work in the lead pigments department at Willow Island encountered the resistance from male workers and the corporate hierarchy that typically awaits women who gain access to jobs traditionally held by men. Production improved in the lead pigments department, as women joined the work force, but resentment among the men grew.

In 1976, the company abruptly stopped hiring women in the department and drafted a "Fetal Protection Policy." The ostensible reason for this policy was the discovery, as a result of a government inspection, that workers were being exposed to levels of lead that were unacceptable by federal standards. The new rule stated that women of childbearing age (under 50) must stop working in jobs where lead was present. Even before the policy was official, the company announced that after May 1, 1978, no fertile woman under 50 would be allowed to work in eight out of 10 of the plant's departments. If women wanted to keep their jobs, they had to undergo surgical sterilization. Five of the seven women left in the lead pigments department did. The other two were demoted to janitorial positions.

The scope, timing, and context of this new policy call into question the sincerity of the company's concern for its employees. Despite a history of hazardous workplace conditions, American Cyanamid had never focused on reproductive health consequences with respect to its male workers, let alone general health ramifications. The Fetal Protection Policy did not even do what the government was demanding: reduce the level of lead exposure for all workers. The high lead levels were dangerous not only to fetuses, but to both male and female workers. (The company could have taken the less restrictive, and gender-neutral, measure of reducing the lead exposure, but concluded that the cost—$700,000—was excessive). The policy covered many more women than was necessary to protect fetuses; it applied to all women workers, whether or not they planned to bear children or were using contraception. And, by forcing the workers to either be sterilized or lose their jobs, the rule was extraordinarily punitive in its effects.

The women workers promptly filed a complaint with the federal Occupational Health and Safety Administration (OSHA). OSHA inspected the plant in 1979 and fined American Cyanamid $10 million. Ironically, lead was not the workplace hazard that OSHA identified; instead, OSHA ruled that the Fetal Protection Policy constituted a hazard because it coerced women to undergo surgery. Rather than pay the $700,000 to reduce lead exposure, the company closed its pigment department. The women who had already undergone surgery lost both their reproductive rights and their hard-won jobs.

A year later, OSHA reversed itself. It set aside the citation, stating that the violation did not "operate directly upon employees." After five years of seeking redress, the women sought the help of their union. (Unlike the early protective labor laws, to which they are often compared, fetal protection policies were strongly opposed by organized labor.) But the federal court ruled in favor of American Cyanamid on the grounds that sterilization was an option, not a hazard. The Supreme Court ruling in the *Johnson Controls* case (1991) that fetal policies violate Title VII came too late to help the women of American Cyanamid. But it will prevent employers from treating other women this way—unless they come up with a different rationale.

Policies that appear to protect women or promote healthy working environments have often been used to do the opposite. They preclude women's active participation in the workplace, especially in higher paying positions traditionally held by men. The early "protective" laws effectively closed many jobs to women. "Fetal Protection Policies" are the most recent variations on this familiar theme. While workplace hazards are serious problems and present grave dangers, these hazards have never generated laws to prevent women from working in traditional low paying female jobs when exposure to chemicals was prevalent such as in dry-cleaning plants. Nor have they ever prevented employers from summoning women workers in national emergencies or wartime, as a reserve labor force for the good of their country.

SEE Employment and Reproductive Rights; Fetal Protection; *International Union, United Auto Workers v. Johnson Controls*; *Muller v. Oregon*; Protective Labor Legislation; Title VII and Reproductive Rights.

Further References. Susan Faludi, *Backlash: The Undeclared War Against American Women* (New York, 1991). Barbara Katz Repa, *Your Rights in the Workplace* (Berkeley, Calif., 1996).

LANA THOMPSON

SIMOPOULOS v. VIRGINIA (462 U.S. 506, 1983), involved a Virginia statute requiring that all second trimester abortions be performed in a licensed hospital. The Supreme Court considered this case along with *City of Akron v. Akron Center for Reproductive Health* and *Planned Parenthood Assn. of Kansas City v. Ashcroft*. But, whereas *Akron* and *Ashcroft* struck down legal requirements limiting the provision of second trimester abortions to acute care (or "full service") hospitals, *Simopoulos* upheld the Virginia law.

Both chronologically and doctrinally, these three cases come about midway between *Roe v. Wade* (1973) and *Planned Parenthood v. Casey* (1992). *Roe*, of course, held that abortion regulations impinge on a constitutionally protected right of privacy. State abortion regulations would thus be strictly scrutinized by courts and upheld only if shown to serve a compelling governmental interest and to employ statutory means that were necessary to achieve that compelling purpose. But *Roe* also held that states have an "important and legitimate interest in the health of the mother"—an interest that legitimately extended to the facilities in which abortions occur—and that this interest becomes "compelling" in the second trimester of pregnancy.

The question the Court faced in *Simopoulos*, as well as in *Akron* and *Ashcroft*, was whether the regulations were drawn narrowly enough to pass constitutional muster. While both *Akron* and *Ashcroft* upheld several regulations, unrelated to hospitalization, the Court concluded that the hospitalization requirements constituted too "significant [an] obstacle in the path of women seeking an abortion" to withstand scrutiny. In contrast, in *Simopoulos* the Court ruled that in permitting use of *outpatient* hospitals for second trimester abortions, Virginia's requirement differed "significantly" from the Akron and Kansas City regulations. Therefore, those two cases were "not controlling" in *Simopoulos*.

In sustaining the Virginia law as a constitutionally permissible means of furthering the compelling state interest in maternal health, the Court granted that a state "necessarily has considerable discretion in determining standards for the licensing of medical facilities" although "its discretion does not permit it to adopt abortion regulations that depart from accepted medical practice." It concluded that the Virginia requirement passed constitutional muster because its "regulations appear to be generally compatible with accepted medical standards governing outpatient second-trimester abortions." The substitution in *Casey* of the "undue burden" test for the "compelling interest" test suggests that similar regulations are even more likely to survive judicial scrutiny than they were in 1983.

SEE *City of Akron v. Akron Center for Reproductive Health* (1983); *Planned Parenthood of Kansas City v. Ashcroft* (1983); *Planned Parenthood of Southeastern Pennsylvania v. Casey* (1992); *Roe v. Wade* (1973); Undue Burden.

JAMES ROGERS

SKINNER V. OKLAHOMA (316 U.S. 535, 1942), involved a constitutional challenge to Oklahoma's Habitual Criminal Sterilization Act of 1935. The act provided for the sterilization of those who committed two or more felonies involving "moral turpitude." Skinner, who had been convicted once of stealing chickens and twice of armed robbery, insisted that the statute violated the U.S. Constitution's guarantees of equal protection of the laws and due process, as well as its ban on cruel and unusual punishment.

Justice William O. Douglas's opinion for a unanimous Court noted that the statute excluded some offenses—violations of prohibition laws or revenue acts, embezzlement, and political offenses—from those that could lead to sterilization. He questioned whether, even if one accepted the inheritability of criminal traits, that inheritability "follows the neat legal distinction which the law has marked out between" crimes as similar as robbery and embezzlement. Subjecting the classification drawn by the state to "strict scrutiny" lest "unwittingly, or otherwise, invidious discriminations are made against groups or types of individuals," he concluded that the classification violated the Equal Protection Clause and ruled the act unconstitutional.

The Court's ruling in *Skinner* must be seen in historical context. Written during a war against an enemy that proclaimed eugenic purity, the opinion of the Court was openly skeptical about the claimed inheritability of criminal traits. But the justices were loath to acknowledge fundamental rights not enshrined in the text of the Constitution, because they had repudiated substantive due process (the idea that the Constitution may protect unspecified rights) less than a decade before. Hence, the Court did not base its ruling on a recognition of reproductive rights. In contrast with *Buck v. Bell* (1927), which upheld a Virginia law requiring the sterilization of institutionalized "mental defectives," *Skinner* does acknowledge that the right to have offspring is "one of the basic civil rights of man" and that sterilization causes "irreparable injury". However, the Court ultimately sidesteps the difficulties associated with identifying and defining fundamental rights by basing its ruling on the Equal Protection Clause.

SEE *Buck v. Bell*; Eugenics; *Stump v. Sparkman*; Sterilization Abuse.

Further References. Robert H. Blank, *Fertility Control: New Techniques, New Policy Issues*. New York, 1991). George T. Felkenes, "Sterilization and the Law," in Harold K. Becker, George T. Felkenes, and Paul M. Whisenand, eds., *New Dimensions in Criminal Justice* (Metuchen, N.J.,1968): 113-201.

G. ALAN TARR

"SQUEAL RULE." SEE *New York v. Schweiker*.

STERILIZATION is the most popular means of fertility control in the United States; about 25 percent of couples report that they have used it. Two common, safe, and simple procedures exist: salpingectomy or tubal ligation (cutting the fallopian tubes) for women, and vasectomy (cutting the *vas deferens*, the spermatic ducts) for men. Both are considered minor surgery, although tubal ligation is slightly more serious. Voluntary sterilization is legal in all states, although some maintain regulations, such as an informed consent requirement, a waiting period up to 30 days, a minimum age, consent of the spouse, or consultation for a second opinion. Federal health policy classifies voluntary sterilization as a method of family planning. Publicly funded hospitals may not refuse to perform them, although private hospitals may do so on moral or religious grounds. Hospital regulations have limited impact on access today because both vasectomies and tubal ligations by laparoscopy are outpatient procedures.

Health providers may impose their own restrictions on patients, based on their personal convictions and fear of malpractice suits. Insurance providers are also free to restrict coverage. Some define voluntary sterilization as a covered medical procedure. Others, however, distinguish between elective and "medically necessary" sterilization and exclude the former. About three-fourths of the states cover the procedure for women on Medicaid.

The history of sterilization in the United States illustrates two recurring issues. First, women who wanted the procedure have not always had access to it. Second, those women who have undergone the procedure have not always done so by choice. As has been true with other methods of birth control, such factors as race, class, gender, and economic vulnerability have played a large part in determining who might be sterilized under what circumstances. Until the late 1960s, many physicians adhered to the "rule of 120" recommended by the American College of Obstetrics and Gynecology: they performed sterilizations on private women patients only if their age multiplied by the number of their living children equaled at least that number. On the other hand, ample documentation exists that women dependent on public assistance have been coerced or tricked into sterilization. The idea of *informed consent*—requiring that individuals have enough information about risks and effects—is gaining support among health professionals. This is an especially sensitive issue for sterilization, because it permanently ends a person's ability to conceive a child (although the operation is sometimes reversible, this is never a certainty) and because of its history of misuse.

SEE Birth Control Movement; *Buck v. Bell*; Class and Reproductive Rights; Eugenics; Federal Sterilization Guidelines; *Skinner v. Oklahoma*; Sterilization Abuse; *Stump v. Sparkman*.

Further References. Robert Blank and Janna C. Merrick, *Human Reproduction, Emerging Technologies and Conflicting Rights* (Washington D.C., 1995). Linda S. Peterson, *Contraceptive Use in the United States: 1982-90* (Washington, D.C., 1995).

DOROTHY MCBRIDE STETSON

STERILIZATION ABUSE occurs when people are subjected to the procedure without their consent or full understanding. In the United States, involuntary sterilization has been used as a method of population control based on the belief that some people are either genetically inferior and should not reproduce or are incapable of taking responsibility for their reproduction. Public officials and health care providers have particularly targeted the poor, people of color, women, the mentally disabled, and the institutionalized. Involuntary sterilization of these populations began early in the twentieth century; the Supreme Court upheld the sterilization of an institutionalized woman in *Buck v. Bell* (1927). But it was not until 1969 that sterilization was approved by the government as a legitimate method of birth control. This policy change resulted in the relaxation of rules and the increased availability of public funds and clinics, which led to further abuse of the procedure among the targeted populations.

Women, particularly welfare and Medicaid recipients, were coerced, deceived, misinformed, or given incentives or disincentives to undergo sterilization (usually by tubal ligation, but sometimes by hysterectomy). Women were rarely provided complete information about the procedure or given information about alternative methods of birth control. Many did not understand that the procedure was permanent, and the use of confusing terminology such as "tied-tubes" misleadingly implied its reversibility. Illiterates and non-English speakers were often deceived into signing papers they could not read. Other women were forced to sign during labor, under heavy sedation, or by threatening to withhold pain medication. Some were told that benefits would be lowered if they did not undergo the procedure, or increased if they did it. Husbands were coerced into giving permission while their wives were in labor.

Some women were not told they were sterilized, only to find out later when unable to get pregnant. Lawsuits, mass protest, and reports of these abuses, particularly between 1973 and 1976, led to drastic federal policy changes by 1979, when the federal government issued strict new regulations. Sterilization has also been proposed as a punishment for crime, but *Skinner v. Oklahoma* (1942) invalidated such a law in terms which discouraged the passage of similar legislation. The forced sterilization of men has never been as common an event as the sterilization of women.

SEE African-American Women and Reproductive Rights; Birth Control and African-American Women; Birth Control Movement; *Buck v. Bell*; Disability and Reproductive Rights; Eugenics; Federal Sterilization Guidelines; Hispanic/Latina Women and Reproductive Rights; Native American Women and Reproductive Rights; *Skinner v. Oklahoma*; Sterilization; *Stump v. Sparkman*.

Further References. Committee for Abortion Rights and Against Sterilization Abuse (CARASA), *Women under Attack: Backlash, Victories, and the Fight for Reproductive Freedom* (Boston, 1988). Betsy Hartmann, *Reproductive Rights and Wrongs: The Global Politics of Population Control* (Boston, 1995). P.R. Reilly, *The Surgical Solution: A History of Involuntary Sterilization in the United States* (Baltimore, 1991).

NILDA FLORES-GONZALEZ

STUMP v. SPARKMAN (436 U.S. 439, 1978) is the most recent Supreme Court case to deal with involuntary sterilization. In mid-1971, 15-year-old Linda Kay Spitler underwent a tubal ligation without her knowledge after her mother petitioned the circuit court of DeKalb County, Indiana, to allow the operation. The mother alleged that Linda was "somewhat retarded" and in "an unfortunate circumstance." Judge Harold Stump issued an order allowing the operation. Linda was told she needed an appendectomy. Subsequently, she married Leo Sparkman and learned that she could not conceive.

The Sparkmans sued Linda's mother, the doctor, and Judge Stump, but the state court dismissed the first two cases because the judge had authorized the operation. In federal court, the couple alleged that the judge had deprived them of their due process and equal protection rights, claiming violations of fair procedure, privacy, and the "right to privacy." Despite support from such *amicus curiae* as the American Civil Liberties Union and the National Center for Law and the Handicapped, the Supreme Court ruled 5-3 against Linda and Leo Sparkman. In doing so, the Court avoided any discussion of the merits of the case. Justice Byron R. White's majority opinion found Judge Stump immune from civil liability under an 1871 federal statute because his order was a valid exercise of his authority. This conclusion was debatable, since no Indiana law authorized judges to order medical treatment on minors whose parents had given consent. Two dissenting opinions stressed the Court's "dangerously broad criteria" and the total absence of judicial remedies rather than questions of individual rights. While *Stump v. Sparkman* had little impact on the development of reproductive rights law, the state and federal rulings allowed several adults to avoid accountability for effectively depriving a teenage girl of her right to procreate.

SEE *Buck v. Bell*; Sterilization Abuse; *Skinner v. Oklahoma*; Youth and Reproductive Rights.

Further References. Virginia Sapiro, "Biology and Women's Policy: A View from the Social Sciences," in Virginia Sapiro, ed., *Women, Biology, and Public Policy* (Beverly Hills, Calif., 1985): 41-64. Sarah Slavin, "Unwanted Pregnancy, Due Process of Law and Justice White," *Women & Criminal Justice* 3, #1 (1992): 41-54. Ann Woolhandler, "Patterns of Official Immunity and Accountability," *Case Western Reserve Law Review* 37 (1986/1987): 396-483.

SARAH SLAVIN

SUBSTANCE ABUSE AND PREGNANCY. In the mid-1980s, prosecutors across the country began bringing criminal charges against women who used drugs or alcohol while pregnant. Mothers whose newborns were exposed to drugs in the womb were charged with crimes such as distributing drugs to a minor, child abuse and neglect, reckless endangerment, manslaughter, and assault with a deadly weapon. By 1995, more than 200 women in 30 states had been prosecuted for prenatal substance abuse. In other cases, pregnant addicts were held in "protective" incarceration until the birth of their babies. The most common penalty for a mother's substance abuse is the temporary or permanent removal of her infant by child protective services. In some states, a positive newborn drug test raises a strong presumption of parental unfitness.

The vast majority of these prosecutions were brought against poor Black women who smoked crack while pregnant. Most drug testing takes place in public hospitals that serve indigent patients and employ protocols that tend to identify

Black women in particular. A study of drug testing of pregnant patients in a Florida county found that, despite similar rates of substance abuse, Black women were 10 times more likely than whites to be reported to government authorities. The racial disparity in prosecutions also stemmed from the media's misleading concentration on crack in its coverage of drug use during pregnancy.

On July 13, 1989, Jennifer Johnson, a 23-year-old Black woman, became the first person in the country to be convicted of exposing her baby to drugs while she was pregnant. The Florida prosecutor successfully argued that Johnson distributed a cocaine metabolite to her two children through their umbilical cords after they were born, in the 60 seconds before the cords were cut. In *Johnson v. State* (1992), the Florida Supreme Court overturned Johnson's conviction on the grounds that the state legislature did not intend to extend the drug delivery statute to this context.

With only one exception, every appellate court to consider the issue has invalidated criminal charges for drug use during pregnancy. Most decisions, like that of the Florida Supreme Court, center on the interpretation of the criminal statute cited in the indictment. A few courts have held that prosecuting a woman for her conduct during pregnancy violates her constitutional right to privacy. But on July 15, 1996, the South Carolina Supreme Court upheld the child abuse conviction of Cornelia Whitner, another Black woman who smoked crack during pregnancy.

Whitner v. South Carolina ruled that a viable fetus is covered by the state's child abuse law and that punishing fetal abuse would further the law's aim of preventing harm to children. It rejected the argument that the conviction violated Whitner's right of privacy, asserting that she had no right to smoke crack while she was pregnant. This reasoning misconceived the constitutional right at stake. The prosecutions infringe on women's constitutional right to reproductive liberty, protected in *Griswold v. Connecticut* and *Roe v. Wade*, by punishing the decision to have a child. The prosecutions center on harm to the fetus, not illegal drug use, and they penalize substance-abusing women who carry their pregnancies to term. Moreover, the government has not met, and cannot meet, its burden of showing that criminal punishment is justified. Every leading medical and public health organization in the country opposes these prosecutions because there is inadequate drug treatment for pregnant women and because the threat of criminal sanctions deters pregnant substance abusers from getting treatment and prenatal care.

The gender and racial disparities in the prosecutions lend support to the argument that they violate the Equal Protection Clause of the Fourteenth Amendment. The prosecutions discriminate against women by making them solely responsible for harm to the fetus. In some states, men have been charged with homicide for killing a fetus, but they have not been charged with child abuse for less harmful conduct when the fetus survives, such as smoking cigarettes near a pregnant woman, distributing drugs to her, or beating her. Black defendants might make a case of unconstitutional racial discrimination by showing the disproportionate number of Black women prosecuted for prenatal crimes, along with the high degree of prosecutorial discretion in selecting which substance-abusing women to subject to criminal charges. An "antisubordination" approach to race discrimination might interpret the prosecutions of Black women as unconstitutional because they reinforce myths of irresponsible Black reproduction and perpetuate the devaluation of Black motherhood. Unfortunately, the U.S. Supreme Court does not interpret the Constitution this way and is unlikely to do so in the near future. Instead, the Court has ruled that facially neutral policies which have a disparate impact on people of a particular race or gender are unconstitutional only if decision-makers intended the biased result.

The criminalization of substance abuse during pregnancy can be seen as part of a trend toward greater state intervention into the lives of pregnant women for the sake of protecting the fetus from harm. This intervention has also included compelled medical treatment, greater restrictions on abortion, and increased supervision of pregnant women's conduct. The holding in *Whitner* that harm to a viable fetus constitutes child abuse potentially makes a wide range of maternal activity criminal. The prosecutions of prenatal crimes are also related to the increasing regulation of reproductive decisions by poor women, particularly minority women, such as "family cap" laws that deny additional benefits for children born to women who are already on welfare.

SEE Fetal Abuse; Fetal Protection; Forced Medical Treatment and Pregnancy; Lifestyle Restrictions and Pregnancy.

Further References. Laura E. Gomez, *Misconceiving Mothers: Legislators, Prosecutors, and the Politics of Prenatal Drug Exposure* (Philadelphia, 1997). *Johnson v. State*, 602 So.2d 1288 (Florida, 1992). Dorothy Roberts, *Killing the Black Body: Race, Reproduction, and the Meaning of Liberty* (New York, 1997). *Whitner v. South Carolina*, 492 S.E.2d 777 (S.C. 1996).

DOROTHY ROBERTS

SURROGATE MOTHERHOOD is the practice by which a woman carries and bears a baby for someone else. It involves a contract between a surrogate mother and the baby's future custodial parents. Traditional surrogacy uses the surrogate's ovum; it involves having the surrogate mother artificially inseminated with the sperm of the man who will become a custodial parent to the resulting offspring. Gestational surrogacy is the practice of implanting an embryo (usually, one produced *in vitro* from the future parents' sperm and ova) into the surrogate. In both instances, the surrogate agrees to surrender the child, at birth, to the custody of the contracting parent or parents. The surrogate mother is usually paid between $10,000-$20,000 for her participation in the arrangement. There are also instances of altruistic surrogacy in which a woman agrees to act as a surrogate without pay, usually for a family member. Surrogacy allows couples to have children who are genetically related to one or both custodial parents when the woman is unwilling or unable to carry the fetus, and men without partners to have genetically related children.

Proponents of surrogacy argue that it allows infertile couples to have genetic offspring and respects the rights of the potential surrogate mother. She enjoys the same reproductive rights that other men and women have: in particular, the same right to bodily autonomy as an ordinary mother or a male semen donor. But surrogacy has also met with strong opposition. Opponents insist that surrogacy for profit constitutes the sale and commodification of babies, pointing out that contracts often stipulate that the surrogate will receive nothing if she miscarries before the fourth month and only a token payment of the baby is stillborn. Further, opponents argue that surrogacy makes it harder for unadopted children to find homes, adds to the problem of overpopulation, and has a bad psychological impact on the surrogate, her family, and the child itself. Another common argument against surrogacy holds that the practice in fact deprives the woman of reproductive autonomy. Since many surrogates are poor and unskilled, opponents fear that women may agree to become surrogates out of financial desperation and become the victims of greedy "baby brokers." Thus, the practice may exploit women and create an underclass of poorly paid baby-makers.

Opponents of surrogacy have won significant victories since the surrogacy issue first received national attention as a result of the 1987 Baby M case. Currently, only three states explicitly hold that surrogacy contracts are enforceable. Nineteen states regulate paid surrogacy contracts; 13 states prohibit the enforcement of contracts; and three states and the District of Columbia ban surrogacy outright. Ten jurisdictions prohibit any compensation for agents or facilitators of surrogacy arrangements.

Surrogacy has raised a host of legal problems. For example, in 1992 a federal appeals court ruled that a surrogate mother could sue the lawyer who arranged her contract for negligence when both she and the unborn child were infected with cytomegalovirus, a sexually transmitted disease, through the semen of the contracting father—even though the child was actually the offspring of the surrogate's husband. Contracts which require the woman to undergo specified medical procedures (as most surrogacy contracts do) have been legally problematic, especially when the contracts require that the surrogate abort the fetus if prenatal tests show abnormalities. The prevalence of lawsuits suggests that surrogacy persists despite legislative efforts to discourage it. Surrogacy undoubtedly serves the interests of infertile women who want children, men who want genetic offspring, and brokers who want money. Judgments about whether, how, and to what extent surrogacy benefits surrogates depend in large part on one's notions of women's reproductive rights.

SEE *Baby M*; *In Vitro* Fertilization; *Johnson v. Calvert*; *Muñoz v. Haro.*

Further References. Lori B. Andrews, "Beyond Doctrinal Boundaries: A Legal Framework for Surrogate Motherhood," *Virginia Law Review* 81 (November 1995): 23- 43. Gena Corea, *The Mother Machine* (New York, 1985).

LENORE KUO

T

_____

TEENAGE PREGNANCY. The feminist and technological revolutions of the 1960s offered women sexual pleasure without the risk of pregnancy. The growth in sexual activity among unmarried females increased the abortion and pregnancy rates among teenagers in the United States until the legalization of contraception for married persons (*Griswold v. Connecticut,* 1965), the extension of this right to single people (*Eisenstadt v. Baird*, 1972) and adolescents (*Carey v. Population Services*, 1977), and the legalization of abortion (*Roe v. Wade,* 1973). The over-all teenage birth rate has steadily declined since the 1970s. But, despite this decline, by the late 1980s teenage pregnancy was widely believed to have reached epidemic proportions. This belief has persisted and intensified in the 1990s. The phenomenon of "children having children" is widely believed to cause crime, poverty, welfare dependency, illiteracy, and a host of other social evils. Teenage pregnancy was one of the concerns which led to the Republican takeover of Congress in 1994 and to draconian cutbacks in the welfare state. What explains the apparent contradiction between political rhetoric and social reality?

Changes in female sexual behavior became visible when fewer pregnant single women of all race, class, and age categories married their babies' fathers or put their babies up for adoption. The rate of pregnancy, childbearing, and single parenting among black teenagers, for whom giving birth signaled entry into adulthood, has been consistently high. But it was overlooked until sexual practices of black teens previously attributed to "natural differences" among the races became increasingly common among white teenagers. Politicians and moralists who sought to reduce the growing number of single women giving birth and raising children alone focused on adolescent female sexual behavior. Fueling a growing commitment to eliminating adolescent sexual activity—and thereby teenage pregnancy, abortion, and childbearing—was the claim that adolescent pregnancy causes poverty.

The over-representation of black teenagers among those who dropped out of school, relied on welfare, and gave birth to small babies at risk for infant death produced what sociologist Kristin Luker called "a story that fits the data." A "family values" political agenda blamed the weakened economy on single, teenage mothers and promoted claims of epidemics of "crack babies" (infants born addicted to crack cocaine) and of "babies having babies" (apparently, the extreme version of "children having children.") However, the supposed increase in the incidence of addiction among newborns was never substantiated, while a steady birthrate of less than one percent among girls aged 15 and under contradicted the belief that the rate of birth to young girls has increased.

By treating teenage sexuality as a social problem, rather than as a developmental stage in the emergence of healthy adult humans, conservatives and liberals inadvertently joined forces to restore female sexual purity. The Hyde Amendment, first enacted in 1976, punished "bad girls" who have sex by virtually eliminating the use of federal Medicaid dollars to pay for abortions for poor teenagers. The 1980s brought the equivalent of Nancy Reagan's "Just Say No" (to drugs) campaign as a way of dealing with teenage sex. Federal legislation supported abstinence-only sexuality education in public schools in order to prevent "good girls" from having sex. The welfare reforms of the 1990s, culminating in the passage of the Personal Responsibility and Work Ethic Act of 1996, included efforts to deny already inadequate cash benefits to unmarried pregnant teenagers under 18.

Legislation to require parental notification of the provision of care to adolescents by the 1970 Title X federal family planning program, which supports confidential reproductive health care to all women regardless of age, failed. Federal courts prevented enforcement of this "squeal rule" throughout the Reagan and Bush administrations. However, state-by-state reforms requiring parental notification for selected aspects of reproductive health care have passed. While a majority of states protect adolescents' rights to continue pregnancy, seek prenatal care, and place their babies for adoption without notifying their parents, only two states and the District of Columbia affirm a minor's right to obtain an abortion without parental notification or consent.

Conservatives claim that laws mandating "parental involvement" account for the decline in teenage pregnancy, abortion, and childbirth rates in the 1990s. But analysis offers little support for this assertion. While a growing minority of American teenagers evince interest in sexual abstinence outside of marriage—a trend that may indeed reflect parental influence—the majority become sexually active by 18 or 19 years of age. For these adolescents, a combination of civil and reproductive rights has supported the decline in U.S. teenage pregnancy and abortion rates. Title IX of the Education Amendments Act of 1972 supports gender equality via equal access to education. Improved educational opportunities have been shown to lead to entry into the formal labor market and to an associated delay in childbearing. The prospect of financial independence for women, paired with knowledge of and access to family planning, is linked with an overall decline in teenage childbearing.

However, limited teenage access to comprehensive reproductive health care is associated with a U.S. teenage pregnancy rate twice that of England, Wales, or Canada, and nine times that of the Netherlands. If conservatives succeed in limiting teenage access to contraception and abortion, the growing use of condoms by teenagers fearing the transmission of AIDS may become the primary method for sexually active adolescents to avoid unplanned pregnancy, abortion, and childbearing.

SEE Abortion and Public Assistance; Class and Reproductive Rights; *Carey v. Population Services*; *Eisenstadt v. Baird*; *Griswold v. Connecticut*; Hyde Amendment; *Roe v. Wade*; Youth and Reproductive Rights.

Further References. Patricia Hill Collins, *Black Feminist Thought: Knowledge, Consciousness, and the Politics of Empowerment* (New York, 1991). Laura Gomez, *Misconceiving Mothers: Legislators, Prosecutors, and the Politics of Prenatal Drug Exposure* (Philadelphia, 1998). Kristin Luker, *Dubious Conceptions: the Politics of Teenage Pregnancy* (Cambridge, Mass., 1996).

ELAINE R. CLEETON

THORNBURGH v. AMERICAN COLLEGE OF OBSTETRICIANS AND GYNECOLOGISTS (476 U.S. 747, 1986) was the last decision in which the Supreme Court strongly reaffirmed its pro-choice abortion ruling in *Roe v. Wade*. At issue were provisions in Pennsylvania statutes that restricted abortions by the following requirements: 1) informed consent, including specific information from the doctor concerning the medical procedure to be used and the risks associated with it, written information provided by the state describing characteristics of the unborn child at two-week intervals and the possibility of the survival of the fetus, and a statement that medical assistance was available and that the father is financially responsible for the child; 2) a doctor must inform a woman of the physical and psychological risks associated with abortion; 3) doctors must report detailed information about each abortion they perform; 4) an additional doctor must care for the fetus in post-viability abortions; 5) a second physician must be involved when the mother's health is endangered without any exception for medical emergencies. The Court, in a 5-4 decision, struck down all of these regulations on abortion. Justice Harry Blackmun wrote for the majority, "The States are not free, under the guise of protecting maternal health or potential life, to intimidate women into continuing pregnancies." Justices William J. Brennan, Jr., Thurgood Marshall, Lewis Powell, and John Paul Stevens concurred, while Chief Justice Warren Burger and Justices Byron White, William Rehnquist, and Sandra Day O'Connor dissented.

The Court's strong support of the right to an abortion was short-lived. President Ronald Reagan, reelected in 1984, had committed himself to appointing judges who opposed abortion rights. By the time the Court heard *Webster v. Reproductive Health Services* (1989), two members of the original *Roe* majority, Burger and Powell, had been replaced, and Rehnquist was chief justice. In *Planned Parenthood v. Casey* (1992), the Court explicitly upheld a provision concerning informed consent.

SEE *Planned Parenthood v. Casey*; *Roe v. Wade; Webster v. Reproductive Health Services.*

SANDRA L. WOOD

TILESTON v. ULLMAN, (318 U.S. 44, 1943) was an early unsuccessful attempt to challenge the Connecticut birth control law eventually struck down in *Griswold v. Connecticut*. One provision of the law prohibited use of birth control drugs or devices, and another prohibited giving assistance or counsel in their use. The law was challenged in state court in 1939 after the state closed a clinic operated by the Connecticut Birth Control League (now the Planned Parenthood Federation). In defense of the persons charged in the clinic raid, counsel argued that the law was unconstitutional as an infringement on the natural right to decide whether or not to have children. The trial judge agreed with this argument, but the Supreme Court of Errors reversed in *State v. Nelson*. The case went back to the lower court for trial, but the state dismissed the charges, leaving no grounds for appeal.

Tileston, a physician, then challenged the law on the grounds that it would prevent him from giving professional advice to patients whose life would be endangered by childbearing, thus depriving them of life without due process of law under the Fourteenth Amendment. The trial court reserved decision for the Supreme Court of Errors, which ruled that the statute was constitutional even though it did prohibit Tileston from giving birth control advice. On appeal, the U.S. Supreme Court held that Tileston lacked standing to challenge the law in federal court because the right being asserted was the right of the patients, who were not parties to the suit. No birth control clinics were opened in Connecticut until 1961, after the Court refused to declare the law invalid in *Poe v. Ullman*.

SEE Birth Control Movement; *Griswold v. Connecticut*; Planned Parenthood; *Poe v. Ullman*.

Further References. Henry J. Abraham and Leo A. Hazelwood, "Comstockery at the Bar of Justice: Birth Control Legislation in the Federal, Connecticut, and Massachusetts Courts," *Law in Transition Quarterly,* 4 (December 1967): 220-245. Walter F. Murphy, James E. Fleming, and Sotirios A. Barber, eds., *American Constitutional Interpretation,* 2d ed. (Westbury, N.Y., 1995). *State v. Nelson,* 126 Conn. 412 (1940).

DARYL R. FAIR

TITLE VII AND REPRODUCTIVE RIGHTS. Title VII of the Civil Rights Act of 1964 is the primary federal law meant to protect minorities and women from discrimination in employment. With respect to women, the law was considerably ahead of its time. Words like "joke" and "fluke" have often been used to describe it. The original draft of the bill forbade employment discrimination on the basis of race, color, religion, or national origin. Opponents amended the bill to include "sex" in the belief—reasonable, at a time when want ads were divided into "Help Wanted, Male" and "Help Wanted, Female"—that such an outlandish idea would doom the provision to defeat. But the few women members of Congress joined liberal Democrats to pass the bill.

Neither Congress nor the federal bureaucracy quite knew what to do with the provision at first, but the courts have taken it seriously and the Equal Employment Opportunity Commission (EEOC) took its cues from them. While Title VII has barely made a dent in the sex segregation of the American workforce, it has protected the interests of many women who challenge employment discrimination.

The statute's meaning in regard to reproductive issues in the workplace—particularly motherhood, pregnancy, and fertility—has been elaborated by courts and by the EEOC. Legal scholars generally agree that Title VII, even as amended by the Pregnancy Discrimination Act of 1978, is a fairly blunt tool for addressing pregnancy-related inequities at work. Title VII makes it unlawful for employers "to fail or refuse to hire or to discharge any individual, or otherwise to discriminate against any individual with respect to his compensation, terms, conditions, or privileges or employment, because of such individual's race, color, religion, sex, or national origin." Title VII applies to private employers of more than 15 workers, labor unions, federal, state, and local governments, and employment agencies. Benefits, seniority, leaves, and disability insurance are among the "terms, conditions, or privileges of employment" covered by Title VII. As originally enacted, Title VII had no language specifically addressing employment discrimination based on pregnancy, motherhood, or fertility.

Title VII authorized the EEOC to create guidelines for employment practices, and those guidelines explicitly address employment practices and policies related to childbirth and pregnancy. The EEOC's regulations state that "[a] written or unwritten employment policy or practice which excludes from employment applicants or employees because of pregnancy is in prima facie violation of Title VII." The regulations describe pregnancy-related disabilities as temporary disabilities, and state that they must be treated as such under health or disability insurance or sick leave plans; leave policies, seniority and other benefits policies, and other employment policies also must treat pregnancy-related disabilities as temporary disabilities. Termination from employment because of pregnancy-related disability is forbidden under the regulations.

The U.S. Supreme Court and lower courts have used a "sex plus" analysis in cases of pregnancy- or fertility-related discrimination under Title VII. Courts and plaintiffs employ the "sex plus" analysis in cases where employers classify employees on the basis of sex plus another, apparently neutral, characteristic. In claiming "sex plus" discrimination one alleges not discrimination against women generally, but discrimination against subclasses of women, like married women or pregnant women. An employment classification that includes a "plus" factor (for example, refusing to hire women with children below school age) is unlawful because it would "present obstacles to employment of one sex that cannot be overcome."

The "sex plus" analysis is generally thought to be derived from the United States Supreme Court case *Phillips v. Martin-Marietta Corp.*, but this may be a misinterpretation. *Phillips* did hold that Martin-Marietta's policy of refusing to hire women with young children violated Title VII, but the Court did not use the term "sex plus" discrimination or even rule that all discrimination against women with young children was illegal. Instead, the Court limited its ruling to policies based on "stereotyped characterizations of the sexes," such as the belief that mothers of young children were unreliable workers. But, since *Phillips*, the Court has applied "sex plus" analysis in declaring several similar kinds of employment discrimination illegal under Title VII. These policies include denial of seniority benefits for women who took maternity leave (*Nashville Gas v. Satty*), limitations on insurance coverage for pregnancy-related medical conditions for spouses of male employees (*Newport News Shipbuilding and Drydock Co. v. EEOC*), and the exclusion of all women of childbearing age from certain job classifications (*UAW v. Johnson Controls*).

Title VII can be a powerful tool for working women, providing a federal remedy for employment discrimination based on reproductive issues. But litigation under Title VII is a costly and lengthy process, and the litigation has resulted in an uneven and inconsistent legal framework for working women. "Sex plus" reasoning offers, at best, a limit on employers' discriminatory uses of stereotypical views of women's roles, without addressing underlying issues of workplace equity.

SEE Employment and Reproductive Rights; *General Electric v. Gilbert*; *International Union, United Auto Workers v. Johnson Controls*; *Muller v. Oregon*; *Newport News Shipbuilding and Drydock Co. v. EEOC*; Pregnancy Discrimination Act of 1978; Protective Labor Legislation.

Further References. E. Christi Cunningham, "The Rise of Identity Politics I: The Myth of the Protected Class in Title VII Disparate Treatment Cases," *Connecticut Law Review*, 30 (Winter 1998): 441-501. Samuel Issacharoff and Elyse Rosenblum, "Women and the Workplace: Accommodating the Demands of Pregnancy," *Columbia Law Review*, 94 (November 1994): 2154-2221. *Nashville Gas Co. v. Satty*, 434 U.S. 136 (1977). *Phillips v. Martin-Marietta Corp.*, 400 U.S. 542 (1971).

RUTH PARLIN

U

—————————

UNDUE BURDEN. A constitutional standard applied to abortion regulations which provides that such a statute is unconstitutional only if it unduly burdens the exercise of the right to an abortion. This standard originated in cases involving state laws that affected interstate commerce; these are valid unless they impose undue burdens on that commerce. The adoption of the undue burden standard in abortion cases was a victory for Justice Sandra Day O'Connor, and may prove to be her major contribution to constitutional jurisprudence. O'Connor first applied the rule in the context of abortion in her dissent in *City of Akron v. Akron Center for Reproductive Health* (1983). In *Akron*, she proposed the undue burden standard as a substitute for the trimester scheme of *Roe v. Wade* (1973), which she described as "completely unworkable" in the light of medical advances which had moved the point of viability earlier and earlier in pregnancy. According to O'Connor, earlier decisions indicated that the constitutionality of an abortion regulation at any time during pregnancy actually turned on whether it "unduly burdened the right to seek an abortion." If not, the Court should determine only whether the regulation was rationally related to a legitimate state interest. An undue burden does not exist if a state regulation merely inhibits an abortion; instead it requires an "absolute obstacle" or "severe limitation" on the abortion decision.

O'Connor also argued for the undue burden standard in *Thornburgh v. American College of Obstetricians and Gynecologists* (1986). Here, she dissented from a ruling that struck down several regulations dealing with informed consent, reporting requirements, and standard of care requirements. In *Webster v. Reproductive Health Services* (1989), she stated that viability testing and its "marginal increase in the cost of an abortion" did not constitute an undue burden. The fact that this was a concurrence rather than a dissent indicated the degree to which the Court was moving away from *Roe* and toward greater acceptance of restrictions on abortion.

O'Connor's plurality opinion in *Planned Parenthood of Southeastern Pennsylvania v. Casey* (1992) effectively wrote the undue burden standard into law. She noted that an undue burden exists if the law's purpose is to place a "substantial obstacle" in the path of a woman seeking an abortion. Although only Justices Anthony Kennedy and David Souter joined this portion of O'Connor's opinion, O'Connor won a majority on several specific rulings applying the undue burden test. Two justices agreed with the plurality that a spousal consent requirement was invalid since it amounted to a veto power. Four justices who voted to reverse *Roe* joined the plurality in upholding provisions dealing with informed consent, a 24-hour waiting period, parental consent, and record-keeping requirements. Three of these justices—William Rehnquist, Antonin Scalia, and Clarence Thomas—remain on the Court with the *Casey* plurality in 2001; presumably, these six will be the winning coalition in abortion cases for the foreseeable future.

The undue burden standard differs from the trimester approach of *Roe* in holding that the state's interest in potential life is compelling throughout the pregnancy rather than simply after viability. Under *Roe*, regulations touching on the abortion decision must survive strict scrutiny; that is, they must be narrowly drawn to serve a compelling state interest. Under the undue burden standard, any regulation which furthers the state interest in protecting potential life or maternal health is constitutional unless it can be shown to place a substantial obstacle on the abortion decision. If it does not, the court must decide only if the regulation is reasonably related to serving the state's interests. Thus, increases in monetary costs, time, and paperwork will no longer be considered an infringement on a woman's right. As a less strict standard than the trimester framework of *Roe*, the undue burden standard allows for significantly greater regulation of the abortion procedure and process.

SEE Abortion as a Reproductive Right; *City of Akron v. Akron Center for Reproductive Health*; *Planned Parenthood of Southeastern Pennsylvania v. Casey*; *Roe v. Wade*; *Thornburgh v. American College of Obstetricians and Gynecologists*; *Webster v. Reproductive Health Services*.

KATE GREENE

W

WEBSTER v. REPRODUCTIVE HEALTH SERVICES (492 U.S. 490, 1989)
was the first major Supreme Court decision to revisit the fundamental holding of
Roe v. Wade. Fifteen years after *Roe*, the Court had become more conservative with
the elevation of William Rehnquist to the chief justiceship and the appointments
of Associate Justices Antonin Scalia and Anthony Kennedy by Republican President Ronald Reagan. Though there was speculation that *Roe* would be overturned,
a majority of the sharply divided Court confirmed a woman's right to choose an
abortion while at the same time increasing the states' power to regulate it.

Webster involved a Missouri law which stated that life begins at conception,
barred the use of state property for abortions, and required physicians to perform
medically appropriate tests to determine the viability of the fetus in cases where,
in the doctor's judgment, the fetus was 20 or more weeks' gestational age. Under
the framework established in *Roe*, 20 weeks fell within the second trimester, when
regulation would only be allowed to ensure the health of the woman.

A bare majority of five justices held that the "life begins at conception" pre-
amble to the bill had no operative legal effect and therefore did not conflict with
the statement in *Roe* that a state could not adopt a particular theory of when human
life begins. This majority also held that at its core, the barring of the use of state
property for abortions was constitutional under *Harris v. McRae*, which had previously upheld a ban on public funding of abortions. But no majority for or against
overturning *Roe* emerged. A plurality opinion, written by Chief Justice Rehnquist
and joined by Justices Kennedy and Byron White, asserted that the state's interest in safeguarding potential human life carried equal weight throughout the
pregnancy. This statement conflicted with the holding in *Roe* that the state's
interest in the fetus increased as the length of the pregnancy increased. While the

plurality's analysis diverged from *Roe*, the opinion refused to go a step further and disturb *Roe*'s central holding. Only Justice Scalia's separate opinion explicitly said that the 1973 decision should be overturned. A majority of justices rejected both Rehnquist's and Scalia's analyses.

In her concurring opinion, Justice Sandra Day O'Connor held that the medical testing provision for viability of the fetus at 20 weeks was constitutional only because there is a four-week margin of error in determining gestational age. O'Connor reasoned that 20 weeks could potentially be 24, putting the fetus in the third trimester and therefore subjecting it to regulation under *Roe*. Many commentators speculated that Rehnquist, Kennedy, and White moderated their position in order to gain O'Connor's vote for increased regulation. Had she voted to overturn *Roe*, many experts believe, the plurality would have adopted Scalia's position.

Justice Harry Blackmun, the author of *Roe*, dissented with Justices William Brennan, Thurgood Marshall, and John Paul Stevens. This dissent argued that the medical testing provision was a second trimester regulation premised on the desire to protect the fetus, and was therefore unconstitutional under *Roe*. Blackmun disagreed with the Court's validation of the medical testing provision. Regretting how close the Court had come to overturning *Roe,* Blackmun wrote, "I fear for the future. I fear for the liberty and equality of the millions of women who have lived and come of age in the 16 years since *Roe* was decided."

Webster had a significant effect on interest-group mobilization in the states. Because the Court upheld Missouri's abortion regulations, state legislatures and election campaigns across the United States became important battlegrounds for both sides in the abortion debate. Those who wanted increased restrictions on abortion argued that *Webster* had increased the states' regulatory power, while supporters of *Roe* portrayed the decision as an assault on women's rights.

Three years later, by the time the Court heard *Planned Parenthood of Southeastern Pennsylvania v. Casey*, Justices Brennan and Marshall had been succeeded by David Souter and Clarence Thomas, nominated by Republican President George Bush. Many observers thought the Court would continue where *Webster* left off and finally reverse *Roe*. Once again, however, Chief Justice Rehnquist fell one vote short of a majority. Souter and Kennedy joined O'Connor, Blackmun, and John Paul Stevens in a joint opinion reaffirming the essential holding of *Roe*.

SEE Abortion as a Reproductive Right; *Beal v. Doe*; *Harris v. McRae*; *Planned Parenthood of Southeastern Pennsylvania v. Casey*; Privacy and Reproductive Rights; *Roe v. Wade*.

Further References. Barbara Hinkson Craig and David M. O'Brien, *Abortion and American Politics* (Chatham, N.J., 1993). Mark A. Graber, *Rethinking Abortion: Equal Choice, the Constitution, and Reproductive Politics* (Princeton, N.J., 1996). Eileen L. McDonagh, *Breaking the Abortion Deadlock* (New York, 1996). Karen O'Connor, *No Neutral Ground? Abortion Politics in an Age of Absolutes* (Boulder, Colo., 1996).

ARTEMUS WARD

Y

YOUTH AND REPRODUCTIVE RIGHTS. Public discourse on youth and reproductive rights, emerging most vocally from the Supreme Court decision in *Roe v. Wade* (1973), is a new phenomenon compared to the ongoing discussion of sexual activity and parenthood among teens, which have existed throughout the course of this country's 225-year history. The term "youth" carries a range of possible interpretations and applications. In the context of reproductive rights, "youth" usually refers to the interval between the attainment of sexual maturity and the age of majority as well as to people within that stage. In this article, the term refers generally to 13- to 17-year olds, unless otherwise specified.

Socially and historically, the topic of youth and reproduction has been addressed mainly in terms of adolescence and puberty, in the context of criminal prosecution of rape, sexual molestation and sexual abuse, and particularly in response to teenage pregnancy and extramarital sex. Reproductive rights have not been common considerations throughout most of U.S. history. In the last generation, however, young people's reproductive issues have entered the public sphere of rights claims, accompanied by an expanding societal understanding of adolescence. In recent years, the United States has seen an increase in the number of medical providers specializing in adolescent health (for example, adolescent pediatrics and adolescent gynecology). These new fields of medical specialization provide a widening cultural context in which to consider the ability of youth to assert claims of autonomy and agency with respect to their own bodies.

Many features of young people's lives work against the exercise of autonomy. Minors cannot vote and consequently lack the political power derived from voting. Minors, unless formally emancipated, have a general legal duty to obey parent(s) or guardian(s). Their lives are subject to the decisions a parent(s) or guardian(s) makes for them. Most minors are financially dependent on their families, a factor that further subjects youth to the power and authority of adult providers and prohibits young people from fully acting on their own behalf. Not only must minors usually get parental consent for medical treatment, but parents can also force treatment on their children if health care providers cooperage. In one instance (*Stump v. Sparkman*, 1978) a mother had her daughter sterilized without the girl's knowledge. While this represents an extreme case, a handful of court rulings and considerable anecdotal evidence reveal numerous instances of parents forcing daughters to continue or terminate a pregnancy, and to keep or surrender the baby for adoption.

The contemporary discourse on youth and reproductive rights displays multiple connections to contemporary discourse on the legality of abortion. However, the phrase "youth and reproductive rights" is not a code solely for the right of adolescent females to obtain abortions. Rather, a discussion of youth and reproductive rights is an integral part of the discourse on adolescence, bodily autonomy, and personal agency. The contemporary and still-emerging notion of rights attached to youth and reproduction offers a broad framework in which to consider the meaning and significance of reproductive rights for youth. As the notions of bodily autonomy and agency remain central to the discourse, the issue of youth and reproductive rights also forces a conscious consideration of adolescent sexuality. The result is a challenge: how do U.S. society and culture accommodate the claims of youth to reproductive rights?

"Youth and reproductive rights" represents a cluster of issues, including access to information about contraception, the availability of low-cost, quality health care, and the freedom to choose when to be pregnant and when not to be. Therefore, much of the political and legal action on youth and reproductive rights has centered around access to contraceptives. Rights activists support policies that make birth control readily available to teens, relying on *Griswold v. Connecticut* (1965), in which the Supreme Court ruled that laws banning contraceptives violated a constitutional right to privacy. Many health care and social welfare professionals, concerned with preventing teen pregnancy, also support access to contraceptives for minors. But many Americans who advocate sexual abstinence for teens insist that access to birth control will encourage teenagers to have sex.

How far does the right of privacy extend to minors? *Carey v. Population Services International* (1977) represented an early victory for the advocates of access. In *Carey*, the Supreme Court invalidated a New York law prohibiting the sale, distribution or advertisement of nonprescription contraceptives to anyone less than 16. However, in 1983, the Department of Health and Human Services, during the Reagan Administration, drafted a regulation requiring federally funded clinics to inform parents or guardians if they provided contraceptives to minors. This "squeal rule" never went into effect since the Department of Health and Human Services allowed the rule to die after a federal court issued an injunction against it. But where regulation is absent, health care providers still may refuse access to minors or require parental involvement.

Abortion remains the most contested facet of the discourse on youth and reproductive rights. Forty-two states now have laws requiring parental consent or notification, although not all of these are routinely, consistently, or strictly enforced. The Supreme Court has never upheld an absolute consent requirement, but each of these current laws permits a "judicial bypass" whereby a minor can get permission from a judge. For pro-choice advocates, preserving the right of female adolescents to elect abortion remains a yardstick measure of the permanence of the right to abortion for all women. Most supporters of reproductive choice argue that parental notification laws violate young women's right to choice and assert that young women should be able to enter a clinic and, if pregnant, get an abortion. Opponents to legalized abortion, on the other hand, view limitations on minors' access to it as limited but significant victories. Anti-choice activists draw encouragement from two features of American law: (a) other matters of private choice, such as recreational use of illegal drugs, are not ranked as fundamental rights; and (b) a long-established legal principle holds that the rights of juveniles are not as extensive as those of adults. The assertion of the constitutional right to privacy as applied to the human female body has been central to the arguments of pro-choice advocates and court decisions affirming *Roe v. Wade* and to the cases regarding access to contraception. The legal principle of private choice remains the cornerstone of the public debate.

If minors are required generally to obtain parental consent for routine and emergency medical treatment, then why shouldn't the rule requiring parental consent for minors' medical treatment apply to abortion, given that, even under the safest conditions, it is a major medical procedure that carries with it a list of serious possible side effects? Consider this scenario: in New Jersey, a 15-year-old suffering from menstrual cramps cannot be administered an over-the-counter painkiller by a school nurse without her parents' consent, yet she can now get an abortion without even telling her parents.

Most states make some important exceptions to the consent rule by allowing female adolescents to act autonomously, making their own decisions about prenatal care and choices about delivery. Often, both males and females receive treatment, without parental consent or involvement, for sexually transmitted diseases. Major inconsistencies persist in the discourse on youth and reproductive rights, and the question of youth's right to choose abortion without consent of a parent or guardian remains a highly contested field, socially, politically, legally, and ethically.

The moral and ethical components of a discussion on youth and reproduction overlap with general moral and ethical considerations with the larger society: What is the appropriate context for sexual relations? Is abortion the appropriate remedy to unwanted or unplanned pregnancy? Should contraceptives be made readily available to young people if it is inappropriate for them to be engaging in premarital sex? Other issues related to bodily autonomy and agency make the debate more difficult to resolve at times. For example, forced pregnancy, rape, incest, sexual abuse, molestation, and harassment are complicating and complicated issues, and men's roles in reproduction, co-creating and co-parenting need also be considered as part of a comprehensive discussion of youth and reproductive rights.

Conceptualizations of both youth and reproductive rights are culturally situated. In other words, the way youth and reproductive rights are conceptualized in the working class neighborhoods of suburban New Jersey is not necessarily the same framework through which they are viewed in East Los Angeles or in Charleston, South Carolina. Each of these locales has distinct social and cultural histories through which ideas emerge and develop. The specificities of race, ethnicity, class, gender, sexual orientation, religious tradition, and region also must be considered consciously since the merging of all these contrasting images into a single pseudo-history risks essentialism (the premise that one viewpoint is shared by all) and results in an oversimplification of complex notions, ideas, and realities.

The history of youth and reproductive rights in the United States remains complex and personal, while at the same time, simple and public. What reproductive rights, if any, do youth have in the United States? There are many questions, and with each set of answers, new questions emerge, subject to close scrutiny and adaptation over time. Rich with inconsistencies and challenging debates, the discourse is filled with undiscovered potential for a genuine understanding of the range and richness of the still-emerging and ever-evolving discourse.

SEE Abortion and Parental Consent and Notification; Abortion and Parental Involvement; *Bellotti v. Baird I* and *II*; *Carey v. Population Services International*; *City of Akron v. Akron Center for Reproductive Health*; *Griswold v. Connecticut*; *H.L. v. Matheson*; *Hodgson v. Minnesota*; *Ohio v. Akron Center for Reproductive Health*; *Planned Parenthood of Central Missouri v. Danforth*; *Planned Parenthood of Kansas City v. Ashcroft*; *Planned Parenthood of Southeastern Pennsylvania v. Casey*; *Roe v. Wade*; Sterilization Abuse; *Stump v. Sparkman*.

Further References. George Creatsas, ed., *The Young Woman at the Rise of the 21ˢᵗ Century: Gynecological and Reproductive Issues in Health and Disease* (New York, 2000). Keith Greenberg, *Adolescent Rights: Are Young People Equal Under the Law?* (New York, 1995). Anita Hardon, ed., *Reproductive Rights in Practice: A Feminist Report on Quality of Care* (New York, 1997). Annette Lawson and Deborah L. Rhode, eds., *The Politics of Pregnancy: Adolescent Sexuality and Public Policy* (New Haven, Conn., 1995). Mary E. Odem, *Delinquent Daughters: Protecting and Policing Adolescent Female Sexuality in the United States, 1885-1920* (New York, 1995).

LISA R. BURKE

Selected Bibliography

Baehr, Ninia. *Abortion without Apology: A Radical History for the 1990s*. Boston: South End Press, 1990.

Baer, Judith A. *The Chains of Protection: The Judicial Response to Women's Labor Legislation*. Westport, Conn.: Greenwood Press, 1978.

————. *Our Lives before the Law: Constructing a Feminist Jurisprudence*. Princeton, N.J.: Princeton University Press, 1999.

————. *Women in American Law: The Struggle toward Equality from the New Deal to the Present*. Second edition. New York: Holmes & Meier Publishers, Inc., 1996.

Bartholet, Elizabeth. *Family Bonds: Adoption and the Politics of Parenting*. Boston: Houghton Mifflin, 1993.

Blank, Robert H. *Regulating Reproduction*. New York: Columbia University Press, 1990.

————, and Janna C. Merrick. *Human Reproduction, Emerging Technologies, and Conflicting Rights*. Washington, D.C.: CQ Press, 1995.

Boston Women's Health Book Collective. *Our Bodies, Ourselves for the New Century*. New York: Simon & Schuster, 1998.

Chesler, Phyllis. *Mothers on Trial: The Battle for Children and Custody*. New York: McGraw-Hill, 1986.

Colker, Ruth. *Pregnant Men: Practice, Theory, and the Law*. Bloomington: Indiana University Press, 1994.

Collins, Patricia Hill. *Black Feminist Thought: Knowledge, Consciousness, and the Politics of Empowerment*. New York: Routledge, Chapman and Hall, Inc., 1991.

Cook, Elizabeth Adell, Ted G. Jelen, and Clyde Wilcox. *Between Two Absolutes: Public Opinion and the Politics of Abortion*. Boulder, Colo.: Westview Press, 1992.

Craig, Barbara Hinkswon, and David M. O'Brien, *Abortion and American Politics*. Chatham, N.J.: Chatham House, 1993.

Daniels, Cynthia R. *At Women's Expense: State Power and the Politics of Fetal Rights*. Cambridge, Mass.: Harvard University Press, 1993.

Davis, Angela Y. *Women, Race, and Class.* New York: Random House, 1981.

D'Emilio, John, and Estelle B. Freedman. *Intimate Matters: A History of Sexuality in America.* New York: Harper & Row, 1988.

Dolgin, Janet. *Defining the Family: Law Technology and Reproduction in an Uneasy Age.* New York: New York University Press, 1997.

Donovan, Patricia. *The Politics of Blame: Family Planning, Abortion and the Poor.* New York: Alan Guttmacher Institute, 1995.

Eisenstein, Zillah. *The Female Body and the Law.* Berkeley: University of California Press, 1988.

Faludi, Susan. *Backlash: The Undeclared War Against American Women.* New York: Crown Publishers, 1991.

Ferguson, Kathy E. *The Man Question: Visions of Subjectivity in Feminist Theory.* Berkeley, Calif.: University of California Press, 1993.

Fine, Michelle, and Adrienne Asch, eds. *Women with Disabilities: Essays in Psychology, Culture, and Politics.* Philadelphia: Temple University Press, 1988.

Fineman, Martha Albertson, and Isabel Karpin, eds. *Mothers in Law: Feminist Theory and the Legal Regulation of Motherhood.* New York: Columbia University Press, 1995.

Flexner, Eleanor. *Century of Struggle.* Revised edition. Cambridge, Mass.: Belknap Press of Harvard University Press, 1970.

Garrow, David J. *Liberty and Sexuality: The Right to Privacy and the Making of* Roe v. Wade. New York: MacMillan Pub. Co., 1994.

Giddings, Paula. *When and Where I Enter: The Impact of Black Women on Race and Sex in America.* New York: William Morrow and Company, Inc., 1984.

Glendon, Mary Ann. *Rights Talk: The Impoverishment of Political Discourse.* New York: The Free Press, 1991.

Gomez, Laura E. *Misconceiving Mothers: Legislators, Prosecutors, and the Politics of Prenatal Drug Exposure.* Philadelphia: Temple University Press,1997.

Gordon, Linda. *Woman's Body, Woman's Right: A Social History of Birth Control in America.* Rev. ed. New York: Viking Penguin, 1990.

Graber, Mark A. *Rethinking Abortion: Equal Choice, the Constitution, and Reproductive Politics.* Princeton, N.J.: Princeton University Press, 1996.

Hartmann, Betsy. *Reproductive Rights and Wrongs: The Global Politics of Population Control.* New York: Harper & Row, 1987.

Hartog, Hendrik. *Man and Wife in America.* Cambridge, MA: Harvard University Press, 2000.

Hoff, Joan. *Law, Gender, and Injustice: A Legal History of U.S. Women.* New York: New York University Press, 1991.

Hooks, Bell. *Feminist Theory: From Margin to Center.* Boston: South End Press, 1985.

Joffe, Carol. *Doctors of Conscience: The Struggle to Provide Abortion before and after* Roe v. Wade. Boston: Beacon Press, 1995.

Kenney, Sally J. *For Whose Protection? Reproductive Hazards and Exclusionary Policies in the United States and Britain.* Ann Arbor: University of Michigan Press, 1992.

Luker, Kristin. *Abortion and the Politics of Motherhood.* Berkeley: University of California Press, 1984.

———. *Dubious Conceptions: The Politics of Teenage Pregnancy.* Cambridge, Mass.: Harvard University Press, 1996.

MacKinnon, Catharine A. *Feminism Unmodified.* Cambridge, Mass.: Harvard University Press, 1987.

———. *Toward a Feminist Theory of the State.* Cambridge, Mass.: Harvard University Press, 1989.

MacNair, Rachel, Mary Krane Derr, and Linda Naranjo-Huebl, eds. *Prolife Feminism: Yesterday and Today.* New York: Sulzburger & Graham, 1995.

Mason, Mary Ann. *From Father's Property to Children's Rights: The History of Child Custody in the United States.* New York: Columbia University Press, 1995.

May, Elaine Tyler. *Barren in the Promised Land: Childless Americans and the Pursuit of Happiness.* Cambridge, Mass.: Harvard University Press, 1995.

McDonagh, Eileen L. *Breaking the Abortion Deadlock: From Choice to Consent.* New York: Oxford University Press, 1996.

McFarlane, Deborah R., and Kenneth J. Meier, *The Politics of Fertility Control.* Chatham, N.J.: Chatham House, 2001.

Mezey, Susan Gluck. *In Pursuit of Equality: Women, Public Policy, and the Federal Courts.* New York: St. Martin's Press, 1992.

Mink, Gwendolyn. *Welfare's End.* Ithaca, N.Y.: Cornell University Press, 1997.

O'Connor, Karen. *No Neutral Ground? Abortion Politics in an Age of Absolutes.* Boulder, Colo.: Westview Press, 1996.

Okin, Susan Moller. *Justice, Gender, and the Family.* New York: Basic Books, 1989.

Petchesky, Rosalind Pollack. *Abortion and Woman's Choice: The State, Sexuality, and Reproductive Freedom.* Rev. ed. Boston: Northeastern University Press, 1990.

Ramírez de Arellano, Annette B, and Conrad Seipp. *Colonialism, Catholicism, and Contraception: A History of Birth Control in Puerto Rico.* Chapel Hill, N.C.: University of North Carolina Press, 1983.

Rapp, Rayna. *Testing Women, Testing the Fetus: The Social History of Amniocentesis in America.* New York: Routledge, 1999.

Reagan, Leslie J. *When Abortion Was a Crime: Women, Medicine, and Law in the United States, 1867-1973.* Berkeley: University of California Press, 1997.

Rich, Adrienne. *Of Woman Born: Motherhood as Experience and Institution.* New York: W.W. Norton & Company, 1976.

Roberts, Dorothy. *Killing the Black Body: Race, Reproduction, and the Meaning of Liberty.* New York: Pantheon, 1997.

Robertson, John A. *Children of Choice: Freedom and the New Reproductive Technologies.* Princeton, N.J.: Princeton University Press, 1994.

Rosenblatt, Roger. *Life Itself: Abortion in the American Mind.* New York: Random House, 1992.

Roth, Rachel. *Making Women Pay: The Hidden Costs of Fetal Rights.* Ithaca, N.Y.: Cornell University Press, 1999.

Rothman, Barbara Katz. *Recreating Motherhood.* New York: W.W. Norton, 1989.

Samuels, Suzanne U. *Fetal Rights, Women's Rights: Gender Equality in the Workplace.* Madison, Wisc.: University of Wisconsin Press, 1995.

Sanger, Margaret. *An Autobiography.* New York: W.W. Norton, 1938.

Schroedel, Jean Reith. *Beyond Conception: Is the Fetus a Person?* Ithaca, N.Y.: Cornell University Press, 2000.

Skocpol, Theda. *Protecting Soldiers and Mothers: The Political Origins of Social Policy in the United States.* Cambridge, Mass.: Belknap Press of Harvard University Press, 1992.

Stetson, Dorothy McBride. *Women's Rights in the U.S.A.: Policy Debates and Gender Roles.* Pacific Grove, Calif.: Brooks/Cole Publishing Company, 1991.

Tribe, Laurence H. *Abortion: The Clash of Absolutes.* New York: Norton, 1992.

Index

Index of Cases

About the Editor and Contributors

Judith A. Baer is professor of political science at Texas A&M University, and is author of *The Chains of Protection: The Judicial Response to Women's Labor Legislation* (Greenwood, 1978) and *Our Lives Before The Law* (1999).

Jilda M. Aliotta, Department of Politics and Government, University of Hartford, West Hartford, Connecticut.

Ángela Pattatucci-Aragón, Division of Clinic and Population-based Studies, National Institutes of Health, Bethesda, Maryland.

Adrienne Asch, Henry R. Luce Professor of Biology, Ethics, and the Politics of Human Reproduction, Wellesley College, Wellesley, Massachusetts.

Von Bakanic, Department of Sociology, College of Charleston, Charleston, South Carolina.

Carrie N. Baker, Institute for Women's Studies, Emory University, Atlanta, Georgia.

Elizabeth N. Baldwin, Esq., Baldwin & Friedman, North Miami Beach, Florida.

Scott Barclay, Department of Political Science, The University at Albany, Albany, New York.

Pauline B. Bart, Center for the Study of Women, University of California, Los Angeles, California.

Joyce A. Baugh, Department of Political Science, Central Michigan University, Mt. Pleasant.

Brigitte H. Bechtold, Department of Sociology, Anthropology and Social Work, Central Michigan University, Mt. Pleasant.

Mary Becker, DePaul College of Law, Chicago, Illinois.

Susan M. Behuniak, Department of Political Science, Le Moyne College, Syracuse, New York.

Sara C. Benesh, Department of Political Science, University of Wisconsin, Milwaukee.

Maria Bevacqua, Department of Women's Studies, Minnesota State University, Mankato.

Gayle Binion, Department of Political Science, University of California, Santa Barbara.

Robert H. Blank, Department of Government, Brunel University, Uxbridge, United Kingdom.

Janet K. Boles, Department of Political Science, Marquette University, Milwaukee, Wisconsin.

Andrea L. Bonnicksen, Department of Political Science, Northern Illinois University, DeKalb.

Adrienne Bousian, California Abortion Rights Action League, San Francisco, California.

Michael W. Bowers, Department of Political Science, University of Nevada, Las Vegas.

Susan Burgess, Department of Women's Studies, Ohio University, Athens.

Lisa R. Burke, Officer of Academic Services for Evening Students, New Jersey City University, Jersey City.

Francis Carleton, Department of Social Change & Development, University of Wisconsin, Green Bay.

George Carr, Esq., Gallagher, Sharp, Fulton & Norman, Cleveland, Ohio.

Glynis Carr, Department of English, Bucknell University, Lewis, Pennsylvania.

Ellen Chesler, Program on Reproductive Health and Rights, The Open Society Institute/Soros Foundations, New York, New York.

Elaine R. Cleeton, Department of Sociology, State University of New York at Geneseo.

Deirdre Condit, Department of Political Science and Public Administration, Virginia Commonwealth University, Richmond.

Christine A. Corcos, Louisiana State University Law Center, Baton Rouge.

Vena Crichlow-Scales, Atlanta, Georgia.

Cynthia R. Daniels, Department of Political Science and Women's Studies, Rutgers University, New Brunswick, New Jersey.

Sue Davis, Department of Political Science, University of Delaware, Newark.

Robbie Davis-Floyd, Department of Anthropology, University of Texas at Austin.

Michelle Donaldson Deardorff, Department of Political Science, Millikin University, Decatur, Illinois.

Kevin R. den Dulk, Department of Political Science, University of Wisconsin, Madison.

Mary Krane Derr, Chicago, Illinois.

Molly Dragiewicz, Department of Cultural Studies, George Mason University, Fairfax Station, Virginia.

J. Shoshanna Ehrlich, Legal Education Center, University of Massachusetts, Boston.

Daryl R. Fair, Department of Political Science, The College of New Jersey, Ewing.

Pamela Fiber, Department of Politics and Policy, Claremont Graduate University, Claremont, California.

Deborah Cordero Fiedler, Cranston, Rhode Island.

Nilda Flores-Gonzalez, Department of Sociology, University of Illinois at Chicago.

Lara Foley, Department of Sociology, University of Tulsa.

Evan Gerstmann, Department of Political Science, Loyola Marymount University, Los Angeles, California.

Betty J. Glass, UNR Libraries, University of Nevada, Reno.

Rachel E. Goldberg, Department of Politics and Government, University of Puget Sound, Tacoma, Washington.

Julianna Gonen, Washington Business Group on Health, Washington, D.C.

Linda Gordon, Department of History, University of Wisconsin, Madison.

Mark Graber, Department of Political Science, University of Maryland, College Park.

Nikki Graves, Institute for Women's Studies, Emory University, Atlanta, Georgia.

Kate Greene, Department of Political Science, University of Southern Mississippi, Hattiesburg.

Susan E. Grogan, Department of Political Science, St. Mary's College of Maryland, St. Mary's City.

Valerie Hartouni, Department of Communication and Critical Gender Studies Program, University of California, San Diego, La Jolla.

Melissa Haussman, Department of Government, Suffolk University, Boston, Massachusetts.

Barbara Hayler, Criminal Justice Program, University of Illinois, Springfield.

Ellen Herman, Department of History, University of Oregon, Eugene.

Jenny Higgins, Institute for Women's Studies, Emory University, Atlanta, Georgia.

Charmaine Jackson, Department of Politics and Policy, Claremont Graduate University, Claremont, California.

Beth Kiyoko Jamieson, Department of Political Science, Haverford College, Haverford, Pennsylvania.

Ted G. Jelen, Department of Political Science, University of Nevada at Las Vegas.

Lakesia D. Johnson, Women's Programs & Affirmative Action, Denison University, Granville, Ohio.

Ronald Kahn, Department of Political Science, Oberlin College, Oberlin, Ohio.

Mary Lou Kendrigan, Social Science Department (Emerita), Lansing Community College, Lansing, Michigan.

Leslie King, Department of Sociology, University of Maine, Orono.

Lenore Kuo, Department of Philosophy and Religion, University of Nebraska, Omaha.

Daniel Lessard Levin, Department of Political Science, University of Utah, Salt Lake City.

Eileen L. McDonagh, Department of Political Science, Northeastern University, Boston, Massachusetts.

Deborah R. McFarlane, Department of Political Science, University of New Mexico, Albuquerque.

Susan Gluck Mezey, Department of Political Science, Loyola University Chicago.

Melissa Moore, Kaiser Family Foundation, New York, New York.

Patricia Murphy, Department of Sociology, State University of New York at Geneseo.

Noelle H. Norton, Department of Political Science, University of San Diego, San Diego, California.

Julie Novkov, Department of Political Science, University of Oregon, Eugene.

Karen O'Connor, Department of Government, American University, Washington, D.C.

Susan M. Olson, Associate Vice President For Faculty, University of Utah, Salt Lake City.

Erica A. Owens, Department of Sociology, University of Florida, Gainesville.

Marian Lief Palley, Department of Political Science, University of Delaware, Newark.

Laura Parisi, Department of Women's Studies, Virginia Polytechnic University, Blacksburg.

Ruth Parlin, Department of Environmental Studies, Green Mountain College, Poultney, Vermont.

Lucinda Peach, Department of Philosophy and Religion, American University, Washington, D.C.

Barbara A. Perry, Department of Government, Sweet Briar College, Sweet Briar, Virginia.

Kirsten Rambo, Institute for Women's Studies, Emory University, Atlanta, Georgia.

Dorothy Roberts, School of Law, Northwestern University, Chicago, Illinois.

James Rogers, Department of Political Science, Texas A&M University, College Station.

Rachel Roth, Department of Political Science and Program in Women's Studies, Washington University, St. Louis, Missouri.

Margaret M. Russell, School of Law, Santa Clara University, Santa Clara, California.

Suzanne Uttaro Samuels, Department of Political Science, Seton Hall University, South Orange, New Jersey.

Jean Reith Schroedel, Department of Politics and Policy, Claremont Graduate University, Claremont, California.

Nelia Beth Scovill, Department of Religious Studies, Carroll College, Waukesha, Wisconsin.

Tracy Sefl, National Clinic Access Project, Feminist Majority Foundation, Washington, D.C.

Mary Lyndon Shanley, Department of Political Science, Vassar College, Poughkeepsie, New York.

Christopher Shortell, Department of Political Science, University of California at San Diego.

Wendy Simonds, Department of Sociology, Georgia State University, Atlanta.

Sarah Slavin, Department of Political Science, State University of New York College at Buffalo.

Viki Soady, Program in Women's Studies, Valdosta State University, Valdosta, Georgia.

Dorothy McBride Stetson, Department of Political Science, Florida Atlantic University, Boca Raton.

Trudy Steuernagel, Department of Political Science, Kent State University, Kent, Ohio.

Philippa Strum, Woodrow Wilson International Center for Scholars, Washington, D.C.

G. Alan Tarr, Center for State Constitutional Studies, Rutgers University, Camden, New Jersey.

Elliot Tenofsky, Department of Political Science, Linfield College, McMinnville, Oregon.

Lana Thompson, Florida Atlantic University, Boca Raton, Florida.

Mary Thornberry, Department of Political Science, Davidson College, Davidson, North Carolina.

Artemus Ward, Department of Political Science, California State University, Chico.

Anne Waters, Department of Philosophy, University of New Mexico, Albuquerque.

David L. Weiden, Department of Political Science, United States Naval Academy, Annapolis, Maryland.

Clyde Wilcox, Department of Government, Georgetown University, Washington, D.C.

Gwyneth I. Williams, Department of History, Politics, and Law, Webster College, St. Louis, Missouri.

Laura R. Woliver, Department of Government and International Studies, University of South Carolina, Columbia.

Sandra L. Wood, Denton, Texas.

Linda Yanney, The University of Iowa Archives, Iowa City.

Fiona M. Young, Women's Studies Program, University of Iowa, Iowa City.

Mary Young, Economics and Women's Studies, Southwestern University, Georgetown, Texas.